PRACTICAL

ALGEBRA

TEACHING WITHIN THE
NATIONAL CURRICULUM

ANNIE OWEN

Published by Scholastic Publications Ltd
Villiers House, Clarendon Avenue,
Leamington Spa, Warwickshire CV32 5PR

© 1993 Scholastic Publications Ltd

Written by Annie Owen
Edited by Juliet Gladston
Sub-edited by Jo Saxelby-Jennings
Designed by Clare Brewer
Illustrated by Sue Hutchison and Clare Brewer
Front cover designed by Anna Oliwa
Front cover illustrated by John Spencer
Photographs by Bob Bray (page 15) and Garry
Clarke (page 73)

Every attempt has been made to trace and acknowledge
the photographers whose pictures appear in this book.
The publisher apologises for any omissions.

Designed using Aldus Pagemaker
Printed in Great Britain by Ebenezer Baylis &
Son, Worcester

British Library Cataloguing in Publication Data
A catalogue record for this book is available from the
British Library.

ISBN 0-590-53091-7

Contents

Introduction

As this book goes to press, all state primary schools in Britain, and by choice very many private schools, are following a national curriculum. This lays down as a statutory requirement (in state schools only) the curriculum content to be followed by children from the age of five to sixteen (in England and Wales) or five to fourteen (in Scotland).

The National Curriculum for mathematics in England and Wales is divided into five areas, one of which is algebra (Attainment Target 3). This attainment target (AT) is further subdivided into three strands: (i) Patterns and relationships; (ii) Formulae, equations and inequalities; and (iii) Graphical representation.

The Scottish curriculum includes the algebra content under two attainment targets: Number, money and measurement; and Information handling.

The inclusion of algebra as a theme within the primary mathematics curriculum came as a surprise to many teachers. Adult memories of the algebra they met at school tends to be of 'finding x' in an equation and manipulating brackets. However, the statements to be found in the Programme of Study (PoS) – at least up to and including Level 4 – look very different. Much of the material is already familiar to the primary classroom, prompting some teachers to marvel that they have 'been doing algebra all this time without knowing it!' For example: *'Find the missing numbers:*
$3 +$ ■ $= x$
● *$+ 3 = 8 ...$'* (AT3 Level 2 Examples).

However, some of the concepts are less familiar, for example: *'Use the difference method to explore sequences such as: 2, 5, 10, 17, 26...'* (AT3 Level 6 Examples).

Are these arbitrary and unconnected ideas or do they lead into the more familiar images of algebra? To answer this question, it is first necessary to attempt to answer the question, 'What *is* algebra?'

There are no formal, comprehensive definitions of algebra which will satisfy everyone! Mathematicians' views of the subject are coloured by what they use algebra for. However, there are two concepts of algebra which are met more often than others and which serve our purpose, of defining algebra for the primary classroom, very well: *algebra as the study of patterns* and *algebra as generalised arithmetic*.

Both these areas are found in Strand (i) of Attainment Target 3 – Patterns and relationships – and this strand could, therefore, be said to contain the fundamentals of algebra as reflected in the National Curriculum. Several concepts straddle across Strands (i) and (ii) (for example, at Level 4a **'Make general statements about patterns'**) but the content of both the second and third strands are both dependent upon and subservient to Strand (i).

Algebra as the study of pattern

Spatial and number patterns

Children are fascinated by patterns, whether these are spatially or number based. 'Growing snowflakes' is an example of a spatial pattern which children enjoy modelling on squared paper. They should begin with a square, for example, of one colour, choose a second colour and add squares of this second colour so that they will only touch *one* side of the first square. They should then choose a third colour and add squares of this colour so that they will only touch one side of the second set of squares and so on. The pattern will build up as shown opposite.

The pattern they get will depend on their initial shape (here a square) and on how many colours are used.

As an example of a number-based pattern, consider the list of the even numbers: 2, 4, 6,

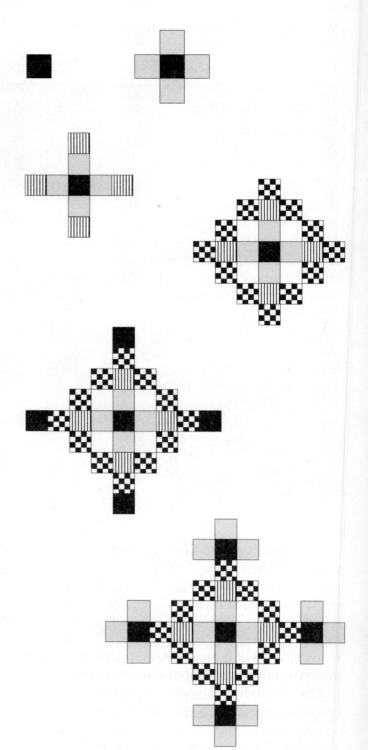

8, 10, 12, 14, 16, 18, 20.... This is a very common pattern to children: 'Two, four, six, eight, who do we appreciate?...', 'The animals went in two by two...' and so on. Socks and shoes also come in pairs.

There is more, though, to this pattern than first meets the eye. Look at the last digit of each number and you will see the cycle of numbers: 2, 4, 6, 8, 0, 2, 4, 6, 8, 0.

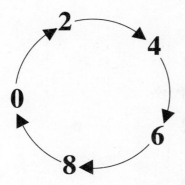

What will happen if we add a different number than two, or if we start with one instead of two? Such questioning gives children scope to choose for themselves what they are going to explore.

Patterns are to be found everywhere in the natural world. The growth of plants and animals obeys mathematical rules, which we observe as pattern. For example, the shape of a snail's shell is a particular mathematical curve called a logarithmic spiral.

The petals of a daisy grow so that the head has symmetry and also the number of petals (34, 55 or 89) forms part of a particular numeral pattern (that is, the Fibonacci sequence).

Children also notice pattern in the manufactured articles surrounding them, for example, in the repeating patterns on wallpaper.

The stitching of a Fair Isle pullover, the patterns in a woven basket and the repetition in a wrought-iron railing also all have basic mathematical structures.

Our ability to understand structures in nature, and to produce patterns in our own craftwork, is therefore dependent upon our grasp of the number patterns underlying them. The study of number patterns is thus a fundamental human activity and takes place on many levels of complexity.

The youngest school children do not have the grasp of number concepts required to study their patterns. However, the habit of recognising, repeating and describing patterns can begin through art, craft, PE and music activities (ideas are provided under 'Structured activities for Key Stage 1' on page 24, Chapter One). In fact, children of all ages will benefit from making and identifying frieze patterns (patterns which only occur along a line), looking at animal camouflage patterns and so on, as other areas of the mathematics curriculum – and cross-curricular links – are involved.

Repeating patterns and sequences

The definition of algebra as the study of patterns is reflected in the sections of Attainment Target 3 which refer to repeating patterns, for example: **'copying, continuing and devising repeating patterns represented by objects/apparatus or single-digit numbers'** (Level 1 PoS) or to sequences, for example: **'follow instructions to generate sequences'** (Level 5a SoA).

A repeating pattern is one which follows a cycle, returning to the beginning over and over again, for example the last digits of the even numbers on page 6, or the two examples quoted for Attainment Target 3 Level 1: *2, 1, 2, 1, 2, 1, 2, 1, ...*

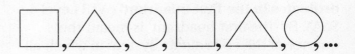

Each repeating pattern has its own rule, which states what is being repeated (in other words, what is in the cycle).

A sequence also obeys a rule, but sequences do not repeat themselves, for example: '*5, 10, 15, 20, ...*' (Level 3 Examples). The rule is 'add five each time', and the sequence goes on for ever.

In both repeating patterns and sequences, the rules cause 'change' to happen. It is helpful for young children to have some focus for what is causing the change, or where it is happening. This is especially valuable when the children need to work backwards, for example to *find* the rule. Function machines are an excellent way of modelling what is happening when sequences are made (see below).

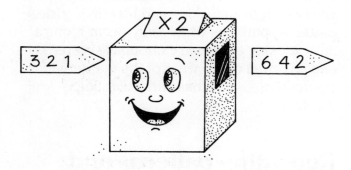

The box may only be a soap powder carton with a silly face, but it helps children to visualise the production of streams of numbers, or the change of an IN number to an OUT number. The rule which the box carries out is called a 'function', hence the name given to such devices.

Graphical representation

For older children, the visualisation of patterns can take the more formal form of a graph, but in order to do this, children first need to understand the co-ordinate system and the way that IN numbers and OUT numbers can be written as co-ordinates.

The co-ordinate system is first mentioned in the National Curriculum at Level 4: **'Use co-ordinates in the first quadrant'** (AT3 Level 4c SoA). By 'the first quadrant' is meant the quarter of the co-ordinate system in which all the numbers are positive.

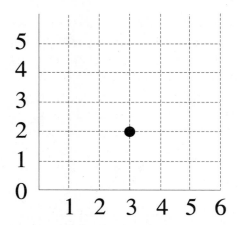

At Level 4, children should understand that, for example, the point shown above has a label (3,2). However, much preliminary work is necessary before the children can hope to reach this stage, as will be discussed later in Chapter 1.

To draw the sequence shown on our function machine opposite, the children need to be able to link the IN numbers and the OUT numbers, perhaps by means of a mapping diagram.

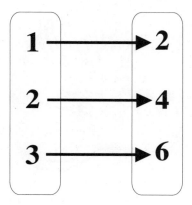

This is then converted into co-ordinates, (1,2), (2,4), (3,6), and plotted on to the first quadrant.

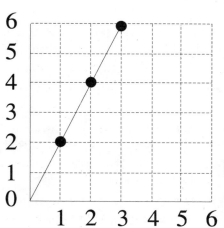

Many readers will remember such drawings from their own school days, and will also recognise that such a graph should have an equation written on it telling the observer what has been drawn. The equation (here it would be y = 2x) represents the 'rule' which changed the 'x' sequence of numbers (the counting numbers along the bottom line) into the 'y' sequence of numbers (the vertical numbers opposite the points).

Generalising sequences

Finding the equation to describe the rule is another way of saying 'generalising' the sequence. Young children are only able to explain what happens to a pattern step by step, for example:
• 1, 3, 5, 7, 9... 'We add two each time.'
• 2, 4, 8, 16... 'We double each time.'
   This is known as the *iterative* description of the sequence.
   Older children should be asked to generalise for any term. For example, taking the first sequence above, the fifth term (9) is 2 times 5 take away 1. The tenth term would be 2 times 10 take away 1 (19). For the second sequence, the fourth term is four lots of 2 multiplied together ($2 \times 2 \times 2 \times 2 = 16$) and so the tenth term would be $2 \times 2 \times 2 \times 2 \times 2 \times 2 \times 2 \times 2 \times 2 \times 2 = 1024$. Symbolic notation of these generalisations is beyond the reach of the vast majority of primary pupils, but is of interest to their teachers as a guide to the direction the work is taking. The symbol used to represent the term of the sequences below is 'n': ***Express in symbols the rules for the following sequences:***

1, 3, 5, ... [2n − 1]
1, 4, 9, ... [n^2]
$\frac{1}{2}, \frac{2}{3}, \frac{3}{4}, ...[\frac{n}{(n+1)}]$ ' (AT3 Level 7 Examples).
   Dealing with number sequences like the ones described here is becoming more and more common in the primary classroom. The major reason is, of course, the growth in importance of mathematical problem-solving, or investigative work. Algebra is an extremely important tool for getting the greatest benefit out of open-ended tasks.
   A popular way of accessing number sequences is through spatial arrangements.

These are not mentioned in the National Curriculum until Attainment Target 3 Level 5, but they are an excellent way for all stages to get involved, for example, 'Put a path around the fish pond.'

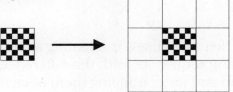

How many paving stones did you need? What about a bigger pond? (adapted from Section 2 'Attainment outcomes and targets: Problem-solving and enquiry' in *Mathematics 5–14*, 1991, The Scottish Office Education Department).

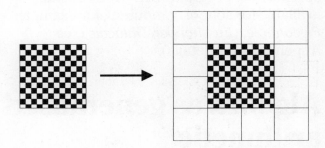

The children will find that they get the pattern 8, 12, 16, 20 and so on, which is well within the grasp of many Key Stage 1 children.
   Not all number patterns are as easy to see as this one; for example, what is happening with this pattern: 1, 11, 27, 49, 77, 111...? Older pupils (Level 6 in the National Curriculum, but accessible to other older juniors) should learn to use the 'difference' method to find how such a sequence is growing.
   Let us take, for example, the sequence above. The rule to generate these numbers is not immediately obvious, but if we look at the difference between each number and the one next to it many children will notice that the second row goes up in 6s:

1   11   27   49   77   111
   10   16   22   28   34

They can then continue the second line and use the numbers to work backwards by adding to get the continuation of the original sequence.

If they still have not seen the pattern, the third row will settle things:

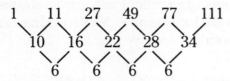

It is helpful to use a calculating aid both for exploring sequences with the difference method and for continuing them once the rule has been identified. Calculators are useful, and in the beginning stages are preferable, as the children understand the process more fully by carrying it out stage by stage, but the more able children at Key Stage 2 will benefit from – and are expected in the National Curriculum (Levels 5 and 6) to use – a spreadsheet program. There are several available for school computers, for example *Pigeonhole, Grasshopper, Datacalc* (see Appendix A for details).

Algebra as generalised arithmetic

The second image of algebra, as generalised arithmetic, encompasses structural patterns and relationships, which lead to the recognition of the properties of numbers and also to the representation of their relationships as equations or formulae.

As we study how numbers behave when we manipulate them, we can notice rules which hold for all cases. For example, if we add two odd numbers together we *always* get an even number:

$$3 + 5 = 8$$
$$7 + 11 = 18$$

This is a rule which children can easily understand spatially (see below) but which mathematicians prove in ways normally beyond the levels of the primary classroom.

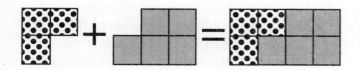

Another example of generalised arithmetic is found in the study of partitions. A partition of a number is a splitting of it into two or more smaller numbers, for example:

$$6 = 3 + 3$$
$$6 = 2 + 2 + 2$$
$$6 = 1 + 2 + 3$$

Through such manipulation children come to recognise the structure of the number (above, for 6, we find it is even, it is made of three lots of two, it is double three and is made from three consecutive numbers). The patterns found in early partitioning help children to remember number facts:

$$1 + 9 = 10$$
$$2 + 8 = 10$$
$$3 + 7 = 10...$$

Partitioning into tens and units enables more complex mental methods:

$$36 + 27 = 30 + 6 + 20 + 7$$
$$= 50 + 13 = 63$$

Such activities give children a 'feel' for the structure of number. Many teachers choose not to make these links explicit, but children do benefit from hearing about other pupils' ways of solving things.

This definition of algebra as generalised arithmetic, is reflected in the sections of Attainment Target 3 which refer to partitions, for example: **'exploring and using patterns in addition and subtraction facts to 10'** (Level 2 PoS) and to the properties of numbers, for example: **'distinguishing odd and even numbers'** (Level 2 PoS).

Also, arithmetic manipulation frequently leads children to discover how the operation itself (for example, addition) behaves and links with other operations. Games like 'Trios' help children to link three numbers in several ways, hence discovering, or reinforcing, the 'opposite' nature of, for example, addition and subtraction: $8 = 3 + 5$ $8 - 3 = 5$

In the game 'Trios', the children are awarded points for the number of different ways they can say the connections between the three numbers, for example:
• 'The difference between eight and five is three.'
• 'Eight is bigger than five by three.'
• 'Five and three make eight.'

Equations

As soon as children begin to play games such as 'Trios', they are also beginning to use equations. The word 'equation' does not occur in AT3 on the whole, until Level 4, where relationships containing some unknown factor are introduced. Even then it is only necessary that such a relationship is expressed in words, for example: ***'Solve a problem such as: "If I double a number then add 1, and the result is 49, what is the number?"'*** (AT3 Level 4 Examples).

However, the need for 'balance' in an equation, and the use of a symbol to stand for an unknown, is introduced much earlier – at Level 2 – in the very form 'finding x' with which most of us are familiar: ***'Find the missing numbers:***

3 + ■ = 10

● + 3 = 8...' (Level 2 Examples).

Some children solve such problems by adding on, others choose to subtract. In doing the latter, children show a grasp of the concept of subtraction being the 'inverse' (or opposite) of addition:

$$10 - 3 = ■ \text{ and } ● = 8 - 3$$

In order to visualise the problem, the function machine is yet again very helpful:

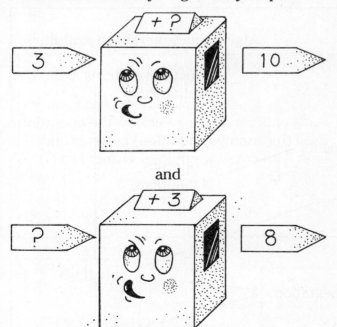

and

These two machines show examples of problems where the children have to 'work back', that is, find inverses.

Children at Level 6 should be able to use the 'trial and improvement' method of solving more difficult equations. Take, for example, the following problem: 'Find two consecutive numbers such that their product is 6162.' Children will initially make wild guesses, but the need to be systematic becomes apparent very quickly. This can be aided by keeping a results table:

1st number	2nd number	Answer	Comments
50	51	2550	Too small
70	71	4970	Still too small
90	91	8190	Too big
80	81	6480	Too big
75	76	5700	Too small
77	78	6006	Better
78	79	6162	Bingo!

Calculators are obviously a boon for such work, though a computer spreadsheet will be not only speedier but also less repetitive. However, children need some experience of the former before moving on to spreadsheet software.

Formulae

The word 'formula' is first introduced in the National Curriculum at Level 4: **'Use simple formulae expressed in words'** (AT3 Level 4b SoA). However, the examples given at this level are not of formulae in the usual definition of the concept.

A formula is a specific case of an equation which involves a relationship that does not change. For example, the area of a rectangle is found by multiplying its length by its width, so we can write:

$$a = l \times w$$

Each letter has a specific meaning, and the relationship between them is set for all time. We say that this is 'the formula for the area of a rectangle', and with a simple move of the letters we can get 'the formula for the length of a rectangle':

$$l = {}^a/_w$$

or 'the formula for the width of a rectangle':

$$w = {}^a/_l$$

11

In other words, the property we are trying to find is usually written first, on one side of the equals sign, and the manipulation of the other properties which is necessary to find it, is written on the other side. Like all equations, it balances, but unlike other equations, the 'x' stands for something specific, often a scientific or economic relationship; such as when finding the area of a circle, $A=\pi r^2$.

Formulae expressed symbolically are introduced at Level 5, and there is then no ambiguity about the understanding required: ***'Use the fact that the perimeter p of a rectangle is given by p = 2(a+b) where a and b are the dimensions'*** (AT3 Level 5 Examples).

Children learn to cope with such abstraction through their work with functions and equations, and should meet formulae through other areas of the mathematics curriculum and the whole curriculum. They should be encouraged to graph the relationships which they discover.

Inequalities

The concept of an inequality is thought to be too difficult for primary children, and indeed is not found in the National Curriculum until Level 7. It is therefore beyond the scope of this book, but teachers who wish to introduce the idea to their older juniors could do so through the concept of a truth set. Some inequalities and their truth sets are listed below to illustrate the concept. All assume that we are only dealing with positive whole numbers.

Inequality	Truth set
❑ < 5	{0, 1, 2, 3, 4}
6 > 4 + ❑	{0, 1}
3 < ❑ < 7	{4, 5, 6}

Teachers may wish to extend such work by asking the children to find the truth set if the numbers can be negative or decimals.

The National Curriculum

How the concepts of the two definitions of algebra relate to the strands of the National Curriculum can be seen through the following diagram:

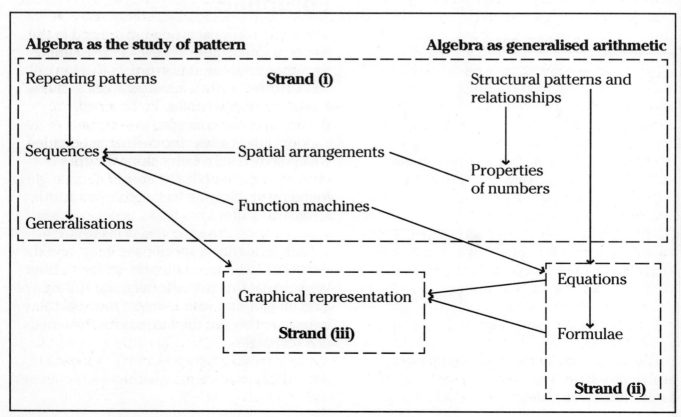

Structure of the book

The first two chapters of this book deal with the *content* of Attainment Target 3 of the National Curriculum. Chapter One looks at algebra as the study of pattern, while Chapter Two deals with algebra as generalised arithmetic. As can be seen from the diagram on page 12, there are interrelated concepts – spatial arrangements, function machines and graphical representation – which will need to appear in both chapters. The introduction to each of these three concepts, and an account of ways of teaching them, is included in Chapter One.

Each concept within Chapters One and Two is introduced through a section of background information. These sections are designed to help any teacher who feels that he or she does not totally understand the content of that particular area of algebra. The descriptions are, therefore, *not* of activities to use with the children, though such work is used as an illustration of ideas.

This background section is followed by specific ideas for activities, divided into Key Stage 1 and Key Stage 2 – although this is often a very loose distinction. Most of these ideas can be adapted for different age groups, and many children move easily between activities for the top of one key stage and the bottom of another.

The activities have also been divided into ones that are 'structured' and ones that are 'open-ended'. Although the most stimulating learning – and some would say the only *true* learning – is found through open-ended or 'investigative' activity, it is recognised that many teachers wish to use closed activities for reinforcement, for revision and consolidation and as an introduction for children who are not used to an open way of working and require a staged approach to it. Also, many games and computer programs which provide stimulating input for algebra are not particularly open-ended.

Closed activities can naturally lead to more open-ended activities and therefore, rather than split an activity into two sections, many parts of the structured sections contain questions to lead children into exploration.

Each activity is mapped to the levels of the statements of attainment and, where relevant, photocopiable pages for teacher use and pupil worksheets are found at the end of the book.

Chapter Three illustrates how the content of Attainment Target 3 can be applied to one particular starting point. The concepts of algebra have been divided into strands in the National Curriculum, and further subdivided in this book, but in many cases they are interdependent. Children should be encouraged to use all the means available to push forward their understanding.

Also, the way that an idea is presented – perhaps being labelled as suitable for a particular age group or implying this through the style of illustration or language – often leads readers to assume that it is *not* suitable for some other group of children. This chapter will show how, very often, one idea can provide all ability levels with a means to learn or practise their algebraic understanding.

Chapter Four draws links between algebra and the rest of the mathematics curriculum. As with Attainment Target 1 (Using and applying mathematics), the algebra concepts should not stand alone if they are to have any true meaning. Teachers may wish to use the activities of Chapters One and Two to introduce and reinforce algebraic concepts, but true understanding comes from the application of an idea to a completely different sphere.

Similarly, mathematics should not stand alone in the overall experience of the children. At the time of writing this book, there is a stated aim of the government to encourage teachers away from a thematic approach. Most schools, however, probably prefer to provide a balanced scheme of work with the curriculum delivered through both subject-based lessons and topic teaching. Certain parts of the curriculum cannot easily be worked into a topic – often the attempt to do so leads to trivialising of the subject and a rather tokenist feel to the lesson planning; for example, 'We have to get some number work out of "Dinosaurs", so let's count their legs – how many legs would three dinosaurs have?' We have all been guilty of such machinations, and it *can* lead to greater motivation for the children, but it is not exactly in the spirit of topic teaching which aims to make all the subjects involved truly relevant. However, some topics do contain obvious and necessary links with mathematics – necessary in that the topic cannot truly be covered without the mathematical input. Chapter Five looks at possible topics where algebra concepts play an integral part.

A glossary of terms is included as an appendix. Concepts can also be traced using the index at the end of the book.

Chapter One
The study of pattern

The concepts found in the study of pattern can be roughly organised under five headings: repeating patterns and sequences; spatial arrangements; generalising; function machines; and graphical representation. These five concepts play an important part in the understanding of algebra for *all* ability levels, even though statements relating to each one might only be found in one or two of the levels of attainment. For example, function machines are mentioned at Levels 3 and 4 of Attainment Target 3, yet they are also an ideal vehicle both for early years logic work (for example, a machine which changes red shapes to blue and vice versa) and for picturing the generation of mapping at Levels 5 and 6 (for example, a machine which doubles the number and adds 4). Therefore, activities involving each concept will be found at both Key Stage 1 and Key Stage 2.

Repeating patterns and sequences

The search for meaning is an essential part of mathematical activity. This search very often involves looking for, exploring and trying to explain patterns. Therefore, by encouraging children always to be on the look-out for patterns you help them develop extremely important skills for their mathematical progress.

Children enjoy playing with numbers and are fascinated by the patterns that appear. For example, children asked to enter a repeating number pattern into a calculator and then manipulate it by, let us say, adding a different pattern over and over or multiplying the pattern by a small number over and over will be intrigued for hours.

For example:

Enter 2, 3, 2, 3, 2, 3, ...

add 1, 2, 1, 2, 1, 2, ... over and over.

The results are: 3, 5, 3, 5, 3, 5, ...

4, 7, 4, 7, 4, 7, ...
5, 9, 5, 9, 5, 9, ...
7, 1, 7, 1, 7, 1, ...
8, 3, 8, 3, 8, 3, ...
9, 5, 9, 5, 9, 5, ...

Children find these patterns fascinating in themselves, but their attention can also be drawn to the following questions:

• What happens if you take the pairs of numbers and add them together? For example:

3 + 5 = 8;
4 + 7 = 11;
5 + 9 = 14;
7 + 1 = 8;
8 + 3 = 11;
9 + 5 = 14....

This gives a new cycle of numbers 8, 11, 14, 8, 11, 14....

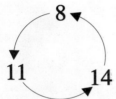

• Will other adding patterns give cycles?

• Why isn't there a line beginning with 6?

Patterns of all kinds are evident around us and children should be given the opportunity to explore them. For example, the manufactured world, that is the world we have created, is full of patterns: from setting the table, through listening to and producing music, to the wallpaper on our bedroom walls. The structure of frieze and wallpaper patterns is a field of mathematical study in itself.

Frieze patterns occur along a straight line (that is, they are one-dimensional) and are often called border patterns. Wallpaper patterns occur across a surface and are hence two-dimensional. Frieze patterns repeat horizontally:

Wallpaper patterns repeat horizontally and vertically (and also in other directions!):

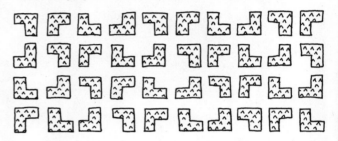

Nature too is steeped in pattern, with growth obeying complex relationships which we see in the beauty of snowflakes, shell spirals, crystals and in the branching of rivers. Noticing and appreciating these patterns can enthuse and motivate children in their maths work.

Attributes

In order to recognise patterns, we need first to be able to recognise the properties, or

attributes, of an object and how they are changing. For example, in the frieze pattern looked at previously, children need to recognise the orientation of the first 'L' shape and how that changes to make the second one, then how the second one changes to make the third one and so on. Some may see a reflection vertically, followed by a reflection horizontally, followed by a reflection vertically and so on. Others may see a quarter turn each time. Both are correct and both, therefore, form a 'rule' to give that pattern. (Such work also provides a link across the maths curriculum to Attainment Target 4: Shape and space.)

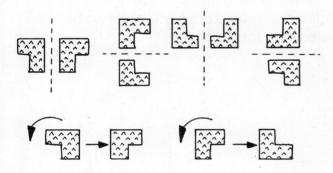

The song 'There were ten in the bed, and the little one said...' is another example of a repeating pattern which children can recognise. Children need to know what the numbers mean and recognise the constant change (one less each time) in order to remember the song. In the example of the necklace pattern shown below, in order to predict what the next bead will look like we need to recognise that the only attribute which is changing is colour, and also *how* the colour changes.

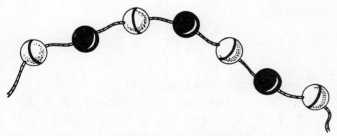

A child may be totally confused by a pattern constructed using logic blocks until it is pointed out that one property (attribute) is thickness/thinness:

It is important, therefore, in the early stages of pattern work to set problems which contain only a small number of attributes and only vary one of them at a time.

Practice at recognising attributes can be gained through sorting activities, decision trees and games such as 'The one-difference game' (see page 18 and 28). The simplest sortings activity is that in which only one attribute is considered; for example, if the red shapes were to be picked out of a set of differently coloured shapes. This can be shown on a Venn diagram:

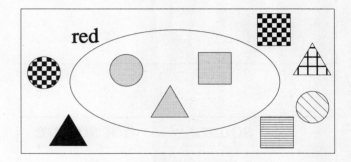

Alternatively, use a Carroll diagram:

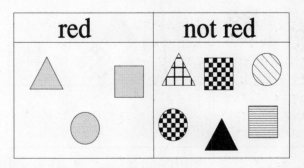

A third representation of the sorting is a decision tree. Children must decide which branch to go down as each shape is led down the tree.

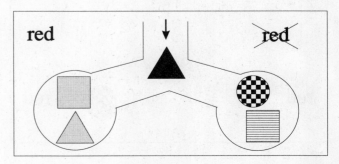

This method can be introduced using 'traffic lights'. Imagine there are traffic lights at the junction. The lights on the left will only allow red shapes through, the ones on the right will let *anything but* red shapes through. Cardboard cut-outs of lights with the instructions 'Red' and 'Not red' can be used to help the children remember.

If two attributes are to be looked at, then the pictures become more complicated:

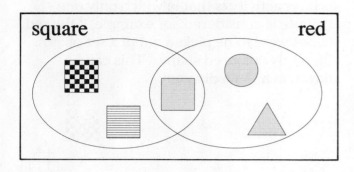

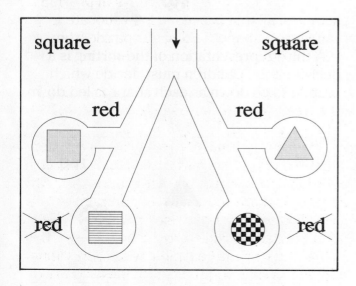

The one-difference game

'The one-difference game' involves the recognition of all the attributes of a shape, and the ability to choose a shape with only one attribute different from another. For example, if a large, yellow, thick circle is laid down, then a shape can be put beside it which is large, yellow and thick, but not a circle. An alternative is a yellow, thick circle, but a small one:

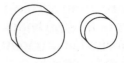

When a third piece is added, it must be different from either of the first two by one attribute, for example:

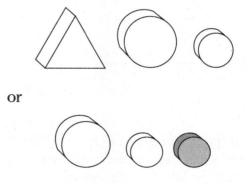

One challenge could be to lay down all the pieces from a logic block set in this way.

Linking patterns

Having recognised the attributes of a set of objects, children can then look for how these might change within a line of the objects. Is there a pattern in the order they are in? For example:

There might be a repeating pattern which could be represented by numbers: '*2, 1, 2, 1, 2, 1, 2, 1,...*' (AT3 Level 1 Examples).

Here is a slightly more difficult example:

18

This pattern could also be represented by numbers: 2, 1, 2, 3, 2, 1, 2, 3, 2, 1....

This pattern might not repeat, but be changing as it grows:

This again could be represented by numbers: 2, 1, 2, 1, 1, 2, 1, 1, 1....

Linking a pattern of shapes to numbers helps to make the number pattern have some relevance to children who are not yet familiar with addition and subtraction. Patterns with the body, with musical instruments and so on, all help motivate the children and reinforce the concept of repeated patterns and sequences. Such ideas can be found in the Key Stage 1 activities on pages 24 and 35.

Patterns can also be made from 'order of size'; for example:

or 'Ten green bottles – 10, 9, 8...' or 'The Three Bears' chairs':

These patterns offer obvious links with measurement concepts.

On a Carroll diagram, or any grid arrangement of information, there will be patterns in more than one line:

In the example shown above, going across, we always have: dog, butterfly, elephant, while going down, we always have the same four colours in the same order. Other examples of patterns on a grid are provided in the 'Graphical representation' section on page 55.

In all cases, children should be asked to explain the rule and try to continue the pattern. They should learn that you can't always tell what a pattern is going to be if you only see a little bit of it; for example, can you say what will happen next?

Can you be sure now?

Now?

You can *never* be really sure how the pattern will continue unless you can prove it, a skill not normally learned until pupils reach 'A' level standard! However, primary children should realise that if they have a lot of information they can be *fairly* sure that their rule is correct but cannot *really* know. Asking the children to try to mislead one another, as in the example above, can be quite illuminating, frustrating and fun. This is also a good opportunity to ask them to make up a non-repeating number pattern. As in previous examples, all that is needed is to allocate a number to a shape. Taking our puzzle from above, let the first counter be 1 and the second counter be 2. The children first see: 1, 2, 1, 2. Can they say what will happen next? (1, 2, 1, 2, 2) Can they now? (1, 2, 1, 2, 2, 1, 2, 1) Now? (1, 2, 1, 2, 2, 1, 2, 1, 2, 2, 1, 2, 1, 2, 2, 1, 2, 1, 2, 2) Were they right? Can they be *really* sure?

Once children are fairly competent at simple addition and subtraction of numbers, they can begin to explore sequences of numbers which are linked by either of these operations. Their first experiences will normally be through their arithmetic work, for example when generating odd numbers: 1, 3, 5, 7, 9... the rule is add two each time, starting at 1. When repeatedly adding three, starting from 0, they will find the three times table: 3, 6, 9, 12, 15.... The rule is add 3 each time, starting at 3.

There are many investigations which produce sequences of numbers. An example which is suitable for Level 2 children is the 'paper tearing' problem on page 33 which gives the number sequence: 2, 4, 8, 16.... The rule is double each time.

A young child will recognise what this sequence is doing (and if she can't, ask her to make the numbers with Multilink cubes or colour in that number of squares, so that she can *see* the doubling), but will not be able to carry the pattern very far because of her limited ability to manipulate numbers. With a calculator, however, there is the possibility of watching how the sequence grows, an activity which children find fascinating, even if the numbers produced are beyond their understanding.

Calculators

A calculator is an essential tool for both generating and exploring sequences. However, there are some problems of which the teacher of young children needs to be aware.

Some infants initially find the numbers shown on a calculator difficult to recognise. The digits shown on the buttons are fine, but the display digits do not look the same. Asking the children to make a frieze of the numbers using headless matchsticks or lolly sticks can help.

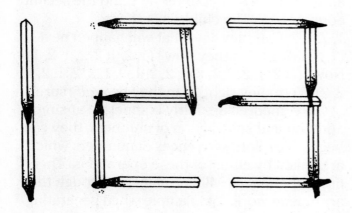

Alternatively draw a series of blank digital numbers and ask the children to colour in their own numbers.

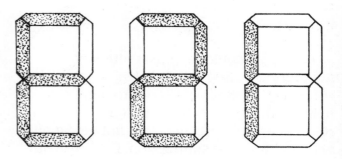

Another problem which young children may have is the order in which to input numbers into a calculator. Often, if they want to put, for example, the number 123 into their calculators, some will start at the 3 and end up with 321. We are to blame to some extent for always insisting children 'begin with the units' (which anyway is *not* the natural way to manipulate numbers). Here they must 'unlearn' that idea and think instead of the calculator 'reading' the numbers just as we read words – from left to right.

Calculators also provide a means to investigation. Many calculators sold for the primary school market have a constant function, which enables the same procedure (function) to be repeated simply by pressing the equals button. For example, try pressing: 2 + = = = = =. The children will see that the numbers progress in twos. They can identify these numbers as even numbers, and look for any patterns. (How can we recognise an even number?) Try pressing 1 + 2 = = = for the odd numbers.

Not all constant functions work with the 'button-pressing' sequence above. On some calculators, it may be + 2 = = = or 2 + 2 = =. You should check the different calculators in your school to find out what facilities they have. Some have a 'k' button, standing for 'constant'. You will also need to experiment – or read the manual – to find out how the other three rules (−, × and ÷) work in the constant mode.

The memory button can also be used for adding and/or subtracting a constant amount or for keeping a running total.

Computers

Computers can also be used to produce sequences. Teachers at Key Stage 1 may wish to use them in order to produce answers more quickly. Even with a constant function on your calculator, it takes a long time to write down all the numbers in order to find any patterns. Also, the children come to learn the speed of the computer.

Computer language

The two languages used at the primary level are LOGO and BASIC. Unfortunately, there are differences in the syntax for both languages depending on the machine you use. This book is limited, by constraints of space, to LOGO and BASIC for the BBC B, BBC Master and Archimedes machines, but the manuals provided with other machines will give the equivalent syntax.

Imagine that you and the children wish to see how repeated additions of threes go, or, for the more advanced, if there is any pattern in the first or last digits of the three times table. With a calculator, this would require writing down the answer each time the equals key is pressed in the sequence. With a short computer program the process needs only to be gone through once, in the writing of the program, and many results can be seen on the screen at one go. The following examples explain how this would be done in BASIC and in LOGO.

BASIC

If you want to show the addition aspect, type:

```
10 LET N = 3
20 PRINT N
30 LET N = N + 3
40 GOTO 20
50 END
```

The program will run when you type RUN. The lines are numbered in tens, so that other lines can be added if you want to change the program later. The computer won't accept any letter (variable) unless you tell it what the value of the variable is or how it is related to other variables. Hence, line 10 tells the computer that, to begin with, N equals 3. PRINT is a command already known to the computer and it will therefore print the number 3. (If asked to print a letter as in line 20, it will print the *value* of the letter. If you want it to print the letter itself, that is N, you must type PRINT "N".)

We now wish to add 3 to N and print out the new N. The command LET as used in line 30 increases N. As we want to continue doing this for some time, it does not make sense to include another PRINT statement and another LET statement, over and over. The power comes in being able to go back through the program using GOTO. In the example above, we GOTO line 20 and travel through the commands again. If we want to do something different other than add 3, then line 30 is the line to change.

This program would go on until the computer's available working memory was exhausted. Children are interested to see this happen, though for an addition program this will take a *very* long time. Therefore, to stop the program so that you can look for patterns you should press the ESCAPE key. It can be difficult to stop the program exactly where you wish, as the numbers come up so quickly. Alternatively, the program can be changed to

contain a counter. It will stop when the counter stops:

```
10 LET N = 3
20 FOR C = 1 TO 20
30 PRINT N
40 LET N = N + 3
50 NEXT C
60 END
```

The computer takes C as 1, works through lines 30 and 40 and, on reading NEXT C, returns to the 'FOR C =' line. It will now count C as 2 and repeat. When C = 20 it makes note not to return. If you want more, or fewer, terms in your sequence (a term is just a member of a sequence, for example 9 is the third term of this sequence) just change line 20.

If the children understand that multiplication by 3 would give the same result as repeated addition of 3, or if you do not want the children to see the program itself but only the results, then the loop idea can be used to produce an even more efficient program:

```
10 FOR N = 1 TO 20
20 PRINT 3*N
30 NEXT N
40 END
```

Only the more able top juniors can write their own programs, though many others can read and understand what a program is doing. It is valuable to let children try making changes to a short program to see what will then happen. Here are built-in investigations of infinite variety. For example:

```
10 FOR N = 1 TO 20
20 PRINT N + N
30 NEXT N
40 END
```

What happens if we change the + to * (multiplication) or – (subtraction) or to / (division)? What if we make one of the 'Ns' in line 20 be (N + 1), or N*N, or 0.5*N?

To save a BASIC program on to disk, type SAVE "NAME". You can name the program anything you like.

LOGO
The program needed in LOGO to produce the repeated addition of 3 is:

```
TO THREES :NUM
PRINT :NUM
MAKE "NUM :NUM+3
THREES :NUM
END
```

The computer learns a procedure – THREES – with which it expects to be given a number – NUM. This is the first number of the sequence (in other words 3). The program won't run if you don't provide the number. To run the program, therefore, you must type: THREES 3 or change the digit if you wish to start elsewhere. :NUM means the value of the variable, "NUM means the variable itself. Hence, the third line means make the variable equal 3 more than it is worth at the moment. To make a different sequence, change this MAKE line.

The fourth line sends the computer back to the beginning again, but this time with the new value for '"NUM'. This is called 'recursion'.

The program will run and run until the ESCAPE key is pressed.

To get a specific number of terms of the sequence, a counter is used, as in the BASIC program.

```
TO THREES
MAKE "N 3
PRINT :N
REPEAT 19 [MAKE "N :N+3 PRINT :N]
END
```

This will give the first 20 terms of the three times table. If you want to show a program using multiplication:

```
TO THREES
MAKE "N 1
PRINT :N*3
REPEAT 19[MAKE "N :N+1 PRINT :N*3]
END
```

As stated earlier, many juniors will be able to explore number sequences through manipulating such short programs. Both the

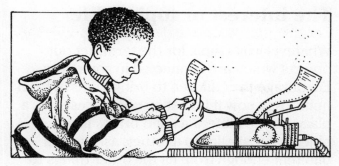

MAKE and the PRINT statements above can be changed to see what might happen.

To save a program in LOGO type SAVE "NAME, for example, here we would type SAVE "THREES. (Note that there are no quotation marks at the end.)

Which language to use

LOGO is a language specifically designed to be used by children and hence, when being used for its original purpose of graphics, causes fewer problems of syntax than BASIC. However, it can be less easy to understand for arithmetic work.

BASIC is felt by many to be easier to use than LOGO for arithmetic work, though this may be a reflection of the teachers' previous experience. BASIC is closer to the types of programs used in commerce and academic programming and therefore is more familiar to anyone with such a background. However, it should be remembered that the children do not have the same advantage, and approach both languages completely fresh.

Many teachers prefer to use LOGO as there is then only one language for the children to learn – LOGO being invaluable for the turtle geometry necessary for Attainment Target 4. Readers must make up their own minds!

Spreadsheets

A spreadsheet is a grid used for storing numbers. Anyone who has experience of accounting or bookkeeping will be familiar with this arrangement. Spreadsheets on a computer, however, are much more powerful than simple devices for the storage and retrieval of figures. Rows and columns can be added or subtracted automatically, multiplied by a constant number, and manipulated in many other ways. Rows can be combined with other rows, and columns with other columns using a simple command, and formulae can be incorporated – the programs doing the calculations for you.

These facilities enable quick and easy generation of number patterns. For example, here the rows are labelled 1 to 10 and the columns A to F. The numbers 1 to 10 have been entered into column A.

	A	B	C	D	E	F
1	1					
2	2					
3	3					
4	4					
5	5					
6	6					
7	7					
8	8					
9	9					
10	10					

Column B can then be programmed to equal Column A + 1:

	A	B	C	D	E	F
1	1	2				
2	2	3				
3	3	4				
4	4	5				
5	5	6				
6	6	7				
7	7	8				
8	8	9				
9	9	10				
10	10	11				

Columns A and B can then be multiplied together and put in Column C:

	A	B	C	D	E	F
1	1	2	2			
2	2	3	6			
3	3	4	12			
4	4	5	20			
5	5	6	30			
6	6	7	42			
7	7	8	56			
8	8	9	72			
9	9	10	90			
10	10	11	110			

Finally, Column D can be made to equal half of Column C:

	A	B	C	D	E	F
1	1	2	2	1		
2	2	3	6	3		
3	3	4	12	6		
4	4	5	20	10		
5	5	6	30	15		
6	6	7	42	21		
7	7	8	56	28		
8	8	9	72	36		
9	9	10	90	45		
10	10	11	110	55		

The numbers in Column D belong to a sequence called the 'triangle numbers', and will be met several times throughout this book. Such manipulation is easy once the children are familiar with the software, and opens up a new avenue for exploration.

The spreadsheet could have been programmed directly, making Column B equal: Column A × (Column A + 1) ÷ 2. However, by spacing the calculation as above the children are able to see every stage of the process. Conceptually, this is much easier than writing the short program, and therefore younger children can create their own number patterns with a computer.

NB These diagrams are not of any particular spreadsheet package, as there are several on the market (see Appendix A on page 203).

Both calculators and computers have further roles to play in primary algebra. The *'difference method'* of exploring sequences (AT3 Level 6 Examples) and the *'trial and improvement'* method of solving equations (AT3 Level 6 PoS and Examples) both require calculating aids. The former is described in this chapter under *'Generalising'* (see page 45), the latter in Chapter Two on page 110.

Structured activities for Key Stage 1

The following short activities can be used as preliminary work on attribute recognition.

The interest or topic table

Whatever your topic for the term, set out objects which are connected in some way. Encourage the children to bring items in from home. Ask how it is that an object deserves a place on the table. If a child brings in an object very similar to another, ask, 'Is this different enough from all the other things to go on the table?' If the children decide that it is and can give reasons, then the object can be added, if not, then it could be swapped for a very similar old one already on the table, and no feelings are hurt!

Tidying time

Everything in the classroom has a home and small objects tend to be stored together with others which are the same in some way. Children new to school have to learn these rules (for example, the top drawer is for sorting, the next drawer is for Multilink, the box for Duplo) and to recognise the differences between the kinds of apparatus. A whole world of sorting activity is therefore present in tidying up.

Out to play

Whenever you have time, send the children out in sets. For example, everyone with trainers on go now, anyone left who has blond hair now, next anyone else who has some red in their jumper and so on.

You can line them up in the same way, hence having many different ways of lining up which is fairer than using the same way (such as alphabetical) all the time.

Sorting

What you need

Sets of sorting equipment such as logic shapes, sets of building shapes, sets of real objects (such as leaves or tins) or ones connected with a class topic; large Venn, Carroll and tree diagrams, or commercially produced logic material.

What to do

Begin with the Venn diagram. Taking one set of objects as an example, point out to the children the attribute you are interested in, such as rolling. Pick one object and check the children can identify the attribute or lack of it (for example, a cube doesn't roll). Place this object on the sorting picture. Let the children try the next object, while explaining to you why they have made particular choices. Let the children finish sorting the set.

As a development, ask the children for a different attribute which the set of objects has and change the heading of the Venn diagram accordingly. Finally, the children should decide among themselves on an attribute, complete the sorting, and then present you with this *fait accompli* asking *you* to identify how they have chosen to do their sorting.

How this activity develops is a matter of personal choice. You may choose to reinforce the Venn diagram with other sets of materials before introducing a different form of sorting arrangement, or you may wish to capitalise on the familiarity the children now have with the present set to introduce, for example, Carroll diagrams.

NC mapping

AT3 – working towards Level 1
AT1 – Level 1 (a) (b) (c)
AT5 – Level 1 (a)

Hot seat

What you need

Sets of sorting equipment such as logic shapes and building shapes; sets of real objects such as leaves and tins; card.

What to do

Show the children a set of sorting objects. Ask them to identify the attributes and then list them in reverse order of importance. The group should write these attributes on cards, in this order; one card for each object.

To play the 'Hot seat', one child must choose a card, unseen by the others, and sit on a seat in front of the group. The sorting material is laid out between her and the group. She reads the first (vaguest) attribute aloud. If the children think they can guess the object, they must put up their hands.

For example, the child may read:
• It doesn't roll.
• It has square corners.
• It has six faces.
• All the faces are squares.

It is not until the last statement that the children can be sure that the shape is a cube. Only one guess is allowed for each attribute read out. If the guess is correct, this child is next in the hot seat, otherwise the next attribute is read out.

NC mapping

AT3 – working towards Level 1
AT1 – Level 1 (a) (b) (c)
AT5 – Level 1 (a)

What's my line?

What you need

Multilink, pegs, pegboards, counters or strings of beads.

What to do

Begin by making a simple repeating pattern for the children to examine. Ask them to continue it. Can they describe it? How could they change it?

The children should now devise their own patterns and ask other children to identify them or continue them.

As an extension, show the children a pattern which has one or two pieces missing. Can they tell you the missing link? Ask them to make patterns and remove pieces for others to identify (start with one missing piece only).

NC mapping

AT3 – Level 1 (a)
AT1 – Level 1 (a) (b) (c)

Telephone lines

What you need

Multilink, pegs, pegboards, counters or strings of beads, toy or pretend telephones, screens.

What to do

With a group of children, ask them to imagine that one of them is far away and wants to tell the others what his pattern looks like. He will have to use a telephone to talk to them. Send one child behind the screen with one set of the pattern-making material. He must make a pattern and describe it to the others only using the attributes and numbers. They must try to make the same pattern with their sets. Remove the screen and see who has got the pattern right.

If there are a lot of mistakes, the child behind the screen will probably have described his pattern wrongly. The children should discuss this and say what *should* have been said.

NC mapping

AT3 – Level 1 (a)
AT1 – Level 1 (a) (b) (c)

Stand in line

What you need

PE mats, PE apparatus (optional), paper, pencils.

What to do

Ask groups of children to stand in line making a pattern with their bodies, for example, holding their hands up/hands down/hands up/hands down, or kneeling, sitting, standing, kneeling, sitting, standing. Can other groups copy the pattern silently? Can they explain it in words? What if a bit is missed out? Can the children find ways of recording their body patterns on paper?

This activity could be tied in with PE sequences, use of apparatus and so on.

NC mapping

AT3 – Level 1 (a)
AT1 – Level 1 (a) (b) (c)

Feel the rhythm

What you need

Percussion or other musical instruments (or anything to make a sound), PE apparatus, pencils, paper.

What to do

Children love silly words and the rhythm of nonsense rhymes. Put them together to make repeating patterns, for example: 'nicky, nacky, noy, polacky, nicky, nacky, noy, polacky...'. Who can make the longest repeating pattern?

Use musical instruments – especially percussion – to make rhythmic patterns. Ask the children to listen carefully to each other and try to copy the sounds.

This work could be integrated with the 'Stand in line' activity and PE sequences.

Can the children find some way of recording their sound patterns on paper?

NC mapping

AT3 – Level 1 (a)
AT1 – Level 1 (a) (b) (c)

Number patterns

What you need

Percussion instruments, calculators, paper, pencils.

What to do

A number pattern, such as that quoted in the National Curriculum document ('**2,1,2,1,2,1, 2,1,**...' AT3 Level 1 Examples), does not have much inherent interest to a young child. However, combining the numbers with other concepts can attract their interest. For example:
• use the numbers to record how often to strike a percussion instrument: 'bong, bong, *pause*, bong, *pause*, bong, bong, *pause*, bong, *pause*...';
• use the numbers to represent which instrument to play, for example 1 for a drum and 2 for a tambourine;
• use the numbers to represent body shapes, for example 1 means stand up straight and 2 means kneel down;
• use the number of syllables in children's names to make patterns: for example: Lisa (2) and John (1) will give a rhythmic pattern: Lisa, John, Lisa, John.... Can the children find some other patterns in the names of their class?

NC mapping

AT3 – Level 1 (a)
AT1 – Level 1 (a) (b) (c)

House numbers

What you need

A trip to look at street numbers or a picture/ photograph of houses showing their numbers or ask the children to look for the numbers on their way to school; calculators.

What to do

Talk with the children about street numbers. Explain how on one side of the street numbers often go: 1, 3, 5, 7, 9... while on the other they go: 2, 4, 6, 8, 10.... What numbers will come next in both sequences? How can the children work it out? (What is the difference between numbers that come next to each other?) What do we call these numbers?

Introduce the names 'odd' and 'even'. Show the children how to get odd numbers on the calculator. How far can they go? When will the odd numbers end? Can they see a pattern in the ends of the numbers (the last digit)?

Can the children tell you how we could get the even numbers on the calculator? Go through the same process as above for even numbers. Follow up with 'Odds and evens: 1' on page 93.

NC mapping

AT3 – Level 2 (a)
AT1 – Level 1 (a) (b) (c)
    – Level 2 (b)
AT2 – Level 1 (a) (b)

Counter

What you need

The 'Counter' computer program (on *SLIMWAM2*, from the Association of Teachers of Mathematics/ATM see Appendix A), paper, pencils.

What to do

This computer program runs through sequences. The sequence is set by the teacher. The computer is pre-programmed to play musical notes; a different note for every number from 0 to 9. You can choose to have the computer play notes relating to the units, the tens, or the hundreds value of the numbers in the sequence. You can also choose to hide parts of the numbers.

Set the program first to play the counting numbers, and check the children can hear the differences. Next try going up in twos. Can they count how many different notes there are before the pattern repeats? What happens with fives?

Set the program to play the notes for the tens, and to count in threes, say. Ask the children to put up their hands when the tens change. Pause the program at this point and discuss what is happening. Hide the tens and units digits and repeat. Can they tell you the whole number when the tens note changes? (This is a good activity for place value and mental methods.)

This program provides a good amount of variety and the level of abstraction varies from Level 1 to beyond primary. The manual to accompany the *SLIMWAM2* programs, *Some More Lessons in Mathematics with a microcomputer*, provides many more ideas for its use (see Appendix A).

NC mapping

AT3 – working towards Level 4 (a)
AT1 – Level 2 (b) (c) working towards
Level 3 (d)
AT2 – Level 1 (a) (b)

The one-difference game

This activity is for older infants and all juniors.

What you need

One set of logic shapes per group, a good deal of space if children use large floor sets of logic shapes.

What to do

'The one-difference game' was introduced at the beginning of the 'Repeating patterns and sequences' section on page 18. Show the children two pieces from the set. Ask them questions such as 'In what ways are these the same?' or 'In what ways are these different?' to establish the attributes. Next ask them to describe an individual piece, lay it down and ask them to choose what to change; for example, they may choose to change the size or the shape. Which piece would it become? Lay the two pieces together; for example:

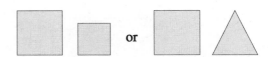

Ask the children if anyone can find another piece which has *one* difference between either of these shapes, for example the colour or the thickness. The new shape is laid down next to the one it differs by one from. This could be:

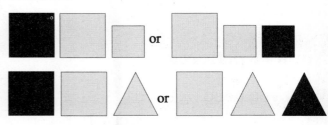

Activities based on this 'one-difference' can be collaborative or competitive, and the number of children involved is flexible. For a competitive game, pieces are shared out between the children and the teacher chooses a starting piece. The children take turns to lay down connecting pieces, missing a go if they cannot match either end of the 'snake' of pieces. The last child able to add to the snake is the winner.

If playing collaboratively, children can be set the following problems:
• Can they use all the pieces from the set?
• Can they put down all the pieces so that the last one joins up with the first one (still with only one difference), that is, can they make the snake bite his tail? (The answer is yes!)
• Can they play with two differences (for juniors)?
• Can they go in two directions (for older juniors), as on a Carroll diagram?

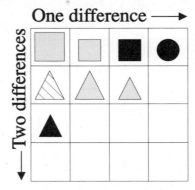

NC mapping

Although the level quoted for the concepts involved in this game is low (working towards

28

Level 1), the game itself is far beyond that level in difficulty. It therefore serves as a revision of attribute work for any age from top infant upwards.

Structured activities for Key Stage 2

Calculator patterns

What you need
Calculators, paper, pencils.

What to do
Ask the children to do the following exercises.
• Put the number 10 in their calculators and keep adding 10. What happens? Ask them to describe it to a friend.
• Put a different starting number in – they could try 1 or 5. What do they think will happen if they keep adding 10 now? They should try it and see.
• Put 5 in their calculators and keep adding 5. Tell them to watch the last digit. What do they notice?

If the children's calculators contain a constant function, the work can be speeded up. For example, 10 + = = = will give a series of additions of 10.

NC mapping
AT3 – working towards Level 3 (a)
AT1 – Level 1 (a) (b) (c)
      – Level 2 (b)
AT2 – working towards Level 3 (a) (b)

Pattern blanks

What you need
Photocopiable page 179.

What to do
Give each child a copy of photocopiable page 000 and discuss with them the first example. Ask them to continue working on the sheet by themselves. The children may return for help with the last two questions (3 to 21 and 24 to 0). These can be visualised as, for example, a frog jumping across a river where 3 is on one side, 21 on the other. The blanks are stones, or lily pads, equally spaced. How big are the frog's jumps?

Those problems devised by the children themselves can be given to others to solve.

NC mapping
AT3 – Level 2 (b)
AT1 – Level 1 (c)
AT2 – Level 1 (a) (b)

Pattern families

What you need
Prepare 32 cards which follow four card sequences, for example:
    1, 3, 5, 7
    2, 4, 6, 8
    5, 10, 15, 20
    3, 6, 9, 12

What to do
Shuffle the cards and teach the children to play the game, which works exactly as 'Happy families'. Each child is dealt four cards. The rest are placed down in a pile in the middle of the table. The first child asks the child next to him (going round in a circle) if she has a 6, for example. If she has, she must hand it over. If she hasn't, the first child must take a card from the pile. This process is then repeated by the second child. The first child to lay down a pattern of four cards and explain it to the others is the winner.

Alternatively, set the game up as before but this time the top card from the pile is turned to face up. If the first child wants this card, he takes it and replaces it with a discard – face up again. Otherwise, he takes the next card from the pile, and again makes a discard. This is repeated by the second child. The first child to lay down a pattern of four cards and explain it to the others is the winner.

NC mapping
AT3 – working towards Level 4 (a)
AT1 – Level 2 (b) working towards Level 3 (c)
AT2 – Level 1 (a) (b)

Multiplication patterns

Readers will be aware of the patterns made on a hundred square when tables are filled in. This activity looks at other patterns.

What you need

Hundred squares (photocopiable page 180), coloured pencils, calculators.

What to do

Ask the children to choose any number either along the top or down the left-hand side of the square and colour it in.

1	2	3	4	5	6	7	8	9	10
11	12	13	14	15	16	17	18	19	20
21	22	23	24	25	26	27	28	29	30
31	32	33	34	35	36	37	38	39	49
41	42	43	44	45	46	47	48	49	50
51	52	53	54	55	56	57	58	59	60
61	62	63	64	65	66	67	68	69	70
71	72	73	74	75	76	77	78	79	80
81	82	83	84	85	86	87	88	89	90
91	92	93	94	95	96	97	98	99	100

Then tell them to colour in all the numbers they get if they repeatedly add 11. Next, they must choose a number along the top or down the right-hand side of the square, colour it in, and then colour in all the numbers they get if they repeatedly add 9.

Can the children explain why they get the patterns? Where do the patterns meet? Is there anything special about the numbers where they meet? Let them try again using different starting numbers.

NC mapping

AT3 – Level 3 (a)
    – Level 4 (a)
AT1 – Level 3 (d)
    – Level 4 (a) (d)
AT2 – from Level 2 (a) to Level 3 (b)

Missing links

What you need

Number sequences of the required difficulty for the group with the numbers written within a chain, so that the children can fill in the 'missing links'.

What to do

Make up some number sequences of the required difficulty, for example:
- 4, 7, 10, 13, 16, 19, 22...;
- 1, 2, 4, 7, 11, 16, 22...;
- 48, 47, 45, 42, 38, 33, 27...;
- 1, 3, 7, 13, 21, 31, 43....

Write the numbers in links of a chain and leave blank links to be completed by the children – either at the end of the sequence or within a sequence. For example:

Can the children describe the sequence in their own words?

NC mapping

AT3 – Level 2 (b)
    – Level 4 (a)
AT1 – Level 3 (a) (d)
    – Level 4 (d)
AT2 – from Level 2 (a) to Level 4(b)

More missing links

What you need

Pencils, paper.

What to do

This is a more difficult version of the 'Missing links' activity (see above). For children who need a more stretching activity ask them to find a rule to fit the following sequences, fill in the gaps and continue the pattern.

1, —, 7, —, —, 16
1, —, —, 7, —, 16
1, —, —, —, 7, 16

Make up some similar problems for your friends.'

NC mapping

AT3 – Level 2 (b)
    – Level 4 (a)
AT1 – Level 3 (a) (d)
    – Level 4 (d)
AT2 – from Level 2 (a) to Level 4 (b)

Monty

What you need

The computer program 'Monty' (on *SLIMWAM2*, from the Association of Teachers of Mathematics), hundred squares (photocopiable page 180), multiplication squares, tracing paper, squared paper, blank 10×10 grid (photocopiable page 180).

What to do

This computer program requires children to identify parts of the multiplication square (and other squares) through recognising number patterns. Grids begin with simple addition patterns, building to quite complex multiplication patterns.

At each level of difficulty, the children are presented with a grid, which they need to study. The grid is removed and a python, 'Monty', moves around the screen. When Monty stops, one of the numbers which is under his body (and part of the hidden grid) is revealed. The children must try to identify the other numbers.

There are many follow-up activities which can be worked on away from the screen. For example, give the children squared paper, on which one of the grid patterns has been copied, and a piece of tracing paper. Ask them to draw a python on the tracing paper and add only one of its numbers. Other children must then try to find the other 'Monty' numbers, having seen the grid on the screen or looked at the grid on paper, but without the copy.

The children must allow others plenty of time to study a pattern before removing it and giving them a Monty puzzle.

NC mapping

AT3 – Level 3 (a)
    – Level 4 (a)
AT1 – Level 3 (d)
    – Level 4 (a) (d)
AT2 – from Level 2 (a) to Level 3 (b)

Open-ended activities for Key Stage 1

Paint prints

What you need

Examples of repeating-shape patterns such as wallpaper offcuts, pottery, fabric and so on; materials for printing, such as potato pieces, cotton reels and sponge pieces; paints, paper or fabric.

What to do

Show the children examples of repeating-shape patterns and ask them to identify the repeat. Can they describe it in words? Do the colours follow a pattern, or is it the shapes that vary? How could the children change the pattern?

Using such things as cut potato shapes, old jigsaw pieces, cotton reels, sorting shapes, their hands and rubber stamps, ask the children to make their own repeating patterns. Can the children describe *each other's* patterns? (Often they will notice new things.)

NC mapping

AT3 – Level 1 (a)
AT1 – Level 1 (a) (b) (c)

Worm walks

What you need

Squared paper, pencils.

What to do

This activity will give repeating number patterns a physical meaning, and hence more interest for the children. Show the children a simple repeating pattern, for example 1, 2, 3, 1, 2, 3, 1, 2, 3.... This can be split into its repeated 'sections', that is into groups of '1, 2, 3'. These sections can then be displayed on squared paper. The 'worm' moves by the first distance, 1, turns anti-clockwise, moves by the second distance, 2, turns anti-clockwise, moves by the third distance, 3, turns anti-clockwise, and then repeats. This gives the following shapes in succession:

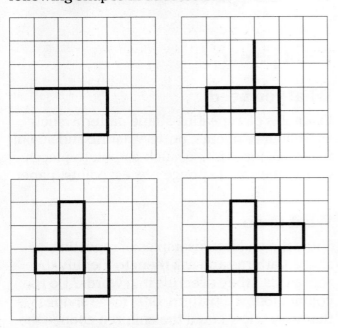

Ask the children to make up their own 'walks'. Which ones return to the starting point? Which worms go off in a particular direction? What if we use negative numbers?

NB: Juniors love this activity, although it doesn't map to high levels of the National Curriculum!

NC mapping

AT3 – Level 1 (a)
AT1 – Level 1 (a) (b) (c)
   – Level 2 (b)
AT4 – Level 1 (b)

Calculator repeats

What you need

Calculators, paper, pencils.

What to do

Ask the children to put a simple repeating pattern, for example 2,1,2,1,2,1, in their

calculators. What happens if they add a different pattern? For example:

212121 + 323232 = 535353.

Let them continue adding 323232. What happens? Can they write down what they get each time? Our example will give:

535353
858585
1181817
1505049
1828281
2151513
2474745
2797977
3121209
3444441
3767673
4090905
4414137
4737369

Such patterns raise a lot of questions, which initially children will need to be made aware of by their teacher, while later they should be encouraged to look for them themselves. For example:
• There are simple patterns until the numbers exceed six digits. Then the pattern is broken by the first and last or last but one number. What if we add these two numbers together? (We get one of the numbers in the pattern!)
• What can they notice about the last digits? (They form a cycle of the odd numbers up to 9.)
• What can they notice about the first digits? (We get three 1s, three 2s, three 3s, three 4s.)
• Do they notice anything else about the numbers?
• Would they get the same sort of patterns if they chose to add a different pattern?

An alternative activity is to multiply the initial pattern by a small number, and record what happens. Let the children 'play' with such patterns, encouraging discussion, recording and the forming of conclusions.

NC mapping

AT3 – Level 1 (a)
AT1 – Level 2 (a) (b) (c)
AT2 – Level 1 (a)

Lots of equals

What you need
Calculators, paper, pencils.

What to do
Ask the children to put a small number in their calculators and then press: + = = =. (The sequence pressed will depend upon the type of calculator used – see page 20.) Ask them to try again and this time write down what they get each time. What happens? Can they see any patterns?

Some calculators work their constant functions: + 2 = = =. Some do it both ways round. Ask the children to experiment to find out all the things their calculators can do.

NC mapping
AT3 – Level 2 (a)
    – working towards Level 3 (a)
AT1 – Level 2 (a) (b) (c)
    – Level 3 (c)
AT2 – Level 1 (a) (b)
    – working towards Level 2(a)
      and Level 3 (b)

Paper tearing

What you need
Large sheets of paper for tearing, pencils, paper, calculators.

What to do
Ask the children to take a piece of paper and tear it in half. How many pieces have they got? Ask them to tear the new pieces in half. How many have they got now? Ask them to continue doing this. Can they describe the pattern? Can they model the way the numbers grow with Multilink?

NC mapping
AT3 – Level 2 (a)
    – working towards Level 3 (a)
AT1 – Level 2 (a) (b) (c)
    – Level 3 (c)
AT2 – working towards Level 3 (b) (c)

Bracelets

What you need
Paper, calculators.

What to do
Ask the children for a starting number and then ask them for an adding number. Show them what happens when you repeatedly add the adding number, but only write down the units. For example, if you have a starting number 7 and add 4 each time you get:
$7 \rightarrow 11 \rightarrow 15 \rightarrow 19 \rightarrow 23 \rightarrow 27 \rightarrow 31 \rightarrow 35 \rightarrow 39 \rightarrow 43...$

The units make a bracelet:

Let the children look for other bracelets. What about subtracting instead? The results of this investigation can be shown graphically by drawing a circle with the circumference marked with 10 equal spaces, labelled 0 to 9. The children can then join up the numbers as they appear in the sequence.

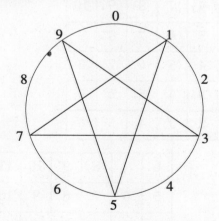

NC mapping
AT3 – Level 2 (a)
    – working towards Level 3 (a)
AT1 – Level 2 (a) (b) (c)
    – Level 3 (c)
AT2 – working towards Level 2 (a) (b)

Addition patterns

What you need

Blank addition squares (photocopiable page 180), pencils.

What to do

Show the children how to fill in the addition square.

+	1	2	3	4	5	6
6	7	8	9	10	11	12
5	6	7	8	9	10	11
4	5	6	7	8	9	10
3	4	5	6	7	8	9
2	3	4	5	6	7	8
1	2	3	4	5	6	7

When the group have all finished, discuss with them any number patterns they can see in it. For example:

Ask how the numbers on one side might be

+	1	2	3	4	5	6
6	7	8	9	10	11	12
5	6	7	8	9	10	11
4	5	6	7	8	9	10
3	4	5	6	7	8	9
2	3	4	5	6	7	8
1	2	3	4	5	6	7

+	1	2	3	4	5	6
6	7	8	9	10	11	12
5	6	7	8	9	10	11
4	5	6	7	8	9	10
3	4	5	6	7	8	9
2	3	4	5	6	7	8
1	2	3	4	5	6	7

changed, for example the horizontal line could become the odd numbers. When the new square is completed, what new patterns appear? Ask the children to find as many different ways as they can to change the horizontal line, the vertical line, or both, and describe their new number patterns.

NC mapping

AT3 – Level 2 (a)
  – working towards Level 3 (a)
AT1 – Level 2 (a) (b) (c)
  – Level 3 (c)
AT2 – working towards Level 2 (a)

Stamps

What you need

Photocopiable page 181, glue, paper, pencils.

What to do

Show the children some cut-out stamps from photocopiable page 181. If they wished to send a letter costing 3p, in how many ways could they stick down the stamps?

What about for 2p, 4p and/or 5p? Can the children see a pattern in the answers?

NC mapping

AT3 – Level 2 (a)
AT1 – Level 2 (a) (b) (c)
  – Level 3 (c)
AT2 – working towards Level 2 (a)

Trains

What you need

Cuisenaire rods, paper, pencils.

What to do

Using Cuisenaire rods, show the children a

3-rod. Explain that this is a 3-train, made from a carriage 3 long. What other trains could they make the same length?

They could have a 2 plus a 1 carriage, a 1 plus a 2 carriage, or three 1 carriages. How many ways are there to make a 4-train or a 5-train and so on? Let the children try to find answers to these questions. Can they see a number pattern in their answers?

The children may decide that the second and the third trains above are the same. It doesn't matter, as long as they are consistent they will get a pattern, though it will be a different one.

NC mapping

AT3 – Level 2 (a)
AT1 – Level 2 (a) (b) (c)
 – Level 3 (c)
AT2 – working towards Level 2 (a)

Open-ended activities for Key Stage 2

There are many practical ways to produce number patterns, each of which can lead on to children setting their own similar problems and carrying out open-ended exploration. Spatial arrangements are both accessible and very popular, and are dealt with fully on page 40. The activities below show a variety of tasks which do not begin with a spatial arrangement.

The dice give it

What you need

Two dice per group, paper, pencils, several copies of the hundred square.

What to do

Demonstrate how a random sequence can be generated by throwing two dice to the children; the first die gives the starting

number and the second die gives the adding number (you could use two differently coloured dice). Write down the first few numbers of the sequence produced. Colour in the sequence on a hundred square. What about subtracting and multiplying?

NC mapping

AT3 – Level 2 (a)
 – working towards Level 3 (a)
AT1 – Level 2 (a) (b) (c)
 – Level 3 (c)
AT2 – working towards Level 2 (a) (b)

The table gives it

What you need

Blank 10 × 10 square grids (photocopiable page 180), lists of sequences which the children have already explored.

What to do

Remind the children of the number patterns that can be seen on a hundred square and on a multiplication square. For example, on a hundred square, vertical lines give numbers ending with the same digit. Can the children explain why?

1	2	3	4	5	6	7	8	9	10
11	12	13	14	15	16	17	18	19	20
21	22	23	24	25	26	27	28	29	30
31	32	33	34	35	36	37	38	39	49
41	42	43	44	45	46	47	48	49	50
51	52	53	54	55	56	57	58	59	60
61	62	63	64	65	66	67	68	69	70
71	72	73	74	75	76	77	78	79	80
81	82	83	84	85	86	87	88	89	90
91	92	93	94	95	96	97	98	99	100

Adding in threes gives the following diagonals. Why? How is this connected to adding in sixes?

1	2	3	4	5	6	7	8	9	10
11	12	13	14	15	16	17	18	19	20
21	22	23	24	25	26	27	28	29	30
31	32	33	34	35	36	37	38	39	49
41	42	43	44	45	46	47	48	49	50
51	52	53	54	55	56	57	58	59	60
61	62	63	64	65	66	67	68	69	70
71	72	73	74	75	76	77	78	79	80
81	82	83	84	85	86	87	88	89	90
91	92	93	94	95	96	97	98	99	100

The digits of numbers which lie on diagonals sloping as above and below always eventually add up to the same number for each diagonal – why?

1	2	3	4	5	6	7	8	9	10
11	12	13	14	15	16	17	18	19	20
21	22	23	24	25	26	27	28	29	30
31	32	33	34	35	36	37	38	39	49
41	42	43	44	45	46	47	48	49	50
51	52	53	54	55	56	57	58	59	60
61	62	63	64	65	66	67	68	69	70
71	72	73	74	75	76	77	78	79	80
81	82	83	84	85	86	87	88	89	90
91	92	93	94	95	96	97	98	99	100

$5 = 1 + 4 = 2 + 3 = 3 + 2 = 4 + 1$

$5 + 0 = 5$

$5 + 9 = 14 \rightarrow 1 + 4 = 5$

$6 + 8 = 14 \rightarrow 1 + 4 = 5$

$7 + 7 = 14 \rightarrow 1 + 4 = 5$

$8 + 6 = 14 \rightarrow 1 + 4 = 5$

$9 + 5 = 14 \rightarrow 1 + 4 = 5$

These are called digital roots.

For the multiplication square, why are the numbers on diagonals like the one below arranged symmetrically?

1	2	3	4	5	6	7	8	9	10
2	4	6	8	10	12	14	16	18	20
3	6	9	12	15	18	21	24	27	30
4	8	12	16	20	24	28	32	36	40
5	10	15	20	25	30	35	40	45	50
6	12	18	24	30	36	42	48	54	60
7	14	21	28	35	42	49	56	63	70
8	16	24	32	40	48	56	64	72	80
9	18	27	36	45	54	63	72	81	90
10	20	30	40	50	60	70	80	90	100

7 12 15 16 15 12 7

Why does this diagonal go up two more each time?

1	2	3	4	5	6	7	8	9	10
2	4	6	8	10	12	14	16	18	20
3	6	9	12	15	18	21	24	27	30
4	8	12	16	20	24	28	32	36	40
5	10	15	20	25	30	35	40	45	50
6	12	18	24	30	36	42	48	54	60
7	14	21	28	35	42	49	56	63	70
8	16	24	32	40	48	56	64	72	80
9	18	27	36	45	54	63	72	81	90
10	20	30	40	50	60	70	80	90	100

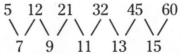

```
5   12   21   32   45   60
 \ /\ /\ /\ /\ /\ /
  7   9   11   13   15
```

What is special about the 'leading' diagonal?

1	2	3	4	5	6	7	8	9	10
2	4	6	8	10	12	14	16	18	20
3	6	9	12	15	18	21	24	27	30
4	8	12	16	20	24	28	32	36	40
5	10	15	20	25	30	35	40	45	50
6	12	18	24	30	36	42	48	54	60
7	14	21	28	35	42	49	56	63	70
8	16	24	32	40	48	56	64	72	80
9	18	27	36	45	54	63	72	81	90
10	20	30	40	50	60	70	80	90	100

Explain to the children that they are going to look for patterns on other grids. If you have been using the computer program 'Monty' (see page 31), then this provides a good source of different grids, otherwise they can be generated as follows:
• count in ones, as in the hundred square, but begin in the centre and spiral round;
• start in the top left-hand corner and add one number each time horizontally and a different number each time vertically;
• as above, but follow any sequence rules the children have met;
• start at the top left-hand corner and write in a sequence to the hundredth term;
• change the size of the grid (and it doesn't have to be square).

Having made new number squares, what new patterns can the children see? Can they explain why these patterns occur?

NC mapping

AT3 – Level 4 (a)
    – Level 5 (a)
AT1 – Level 3 (c) (d)
    – Level 4 (d)
AT2 – from Level 2 (a) to Level 4 (b)

Digital roots

What you need

Paper, pencils.

What to do

Ask the children to take the answers from a multiplication table and add the digits together. If the new number is over 9, they should add the digits again. When a single digit is left, this is the 'digital root'. For example, for the eight times table:

8	8	
16	1 + 6 = 7	
24	2 + 4 = 6	
32	3 + 2 = 5	
40	4 + 0 = 4	
48	4 + 8 = 12	1 + 2 = 3
56	5 + 6 = 11	1 + 1 = 2
64	6 + 4 = 10	1 + 0 = 1
72	7 + 2 = 9	
80	8 + 0 = 8	

Are there any patterns in the digital roots of the tables? Are there any connections between different tables?

NC mapping

AT3 – Level 4 (a)
    – Level 5 (a)
AT1 – Level 3 (c) (d)
    – Level 4 (d)
AT2 – Level 2 (a)
    – Level 3 (b)

Escape

What you need

Paper, pencils, sugar paper for display (optional).

What to do

Using the flow chart shown below work through with the children how a few numbers would behave when fed into this machine. For example, if 10 is fed in, we would get: $10 \rightarrow 5 \rightarrow 16 \rightarrow 8 \rightarrow 4 \rightarrow 2 \rightarrow 1$

If 13 is fed in we get: $13 \rightarrow 40 \rightarrow 20 \rightarrow 10 \rightarrow 5 \rightarrow 16 \rightarrow 8 \rightarrow 4 \rightarrow 2 \rightarrow 1$

This means that 13 'feeds into' the 10 string of numbers. Ask the children to investigate how all the numbers from 1 to 100 will feed in. What is special about the main string, which all the others feed into?

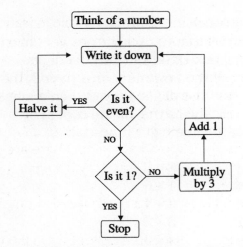

This activity can make an attractive display by showing the main string as the trunk of a tree, the smaller strings as the branches and the numbers as the leaves.

NC mapping

AT3 – Level 4 (a)
  – Level 5 (a)
AT1 – Level 3 (c) (d)
AT2 – Level 2 (a)
  – Level 3 (c)

The chessboard problem

What you need

A chessboard, paper, pencils, tracing paper, squared paper.

What to do

Show the children a chessboard and ask them, 'How many squares are there on a chessboard?' The answer is not 64, nor is it 65 (the usual two attempts). Show the children where there are other squares:

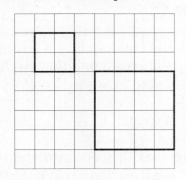

Ask them to see how many they can find. They may need help to get started – for example, moving tracing paper, on which they

have drawn one size of square, over the board can help. It is even better to start with a small square and then build up. How many squares are there in a 1×1 square? How many are in a 2×2 square? This will give an interesting number sequence.

NC mapping

AT3 – Level 4 (a)
  – Level 5 (a)
AT1 – Level 3 (c) (d)
  – Level 4 (d)

Handshakes

What you need

Paper, pencils.

What to do

Tell the children the following story and ask them to solve the problem, reminding them that it is better to start small!

The leaders of the most powerful countries in the world held a conference to promote world peace. A party was held at the start of the conference and the leaders decided that, as the conference would be more successful if everyone was friendly, no one could eat or drink until everyone present had shaken hands with everyone else!

If 100 people turned up at the party, how many handshakes must there be before everyone can eat or drink? (The answer is 4950.)

Children can use a series of circles to help them order their work, though it is better initially to let them try to find their own way of recording the information.

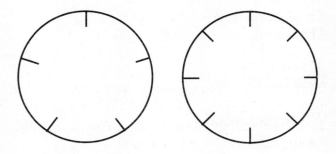

NC mapping

AT3 – Level 4 (a)
  – Level 5 (a)
AT1 – Level 3 (c) (d)
  – Level 4 (d)

Counter get-together

What you need

Two sets of differently coloured counters, grids as drawn below.

What to do

Ask the children to arrange their counters as shown below.

They should not leave any blanks and they should alternate the counters. By exchanging *adjacent* counters only, can they get all the white counters on to the left-hand side and all the black counters on to the right?

The children will find it easier to start with a small number, two of each colour, say. How many moves are needed for one of each colour, two of each colour, three of each colour? The answers give a number pattern!

NC mapping

AT3 – Level 4 (a)
  – Level 5 (a)
AT1 – Level 3 (c) (d)
  – Level 4 (d)

The Tower of Hanoi

What you need

Cardboard discs of different sizes, peg abacus.

What to do

This story has been around for so long that there are many variations of it. The following story will suffice, though the children should be told that it is *only* a story.

In an ancient Buddhist temple in Hanoi, there is a tower made from 100 different-sized golden discs which were originally arranged on one of three poles with the largest disc at the bottom. The priests in the temple have a task. They must eventually move all the discs from one of the poles to another, but there are strict rules about *how* the discs can be moved:

• only one disc can be moved at any one time;
• a larger disc must never be placed on top of a smaller one;
• all three spikes can be used.

The legend goes that when the priests finish their task, the world will end. Is this likely to be soon?

Ask the children to try to solve the puzzle using only three discs, then four and so on. How many moves are needed in each case? The number of moves will produce a number pattern.

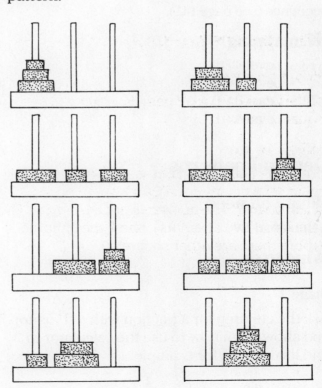

NC mapping

AT3 – Level 4 (a)
  – Level 5 (a)
AT1 – Level 3 (c) (d)
  – Level 4 (d)

St Paul's staircase

What you need

Calculators.

What to do

There are 617 steps to the top of St Paul's Cathedral. If you can go up them one at a time, two at a time or any combination of these (but never more than two at a time), how many ways can you get to the top?

Demonstrate the problem to the children using a small step ladder. To reach the third step, there are three ways:

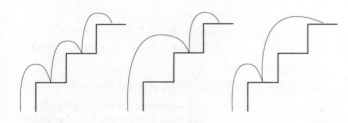

This investigation gives the Fibonacci sequence (see page 141).

NC mapping

AT3 – Level 4 (a)
      – Level 5 (a)
AT1 – Level 3 (c) (d)
      – Level 4 (d)

Decimal patterns

What you need

Calculators.

What to do

Stage 1

Ask the children for a fraction with a '1' on top and show them how to use the calculator to find its decimal, for example:

$$\frac{1}{4} = 0.25$$
$$\frac{1}{3} = 0.33333333$$
$$\frac{1}{7} = 0.1428571428$$

What do the children notice? Some fractions stop, some go on for ever with the same number and some have a repeating pattern. Let the children explore these fractions.

Stage 2

Ask the children to take a decimal which repeats a pattern. What happens if we try '2 over', or '3 over' instead of 1? For example:

$$\frac{1}{7} = 0.1428571428$$
$$\frac{2}{7} = 0.28571428571$$
$$\frac{3}{7} = 0.4285714285$$

What is happening? The cycle 142857 is moving along:

0.1428571428
0.2857142857

Try for other decimals.

NB: the children will need to understand rounding on the calculator, as the pattern is often spoilt by the last digit, for example: $\frac{2}{3} = 0.666666667$.

If your calculator cannot hold enough digits to see the pattern, try a computer program:

BASIC

```
10 PRINT "TOP NUMBER?"
20 INPUT X
30 PRINT "BOTTOM NUMBER?"
40 INPUT Y
50 PRINT X/Y
60 END
```

LOGO

```
? TO DEC :T :B
> PRINT :T/ :B
>END
```

NC mapping

AT3 – Level 5 (a)
AT1 – Level 3 (c) (d)
      – Level 4 (d)
AT2 – Level 4 (c) (d)

Spatial arrangements

If given a choice, most children will choose to try a mathematical problem which is represented spatially before they will opt for one presented through words alone, or through numerals. Shapes are attractive and they promise practical activity – perhaps some building or modelling. Children also approach spatial problems with more confidence, as they will have learned that they often understand concepts better if they are explained with a diagram or a model.

Very many spatial arrangements of objects lead to number sequences. For example, watch how this arrangement grows:

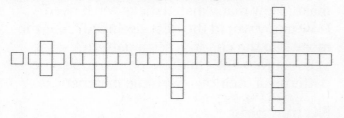

How many squares are needed for each shape? (1 5 9 13 17)

As the children are led into numbers gradually, and usually into finding them out for themselves, the work is more accessible to the less-secure child. He will find success through being able to repeat the pattern, or let it grow, and count the objects. In the example above, he will be able to find the number sequence, even if he cannot describe it or continue it. The older or more-able child, however, will recognise the rule and quickly discard the diagram in favour of writing out successive terms of the sequence, continuing on a calculator. Hence, the spatial arrangement of a sequence enables children of *all* abilities to join in at different levels.

An infinite number of spatial arrangements can be devised, each giving a number sequence (though not all unique). For example we can use small squares:

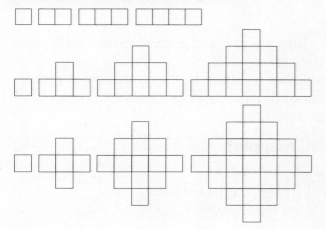

We can use headless matchsticks (available from educational suppliers) in a variety of arrangements:

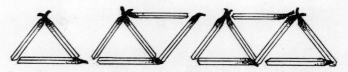

We can draw on circled paper (provided by several educational suppliers):

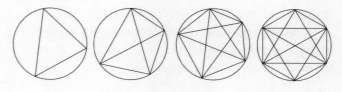

We can vary the questions: how many bricks, sticks, lines? How many regions? How many crossings?

It helps to give the investigation a real setting; for example, building a staircase, a snowflake, or (from the last example) children standing in a circle throwing a ball – How many different throws can there be? (You can then introduce the problem physically.)

Some spatial arrangements are well known by children through measurement work, for example the sequence of square numbers:

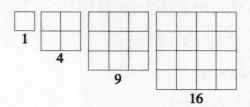

And the sequence of cubed numbers:

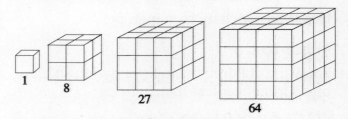

An interesting sequence, which occurs again and again in investigational work, is that of the triangle numbers: 1, 3, 6, 10, 15, 21, 28. (As an example of a problem leading to this sequence, try 'Handshakes' on page 38.)

Triangle numbers get their name simply because they can be arranged as a triangle:

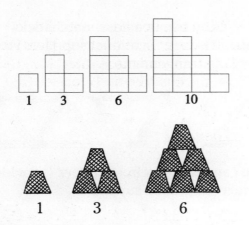

1   3   6   10

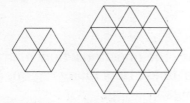

1   3   6

Readers may also be interested to explore hexagonal numbers:

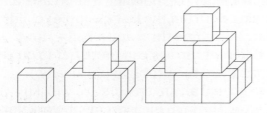

And pyramid numbers:

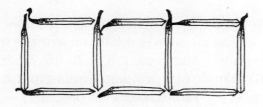

Open-ended activities for Key Stage 1

Match trains

What you need

Headless matchsticks, paper, pencils.

What to do

Show the children the following train shape made from headless matchsticks:

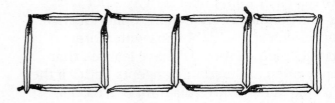

Ask them how many matchsticks were used. Show them how to make the shape bigger:

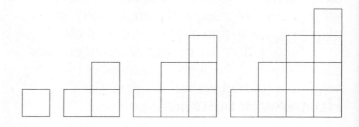

Ask the children to build other, different trains. What is the smallest train they can make? How many matchsticks will it need? How many would the next size need? And the next? Can the children see a pattern?

Encourage the children to make up some patterns of their own with the matchsticks.

NC mapping

AT3 – Level 2 (a)
AT1 – Level 1 (a) (b) (c)
    – Level 2 (c)

Match staircase

What you need

Headless matchsticks, squared paper, pencils, calculators (optional).

What to do

Show the children how to make a staircase with headless matchsticks:

How many matchsticks are needed to make the perimeter of each staircase? Ask the children to build their own staircases and count the matchsticks. Can they find a pattern?

NC mapping

AT3 – Level 2 (a)
AT1 – Level 1 (a) (b) (c)
AT4 – working towards Level 4 (d)

Crossings

What you need

Paper, pencils, rulers.

What to do

Draw two straight lines on paper. Cross them with two more lines:

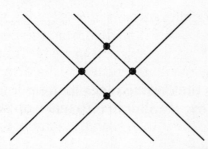

Ask the children how many crossings there are. Now draw two lines crossed by three lines. How many crossings are there now?

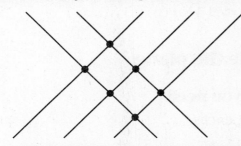

Let the children draw their own crossings. Can they find a pattern in the number of lines and corresponding crossings?

NC mapping

AT3 – Level 2 (a)
AT1 – Level 1 (a) (b) (c)
　　 – Level 2 (c)

How many squares?

What you need

Squared paper, pencils.

What to do

Show the children this growing shape sequence:

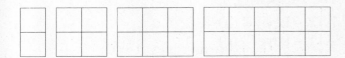

How many squares are there in each pattern? Beware, there are more than four in the second term and more than six in the third. Can the children find a pattern?

NC mapping

AT3 – Level 2 (a)
AT1 – Level 1 (a) (b) (c)
　　 – Level 2 (c)

Open-ended activities for Key Stage 2

Growing triangles

What you need

Isometric (triangle) paper, pencils.

What to do

Children may be familiar with the pattern of little squares one finds as squares grow (1, 4, 9, 16...). If not, they should be reminded of it before attempting 'growing triangles'.

Show the group how triangles can grow on isometric paper. How many little triangles do they think will make each big one? Let them experiment and discuss their findings.

1st triangle		1 little triangle
2nd triangle		4 little triangles
3rd triangle		9 little triangles
4th triangle		16 little triangles

NC mapping

AT3 – Level 4 (a)
AT1 – Level 3 (c)
　　 – Level 4 (a) (b) (c) (d)

Dominoes

What you need

Dominoes, squared paper, pencils.

What to do

Let the children take two dominoes. Tell them to put them together, and draw round them.

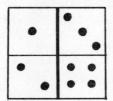 

Are there any other ways they could fill the same space with the two dominoes?

The answer shows that we have two ways of putting together two dominoes in a '2 × 2' rectangle:

What about a '2 × 3' rectangle?

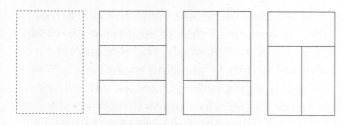

What about a '2 × 4' rectangle?

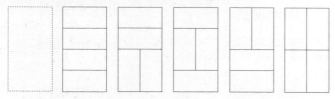

Can the children find a pattern in the number of ways?

NC mapping

AT3 – Level 4 (a)
AT1 – Level 3 (c)
    – Level 4 (a) (b) (c) (d)

Pyramidal numbers

What you need

Cubes (not Multilink) or cylinders, paper, pencils.

What to do

Show the children how a pyramid can be made from five cubes (the second term of the sequence shown below):

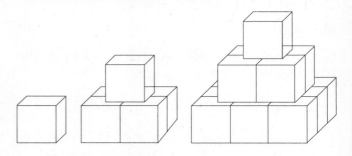

Ask the children to make larger pyramids, counting the number of cubes needed each time.

NC mapping

AT3 – Level 4 (a)
AT1 – Level 3 (c)
    – Level 4 (a) (b) (c) (d)

Divide the plane

What you need

Paper, pencils.

What to do

Draw three intersecting lines on paper.

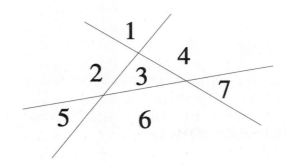

Ask the children how many regions this divides the plane (the surface) into – can they repeat this activity for different numbers of lines? Can they find a rule for the number of regions?

NC mapping

AT3 – Level 4 (a)
AT1 – Level 3 (c)
    – Level 4 (a) (b) (c) (d)

Skeletal cubes

What you need

Multilink cubes, paper, pencils.

What to do

Build a cube with Multilink, using the Multilink cubes to make only the edges.

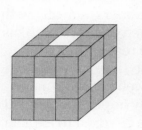 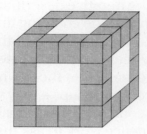

Ask the children to make similar, larger cubes and count how many Multilink cubes they need. Can they find a pattern?

NC mapping

AT3 – Level 4 (a)
AT1 – Level 3 (c)
     – Level 4 (a) (b) (c) (d)

Painted cubes

What you need

Small wooden cubes (not Multilink), paper, pencils.

What to do

Make a $2 \times 2 \times 2$ cube, and mark the six sides with either felt-tipped pen, paint or sticky paper. Show it to the children and then take it apart in front of them. How many of the small cubes used have three faces coloured? How many have two faces coloured? How many have one face coloured and how many have none?

Ask the children to record these answers and then make a $3 \times 3 \times 3$ cube, a $4 \times 4 \times 4$ cube and so on, painting them and then, when dry, taking them apart and counting.

This activity gives several number patterns.

NC mapping

AT3 – Level 4 (a)
AT1 – Level 3 (c)
     – Level 4 (a) (b) (c) (d)

Generalising

We have talked, until now, rather loosely of 'finding the rule' of a sequence. There are, however, two meanings of 'rule' in this context, one is the *iterative* description of the sequence, the other is the *generalisation*.

Iterative description

An iterative description tells the reader what is done to one term in the sequence in order to get the next. For example, for the even numbers 2, 4, 6, 8, 10... we add 2 to 6 to get 8, add 2 to 8 to get 10 and so on, therefore the iterative description contains 'add 2 each time'. This description would be perfect to describe the sequence of odd numbers too: 1, 3, 5, 7, 9...; therefore, we must also state at what point the sequence begins. So, the even numbers are described as 'add 2 each time, starting at 2', while the odd numbers 'add 2 each time, starting at 1'.

As soon as Key Stage 1 children (Level 2 of the National Curriculum) begin to recognise number sequences, they are finding the iterative description quite naturally. Let's return to the spatial arrangement from page 41:

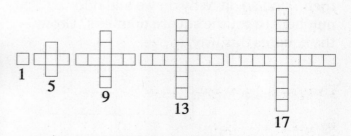

1   5   9   13   17

This sequence goes up by 4 each time, starting at 1. Some children in Year 2 will find

45

this out for themselves, others will understand it if helped, and, of course, some will not yet be ready for the concept. For those that are, find out whether any child can tell you or the group *why* it goes up by four each time. If not, suggest that they make the fifth shape, with 17 squares, into the next one in the sequence. What will they need? Many will realise that they need four more squares, one for each arm of the cross.

Similarly, for the other spatial patterns described earlier, we have 'add 1 each time, starting at 1'; 'add the next odd number each time, starting at 1'; 'add the numbers from the four times table each time, beginning at 1':

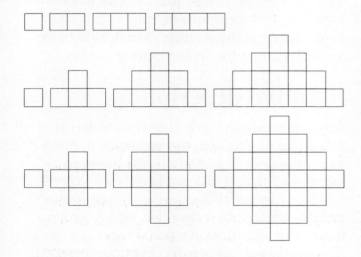

Sometimes, the iterative description can come as a great surprise:

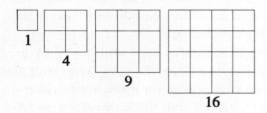

What is added each time? We add 3, then 5, then 7 and so on. Why do we add odd numbers to get the square numbers? Grow the squares this way, to see:

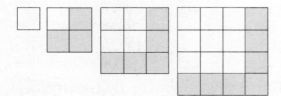

Taking the triangle numbers:

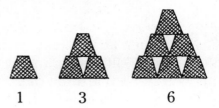

The iterative description is 'Begin with 1, then add the counting numbers, starting with 2'. So we add 2, then 3, then 4 and so on. This may seem obvious to the reader, but young children – even those who have been building towers with cups – may well not have made the connection. It is vitally important with all sequence work to ask the children to explain, in their own words, what is happening.

Older children should meet sequences where the iterative description is not as obvious as a repeated, simple addition or a doubling. For example, let us look at three sequences:

• 1, 3, 7, 15, 31....
• 1, 2, 5, 14, 41, 122....
• 1, 1, 2, 3, 5, 8, 13, 21....

Some children may be able to see the rule by inspection, but others need to use a manipulative technique called the 'difference method'. Write out the sequence, and by the side write the difference between the pairs of numbers. A pattern may appear which will then help to find more of the sequence. If it doesn't, then take differences again. For example, with the first sequence:

Some children may notice that the numbers in the second column double each time. One way of stating the rule could be, 'Starting with 1 and adding 2, the number you add each time doubles.' Other children may notice that, 'The number you add is one more than the last number in the sequence'. Whichever way they see it, they can now work backwards to find the next numbers in the sequence. First work out the differences using the rule you have noticed, and then add to it:

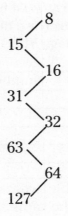

Looking at the second sequence we find:

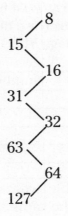

Again, there are at least two ways of seeing what is happening. Some may notice that the differences go: 1, 3, 3×3, 3×3×3, 3×3×3×3. Others may notice that the difference is one less than double the last number, for example 27 = (14×2) − 1. Either way, we have a means of continuing the sequence.

Finally, the third sequence gives us:

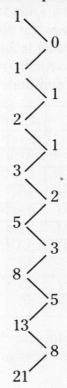

We get the same numbers again! The difference is the next to last number we wrote down.

The difference method is not mentioned until Level 6 of the National Curriculum: *'Use the difference method to explore sequences such as: 2, 5, 10, 17, 26,…'* (AT3 Level 6 Examples). However, the method is within the reach of most Year 6 children, and many from Year 5.

Such work obviously begs the use of a calculator, both to speed up the process and to avoid any small errors which would wreck the pattern. By Level 6, children should also be accessing computer software to do the manipulations for them. Spreadsheets are excellent for this method.

Spreadsheets were met earlier on page 23, where the final sheet showed the generation of the triangle numbers. To find the differences, then, all that is needed is to program Column E to find the difference between successive numbers in Column D:

	A	B	C	D	E	F	G
1	1	2	2	1			
2	2	3	6	3	2		
3	3	4	12	6	3		
4	4	5	20	10	4		
5	5	6	30	15	5		
6	6	7	42	21	6		
7	7	8	56	28	7		
8	8	9	72	36	8		
9	9	10	90	45	9		
10	10	11	110	55	10		

All that remains is for the children to explain why the differences are what they are!

Generalisation

The second form of description of a number sequence is that of a *generalisation*. Here, a number in a sequence is described in terms of its position in the sequence. To illustrate, let's imagine a spatial arrangement which grows in the following way:

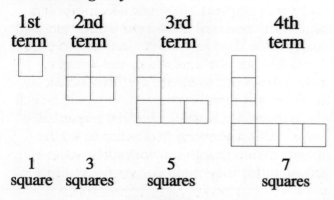

1st term — 1 square
2nd term — 3 squares
3rd term — 5 squares
4th term — 7 squares

How many squares would we need to make the hundredth term?

Many Year 1 and Year 2 children can recognise that the number of squares you need goes up in twos (the iterative description). Many will be able to continue the pattern. Some will be able to work out what the tenth term will be. Some will be able to explain *why* it is going up in twos: 'We add on one to each "leg" each time'.

But what about the hundredth term? Often children will suggest going away and working this out. If they do, then let them try as they will either spot a quicker way to get the answer (the *generalisation*) or return frustrated for some extra help. What if we wanted to know the millionth term!?

In order to answer such questions, we need to find a way that doesn't require us to find every term along the way. We need to link the 'term number', for example, the hundredth or the millionth, with the answer.

To see more clearly what is happening, we can draw a table thus (or a mapping diagram if you prefer – see page 51):

Term	Number of squares
1	1
2	3
3	5
4	7
5	9

Looking at the table, what could we do to the 2 to get 3? Is it the same as we do to 3 to get 5? We need a rule which is the same each time. What do we do to 1 to get 1, and is it the same as we do to 3 to get 5 and is it the same as we do to 5 to get 9?

The language the children will use can vary. Let them tell the others in their group *their* way of doing it. For example: 'It's the number plus itself, take away 1' or 'You take the number and add one less than the number'. Do the others agree? Can they explain their way satisfactorily to the others?

Let us return again to the set of spatial arrangements for which we have already found the iterative description.

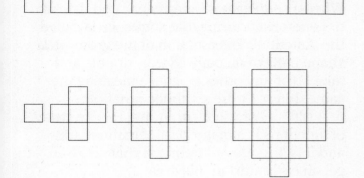

For the first sequence:

Term	Number of squares
1	1
2	2
3	3
4	4
5	5

This is an easy one! The generalisation is that the number of squares we need is the same as the term number. The hundredth one would have 100 squares.

For the second sequence:

Term	Number of squares
1	1
2	4
3	9
4	16
5	25

The generalisation is 'the number of squares we need is the square of the term number'. Did you notice that these were square numbers before? Why are they? (If you split each picture you can make a square and so on).

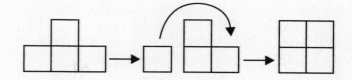

Could we rearrange the spatial arrangements to make squares? The hundredth one would have 100×100 (= 10,000) squares.

Finally, the third sequence:

Term	Number of squares
1	1
2	5
3	13
4	25
5	41

This is definitely not an easy one, and beyond all but the very able junior pupil. The generalisation in words is rather cumbersome: 'Square the term number and then double the answer. Take away double the term number, and then add 1'. Alternatively, 'Square the term number and take away the term number from that answer. Double this and then add 1'. Not very clear, is it? It is easier for an adult to read if written symbolically: $2n^2 - 2n + 1$. The hundredth term would have:
$2 \times 100 \times 100 - 2 \times 100 + 1 = 19,801$ squares!

This is an important lesson for anyone embarking on sequence work with primary children. If they are free to explore, they may meet sequences which they cannot fully understand. Children should not be worried by this, but be reassured that there is a lot of mathematics around them that they can't understand yet. We give them a very false view of the world if they think all is already within their grasp!

They will also sometimes meet sequences where the generalisation is easier than the iterative description. For example, for cube numbers:

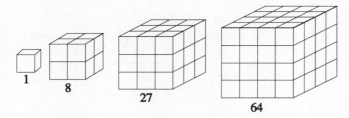

The generalisation 'Multiply the term number by itself, and then by itself again', is much easier to understand than the pattern we get from looking at the differences:

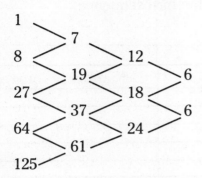

Returning to our third spatial arrangement, which gave $2n^2 - 2n + 1$, this symbolic notation is not required until Level 7, but as children are expected to use symbols at Level 6 for other algebra work (equations and mappings) this appears to be inconsistent. If a child can understand: '$x \rightarrow 2 - x$' (AT3 Level 6 Examples) which means a number is changed to 2 minus that number, then they can also understand simple generalisations written in terms of a symbol. The letter chosen for this work is usually 'n', to stand for the term 'number', but any letter would do. Our first generalisation, 'the number of squares we need is the same as the term number' now becomes: the nth term = n. Our second generalisation, 'the number of squares we need is the square of the term number', becomes: the nth term = n^2. The first arrangement of this section, the growing 'L' shapes, for which we found 'It's the number plus itself, take away 1' or 'You take the number and add one less than the number', becomes: 'the nth term = 2n – 1'.

Such work is recognised at Level 7 thus: **'Express in symbols the rules for the following sequence: 1,3,5,...[2n – 1]...'** (AT3 Level 7 Examples). You should keep an open mind about what able top juniors can do.

No extra activities are included for this 'Generalising' section, as all the number sequences we have met so far can be generalised. You should encourage children to find the iterative description, or the generalised function if they are of that ability level, for all problem-solving activities.

Function machines

When a sequence is being generated the rule, or generalisation, for that sequence is called the 'function'. The function of the growing 'L' shape pattern on page 48 was 'double and take 1' (or any other language meaning the same thing), or the symbolic notation: $n \rightarrow (2n - 1)$ or nth term = $(2n - 1)$. The study of functions is a major part of mathematics and it is, therefore, important that children get an early start in this area.

A function, therefore, stands for a 'change' and can be introduced to the youngest school children in this form. For example, when playing 'Simple Simon says...' the speaker makes the other children 'change' in some way. If Simple Simon is a function machine then when the speaker doesn't say, 'Simple Simon says...' the machine is not turned on.

Changing shapes or numbers can be done through a toy 'machine', made from a large washing-powder box, with slits cut in the sides. The teacher – or a child – has to think for the machine, feeding in the 'IN' pieces, or numbers cards, working out the answer and feeding out the 'OUT' pieces or number cards.

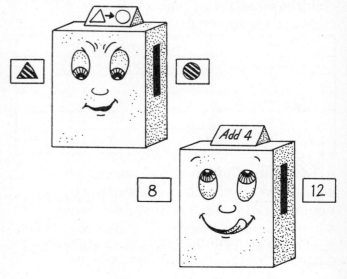

It is obviously necessary to make sure in advance that you have all the pieces, cards, or whatever, hidden behind the box. Young children will need an adult helper.

Work with the function machine can be made into a game, the first child to spot the rule being the next to 'program' the machine.

Function machines can also be represented diagrammatically:

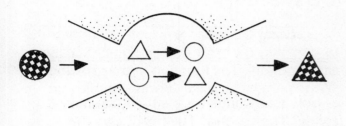

If a square is fed in to the machine above, then it will not change in any way.

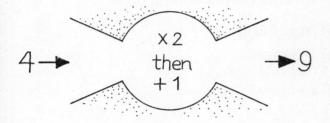

If children have used logic boards, this will not be a difficult concept to understand. Others may need more explanation and examples before they can work out the 'outputs'.

Inputs and outputs need to be recorded, whatever level the children are working at. A good introduction, and one which will help children when they progress on to results tables, is a mapping diagram:

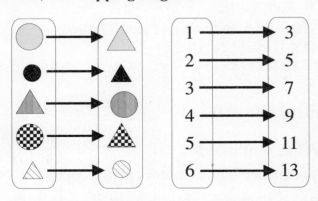

The above examples show mapping diagrams for the two function machines shown on page above. Many mathematics schemes use mapping diagrams for such things as one-to-one correspondence in early number work, so this idea will not seem strange to most children.

The corresponding results table for the second example is:

IN (or x)	OUT (or y)
1	3
2	5
3	7
4	9
5	11
6	13

The pairs of numbers from a mapping diagram or a results table are converted into co-ordinates: (1,3) (2,5) (3,7) (4,9) (5,11) (6,13) and then plotted on to squared paper.

The graphical representation of a sequence – and hence of a function – is vitally important. This work is developed in the next section.

If function machines are to be used to model the production of sequences, then the counting numbers (1, 2, 3...) must be in input. Otherwise, arbitrary members of a sequence would be produced, and finding the iterative description would be more difficult. For example:

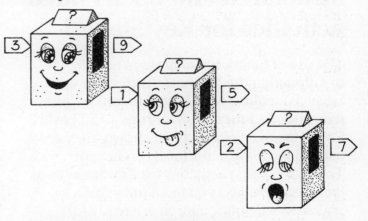

It is difficult for children to see the rule when the inputs have no pattern. Older children can see the generalisation if they have enough examples – here it is 'double and add three' – but children still working iteratively (that is, looking for a sequence in the outputs) will find the example above difficult. If the machine is fed numbers in counting order, the pattern becomes clear:

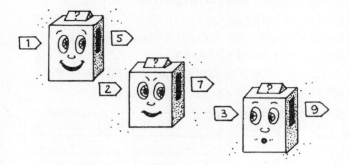

It is even easier to see if the inputs and outputs are shown on 'ticker-tape':

Notice the order of the numbers – they are written so that 1 is fed in first, and the output for 1 comes out first.

This way of showing a sequence with a function machine is the method used in the following activities.

Structured and open-ended activities for Key Stage 1

The use of function machines is not mentioned in the National Curriculum until Level 3: **'dealing with inputs to and outputs from simple function machines'** (AT3 Level 3 PoS). However, as has been shown, they are useful long before this level is reached. Therefore, some activities for Key Stage 1 are included here and you must judge for yourselves if your children are ready for them.

Conveyor belt

What you need

A long strip of paper to act as a conveyor belt, some mechanism to add Multilink to the belt (could just be your hand, or a dumper truck, or a mechanism built with LEGO), Multilink.

What to do

Explain to the children that this machine makes sticks of toffee longer by adding another colour toffee:

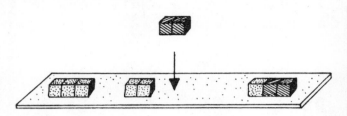

How many units long is the first stick of toffee? The second? The third? Can the children see a pattern? How long will the fourth stick in the sequence be? What about the seventh and tenth? Ask the children to try to work out the answers on paper.

NC mapping

AT3 – Level 2 (a)
AT1 – Level 1 (a) (b) (c)
AT2 – Level 1 (b)

Find the OUT number

What you need

Photocopiable page 182.

What to do

Distribute copies of photocopiable page 182 and ask the children to fill in the OUT numbers.

NC mapping

AT3 – working towards Level 3 PoS
AT1 – Level 1 (a) (b) (c)
AT2 – Level 2 (a)

Find the rule

What you need

A sequence blank, photocopiable page 183.

What to do

Show the children an example of a function

machine where they can see the OUT numbers.

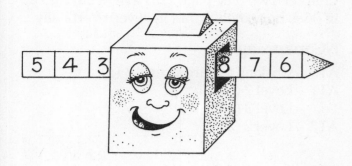

Can they work out what the machine is doing? Distribute copies of photocopiable page 183 and show the children where to write the rule each time.

NC mapping

AT3 – working towards Level 3 PoS
AT1 – Level 1 (a) (b) (c)
AT2 – Level 2 (a)

Cannon machines

What you need

A model of a cannon, perhaps made from LEGO, a marble to act as the cannon-ball, a long strip of numbered paper, photocopiable page 184.

What to do

Explain to the children that this pretend cannon can be set to fire 'cannon-balls' to different distances. Set up the machine on a number line at, for example, 3. Say the machine is going to fire four places. Where will the ball land? After several goes, the children can make up their own co-ordinates.

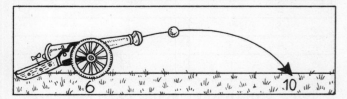

Explain that the cannons will also fire bouncy cannon-balls. These will keep bouncing a certain distance once they have been fired; for example, they might always bounce two numbers or three numbers. The cannon can be set to fire the cannon-balls to bounce any number.

If we start a '3' cannon at 0 what numbers will the cannon-ball land on?

If a cannon-ball lands on 18, what number was the cannon set on? (This activity is a preparation for multiplication – the cannon could have been set on 1, 2, 3, 6, 9, or 18.) Ask the children to work out where the cannon-balls will bounce for the examples on photocopiable page 184.

This activity could also be used to introduce a variety of other concepts. For example, if we turn the cannon around, the numbers will become negative:

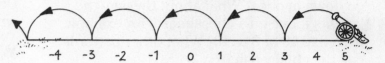

NC mapping

AT3 – working towards Level 3 PoS
AT1 – Level 2 (a) (b) (c)
AT2 – various, depending upon the task the teacher sets using the cannon.

Structured and open-ended activities for Key Stage 2

Machine table

What you need

Large squared paper, photocopiable page 185.

What to do

Two function machines, for example 'Add 3' and 'Add 4', can be combined together and re-entered as often as one likes. If we only use the 'Add 3' machine, we would get the bottom row of the table on shown below, and if we only used the 'Add 4' machine we would get the left-hand column. If we start by feeding in 1, two goes with 'Add 3' followed by one go with 'Add 4' would give 11. This is located on the results table as two moves along, followed by one move up. Show the children a couple of examples on squared paper.

17	20	23	26	29
13	16	19	22	25
9	12	15	18	21
5	8	11	14	17
1	4	7	10	13

Add 4 (vertical, left)

Add 3 (horizontal, bottom)

Can the children see any patterns in the diagonals on this table; for example, 5, 12, 19, 26 or 7, 14, 21 – why does this go up in sevens? Why do the diagonals the other way go down in ones? What about the way the knights move on a chessboard; for example, from 8 to 18 or 8 to 13? What other patterns can the children find?

You can also bring out questions which reinforce number structure. What if the children consider a small square of the pattern; for example:

12	15
8	11

Add the diagonally opposite numbers: 12 + 11 and 8 + 15. What do the children notice? Now multiply the diagonally opposite numbers, 12 × 11 and 8 × 15. Try again for the two other small squares. What do the children notice this time? What about other sizes of square for both problems?

Take out a cross shape:

	20	
13	16	19
	12	

What patterns/rules can the children find here? Try other sizes and other shapes.

Distribute photocopiable page 185 and ask the children to look for the types of patterns

above on their completed sheets. If they need further experience of explaining moves of different meaning, try 'Calendar capers' in Chapter Two (see page 123) where days go up in ones horizontally, but in sevens vertically.

NC mapping

AT3 – working towards Level 3 (a)
AT1 – Level 2 (c)
  – Level 3 (c)
AT2 – Level 2 (a)

Clever machines: 1

What you need

Double machine blanks on which you can write the functions, photocopiable page 186.

What to do

By the time they reach Level 4, children should be able to combine machines, in preparation for solving more difficult equations:

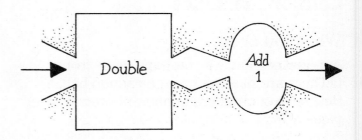

Explain that some machines can do more than one function at a time. Ask the children if they can see what the following 'clever' machine is doing:

IN	OUT
1	3
2	5
3	7
4	9
5	11

What is the pattern in the 'OUT' numbers? Why do we get only odd numbers? What is the 'rule' for the sequence?

Let the children make up their own clever machines and list their sequences. Finally, distribute photocopiable page 186 and ask the children to find the rule each time.

NC mapping

AT3 – Level 4 (a)
AT1 – Level 4 (b) (d)
AT2 – various, depending on the functions provided by the teacher, or devised by the children.

Graphical representation

There is no mention of graphical representation in Attainment Target 3 until Level 4, yet there are many opportunities for the pictorial and graphical display of relationships long before this. Also, it is expected that by Level 4 children can cope with formal co-ordinate representation. You will be well aware that much preliminary work is necessary to reach this point, though this is not recognised in the document. Therefore, this section will consider activities for the early years upwards as 'working towards' Level 4 and, as necessary, for the understanding of the subject.

There are two main concepts for the children to tackle. First, that *every point on the space of the grid can carry information and has its own label*, and second, that *we always look along before we look up*.

For very young children, labels on graphs take the form of attributes as in, for example, Carroll diagrams:

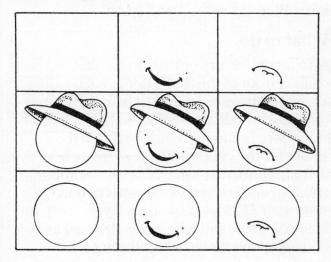

Children may be shown an empty square in a Carroll diagram and asked to find, for example, a picture to fit the space, in which case they must look to the axes for the required attributes. Or they may be given a picture, recognise the attributes and then locate its position on the grid. In both cases, the fact that two pieces of information combine to make an *exclusive* set of attributes which always go in one particular square – and the method of finding that square – are emphasised. At this stage, it is not important which attribute the child locates first.

From this initial stage, children advance to using grids with labels of letters and numbers. These are used only to say which square we are looking at; for example, in the game 'Fishing', where all the squares are covered with card and 'fish' have been hidden under a few squares. The children must guess where a fish may be hidden and say the correct position. If they are right, and that square contains a fish, they collect the fish.

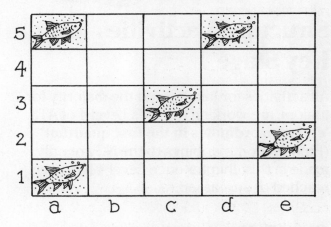

Although it is still unimportant which part of a label is given first – 3a, for example, will indicate the same square as a3 – children should be encouraged always to say the letter before the number, in preparation for the second concept that *we look along before we look up*. You may find it helpful to introduce this labelling idea on a larger scale, for example through body games. (There are ideas for such games on pages 56 and 57.)

In the next stage of the development towards formal co-ordinates, children should learn to use numbers on both axes. Any problems they have remembering to look first along the bottom line will become apparent as they show confusion over position. Well into the secondary school, many pupils have problems remembering that the 'x-axis' is visited first, and therefore muddle the position of (x, y). Use mnemonics such as 'along the corridor, up the stairs' to help children remember the order. A group of students at Homerton College, Cambridge, came up with: 'We always say snakes and ladders, never ladders and snakes'. Snakes slither along the ground and ladders go up.

Combine the two to give the children a more memorable idea:

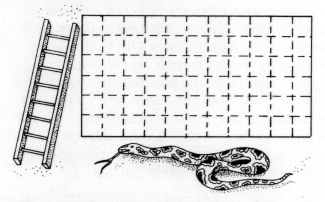

Structured activities for Key Stage 1

All activities for infants, and the majority for juniors, are working towards Level 4 of AT3: **'c) Use co-ordinates in the first quadrant'** (PoS). Hence, mappings to the NC are only made in this chapter once Level 4 has been reached or surpassed.

Carroll diagrams

Any set work with Carroll diagrams – such as the 'Faces' grid on page 55 – will introduce and reinforce the idea of information stored in a grid. Many school suppliers provide logic cards to set up Carroll diagrams and logic dice are also available to make chance games such as 'logic bingo' possible:

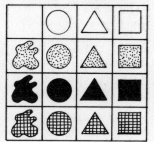

To play logic bingo the children should throw the two dice. They must use the information from the dice to identify the combined shape and then check their bingo card for this shape. The activity is made a little more difficult by the removal of the attribute labels from the cards.

Weather charts

Recording the weather is often done on a grid:

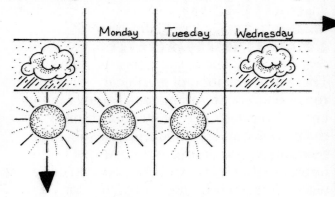

Asking the children, 'Did it rain on Wednesday?' or 'It's sunny today, where shall we stick the picture?' requires them to access information in the form of 'block' co-ordinates.

Any other form of information-gathering on a grid will provide similar cross-curricular links.

Chair grid games

What you need

Chairs or mats (for hall/PE work), large pieces of coloured paper, a ball, a bag containing cards on which are written co-ordinates in the form: Blue 4; Yellow 2; and so on.

What to do

Arrange the chairs or mats in a grid. Give each child in front of the first chair in each column a piece of coloured paper to hold (or give them each a different-coloured hat). Make sure there is enough space between the chairs for the children to move freely between them (mat work is safer). Check that the children understand what each column stands for ('Put your hand up if you are in the blue column'), and which row they are in ('Stand up everyone in row three').

The child who is 'it' then walks between the chairs and at a convenient point (the children will learn when is convenient) says the co-ordinates of two children, for example, 'Red 2 and Yellow 3'. When she also says 'Go!' the two children must try to swap places before the person who is 'it' can sit on one of their chairs. The child left without a chair is 'it'.

Alternatively, the children can use a ball, throwing it to each other according to co-ordinates either chosen by a child at the front, or picked out of a bag.

A game which can cause much commotion is 'Cat and mouse'. To play this game all the chairs are initially occupied and the cat and mouse circulate around them. When a co-ordinate is called, the child on that chair must move away quickly, as it now represents a safe 'hole' for the mouse. If the mouse can get there ahead of the cat, the displaced child becomes the new mouse, otherwise the displaced child becomes the new cat.

When the children are familiar with this concept, ask them to write down (or try to remember) their position. The chair plan can be drawn out on paper or on the board, and the children can then draw and stick on a picture of themselves in the correct positions.

Body puzzles

What you need

Photocopiable page 187, scissors.

What to do

Give the children a copy of photocopiable page 187 to look at, individually or in pairs. Explain that the parts of pictures can be put together to make proper pictures of people. Can anyone point to the head that goes with

the clown's coat? Can they tell by *looking only* in what order the rectangles should go? Can they tell you by using the letters and numbers, rather than pointing? If they cannot, then cut up the puzzles and let them put the jigsaw together. Can they now tell you – using the original and the solved puzzle side by side – the 'names' of the rectangles which, for example, make the nurse?

Advent calendars

Next time you make advent calendars, make one large one for the class with the advent windows arranged on a grid. Where is 16 December? Which day is in C5?

Sprite bingo

Sprites are small pictures drawn on a computer screen using co-ordinates. These little pictures can then be animated using LOGO commands (a 'Sprite' program is necessary). However, classes without the program can have fun designing sprites for a 'computer' poster. As they tend to look like the characters from arcade games, designing their own 'space invader' type games could be attempted.

What you need

Sprite boards (see below), pieces of paper the same size as the grid squares on the boards, 20 blank playing cards.

What to do

Ask the children to design sprites which all use the same number of squares. Here is an example which uses 22 squares:

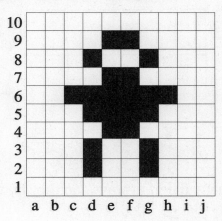

Make these designs into bingo cards. Label the 20 blank playing cards as two sets (one a to j, the other 1 to 10). Shuffle the packs and turn over the top card of each pack. Children with this square coloured on their bingo cards, cover the square with a blank piece of paper. Continue turning over cards until all ten of each pack are turned over, shuffle and begin again. The first child to hide all of her sprite is the winner.

If this game lasts too long for the age group you teach, cut down the size of the sprites and boards.

To avoid arguments, it is helpful to have one child act as 'scribe' and record all the co-ordinates called. In this way, the winning bingo card can be checked.

There are more activities using sprites on page 61.

Zoo

What you need

Toy animals, for example from a sorting set, or pictures of animals, a grid drawn as below.

What to do

Ask the children to put the animals in their cages. To make the zoo more interesting, they mustn't put any of the same animals in the same row or column:

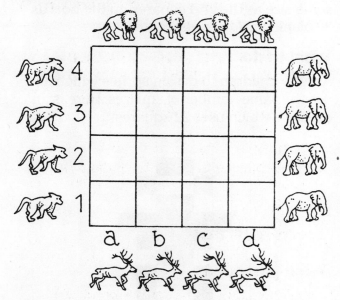

How many different ways can they find to do it?

Code breakers: 1

What you need

Code breaker grids as shown below.

What to do

Use a word or short sentence to demonstrate to the children how the code breaker works. Breaking a code like the one below will reinforce the idea that the letter must come first.

	A	B	C	D	E	F
4	g	p	u	c	y	h
3	t	a	k	w	r	e
2	l	s	i	f	m	o
1	n	d	q	v	b	j

D3 F4 B3 A3   B1 F2 F3 B2   A3 F4 C2 B2
B2 B3 E4?

Ask the children to make up their own hidden sentences. No one will know what they are saying unless they have the code breaker!

Line families

A game for four top infants or lower juniors.

What you need

One blank grid labelled a to d and 1 to 4 (make sure it is large enough to take playing cards in the squares), 48 blank playing cards on each of which is written a1, a2, a3, a4, b1 and so on up to d4 (there will be three of each).

What to do

Sit the children around the blank grid and show them how the squares a1, a2, a3, a4 are in a line, as are a2, b2, c2, d2 and so on. Explain that they are going to play a game similar to 'Happy families' where they have to collect a family of cards. Their families will make a line on the grid.

Shuffle the cards and deal four cards to each child, placing the rest of the cards face down in the centre. Choose who is to begin

58

and which way you are going. The first child asks the child next to him if she has any twos, say. If the other child has some, she must hand them over. If not, the child who asked the question must take a card from the top of the pile and the game continues round. As soon as a child thinks he has a line family, he must say so and put them on the grid to prove it. He can then collect them up and put them on one side. Play the game until there is an impasse. The child with the most families is the winner.

Structured activities for Key Stage 2

Code breakers: 2

What you need

Code breaker grids (see page 58).

What to do

This game is played in a similar way to Key Stage 1 'Code breakers' (see page 58), but using numbers in both directions. The children will need to concentrate hard on the rule 'along, then up'.

Password codes

What you need

Paper, pencils.

What to do

Write a password over and over. For example, if the password was 'dinosaur', write:

DINOSAURDINOSAURDINOSAURDINOSAUR

Underneath this write the message:

D I NOS AURDINOSAURDI NOSAURDINOSA
MEETMEBYTHEGREENGATEATELEVENAM

We then have a set of pairs of letters which can be used as co-ordinates to produce a code:

	A	B	C	D	E	F	G	H	I	J	K	L	M	N	O	P	Q	R	S	T	U	V	W	X	Y	Z
Z	Z	A	B	C	D	E	F	G	H	I	J	K	L	M	N	O	P	Q	R	S	T	U	V	W	X	Y
Y	Y	Z	A	B	C	D	E	F	G	H	I	J	K	L	M	N	O	P	Q	R	S	T	U	V	W	X
X	X	Y	Z	A	B	C	D	E	F	G	H	I	J	K	L	M	N	O	P	Q	R	S	T	U	V	W
W	W	X	Y	Z	A	B	C	D	E	F	G	H	I	J	K	L	M	N	O	P	Q	R	S	T	U	V
V	V	W	X	Y	Z	A	B	C	D	E	F	G	H	I	J	K	L	M	N	O	P	Q	R	S	T	U
U	U	V	W	X	Y	Z	A	B	C	D	E	F	G	H	I	J	K	L	M	N	O	P	Q	R	S	T
T	T	U	V	W	X	Y	Z	A	B	C	D	E	F	G	H	I	J	K	L	M	N	O	P	Q	R	S
S	S	T	U	V	W	X	Y	Z	A	B	C	D	E	F	G	H	I	J	K	L	M	N	O	P	Q	R
R	R	S	T	U	V	W	X	Y	Z	A	B	C	D	E	F	G	H	I	J	K	L	M	N	O	P	Q
Q	Q	R	S	T	U	V	W	X	Y	Z	A	B	C	D	E	F	G	H	I	J	K	L	M	N	O	P
P	P	Q	R	S	T	U	V	W	X	Y	Z	A	B	C	D	E	F	G	H	I	J	K	L	M	N	O
O	O	P	Q	R	S	T	U	V	W	X	Y	Z	A	B	C	D	E	F	G	H	I	J	K	L	M	N
N	N	O	P	Q	R	S	T	U	V	W	X	Y	Z	A	B	C	D	E	F	G	H	I	J	K	L	M
M	M	N	O	P	Q	R	S	T	U	V	W	X	Y	Z	A	B	C	D	E	F	G	H	I	J	K	L
L	L	M	N	O	P	Q	R	S	T	U	V	W	X	Y	Z	A	B	C	D	E	F	G	H	I	J	K
K	K	L	M	N	O	P	Q	R	S	T	U	V	W	X	Y	Z	A	B	C	D	E	F	G	H	I	J
J	J	K	L	M	N	O	P	Q	R	S	T	U	V	W	X	Y	Z	A	B	C	D	E	F	G	H	I
I	I	J	K	L	M	N	O	P	Q	R	S	T	U	V	W	X	Y	Z	A	B	C	D	E	F	G	H
H	H	I	J	K	L	M	N	O	P	Q	R	S	T	U	V	W	X	Y	Z	A	B	C	D	E	F	G
G	G	H	I	J	K	L	M	N	O	P	Q	R	S	T	U	V	W	X	Y	Z	A	B	C	D	E	F
F	F	G	H	I	J	K	L	M	N	O	P	Q	R	S	T	U	V	W	X	Y	Z	A	B	C	D	E
E	E	F	G	H	I	J	K	L	M	N	O	P	Q	R	S	T	U	V	W	X	Y	Z	A	B	C	D
D	D	E	F	G	H	I	J	K	L	M	N	O	P	Q	R	S	T	U	V	W	X	Y	Z	A	B	C
C	C	D	E	F	G	H	I	J	K	L	M	N	O	P	Q	R	S	T	U	V	W	X	Y	Z	A	B
B	B	C	D	E	F	G	H	I	J	K	L	M	N	O	P	Q	R	S	T	U	V	W	X	Y	Z	A
A	A	B	C	D	E	F	G	H	I	J	K	L	M	N	O	P	Q	R	S	T	U	V	W	X	Y	Z
	A	B	C	D	E	F	G	H	I	J	K	L	M	N	O	P	Q	R	S	T	U	V	W	X	Y	Z

From the message: D, M = P
                        I, E = M

The message can then be written out as a code which cannot be broken without the password.

Ask the children to try setting and breaking such messages. For example:

H Z R I M O E Z I E X W L T R E I D G D W E

The code word is 'elephant'. To solve the code the word 'elephant' must be written out repeatedly above the code:

E L E P H A N T E L E P H A N T E L E P H A
H Z R I M O E Z I E X W L T R E I D G D W E

You can then use the grid:
(E, ?) = H   ? = D
(L, ?) = Z   ? = O
Ask the children to continue finding the message.

Treasure trails

What you need

A scale diagram of the school, number puzzles (see below), sweets or some substitute prize.

What to do

Draw a grid on a scale diagram of the school grounds (if the school is not very old, the architects' plans should be available). Hide clues to a co-ordinate puzzle at several places, for example, 'My first is a prime between 13 and 19, my second is the second square number, gives the next place to look': (17, 4).

The children can win a sweet (or something else) when they find the final note. Ask the children to make up such clues for different teams – or for parents. (You *must* check these before they are set up around the school.)

Radar game

This is a good alternative to 'battleships', which is rather bloodthirsty.

What you need

Something to act as a screen between the opponents, squared paper, pencils.

What to do

Ask the children to work in pairs. They should sit opposite each other with a screen between them. Each draws aeroplanes (rectangles) of different sizes (for example three of two squares, two of three squares and one of four squares) on their grids.

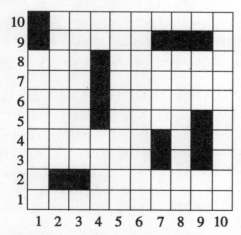

Taking turns, they each pretend to be an air traffic controller sending a radar beam to search for aeroplanes. They send the beams to particular squares by saying the co-ordinates of the square to their partners. The other child must say if the beam finds a part of any of their planes, though not where on the plane or which plane. Each should keep a

record of their own guesses and also mark on their planes where the opponent has succeeded. The first child to correctly identify all the other's planes is the winner.

Towering infernos

What you need

An eight-sided die labelled a to d (twice), or a six-sided die with two blanks; a six-sided die labelled 0,1 and 2 (twice); counters; photocopiable page 188.

What to do

Distribute the photocopiable sheets so that each pair of opponents has a sheet and ask each child to choose a counter. Then explain how to play the game. Ask the children to imagine that they are on the top floor of the skyscraper. A fire has broken out on the roof and they must try to get down as quickly as possible.

Demonstrate how they get down by placing a counter on the roof and throwing the two dice. The numbered die will tell the children how many flights of stairs to go down. The lettered die will tell them which flat to go into in order to telephone for the fire brigade.

The first child to reach the bottom flight of stairs is the winner – in other words, the one who ran for help.

Noughts and crosses/OXO/ Connect three: 1

A game for two children.

What you need

Two dice of different colours, each labelled 1, 1, 2, 2, 3, 3; 3×3 square grids.

What to do

Ask the children to decide which colour is to represent the horizontal number, and which the vertical number. They must also decide how to choose who will start. The first to go is 'O', the other child is 'X'.

The first child throws both dice, works out the square this represents and writes an 'O', the second child repeats this process but writes an 'X'. They continue until one of them completes a line of three 'Os' or 'Xs'.

The game can be widened by using differently labelled dice and larger grids. The game can also be changed to 'OXO', where the first child to complete a line with the word 'OXO' is the winner.

Open-ended activities for Key Stage 1

Sprites

Sprites were first introduced under 'Sprites bingo' on page 57.

What you need

Squared paper, coloured pens, poster material, toy telephones (optional), screens (optional).

What to do

If you have the LOGO sprite program, follow the directions to draw a screen sprite and show how the sprite can move around the screen. Ask the children to draw their own sprites on paper. These can then be transferred on to the computer. Otherwise, show the children a sprite drawn on squared paper (for example the one shown on page 57). Ask them if they have seen little figures like this before (on a computer program or arcade game). Explain that they are going to make a poster of different sprites as though in a computer game. The children can then design their sprites.

Match the sprite

Ask the children to write down the labels of the squares they coloured in. They should not put their names on their pictures. When the sprites are mounted on the wall, give one group of children the co-ordinates of another group's pictures. Can they match them up with the correct picture? The co-ordinates can then be pinned alongside the picture.

Telephone sprites

Ask half of the group of children to imagine they work for a company which makes computer games. The other half are designers who work in a different town. The computer company needs to know new designs quickly. Can the designers tell the company their sprite designs over the phone? Show the children how this could be done, with them recording the conversation on squared paper. The children can then work in pairs, with a screen between them, to draw the designs.

Addition squares

What you need

Addition squares blanks, two ordinary dice, pencils.

What to do

Ask the children to take turns throwing the two dice and adding the scores. They must then find where the total goes on an addition square and write in the number.

6						
5						
4			7			
3						
2		4			7	
1						
+	1	2	3	4	5	6

Where are all the 'double' numbers? Where are all the 7s? Can the children use the patterns they have noticed to fill in the rest of the square to 10 + 10?

This process can be repeated for multiplication and subtraction (if the children have not already met negative numbers, they will need explanation using a number line). If you introduce a calculator at the same time, the minus sign in the answer can be pointed out and explained.

Open-ended activities for Key Stage 2

A to Z

What you need

Real A to Z maps of your area, or town maps, on which you have superimposed a grid, or real Ordnance Survey maps.

What to do

Begin by identifying places known to the children, showing them where these places are on the map and how to read the grid references. Make up and read out a route, using co-ordinates, which a person might take. For example, a journey from a house to a school to an office, back to the school and then back to the house (this would go something like: 'Page 10, E6; page 13, A3; page 12, C3...' and so on). Who might be making this journey (not a named person, but it could be a parent taking their child to school and then going to work, and so on)? Ask the children to plan routes for others to identify.

Draughts

What you need

Draughtboards labelled with numbers along the sides, draught pieces, squared paper, pencils.

What to do

Let the children play draughts, but they must

say the co-ordinates of the square to which they wish to move. If they then move to a different square, they must go back and miss a go.

Alternatively, ask the children to set up draughts positions. Pairs of children can then write down the positions which the draughts might take for successive moves. They can then follow each other's games and discuss strategy.

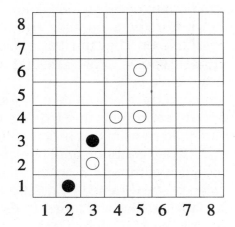

The children might be interested to look at chess games as described in newspapers:

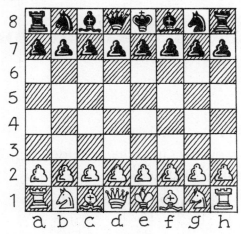

The following account of the start of a recent game between Anatoly Karpov (Russia) and John Nunn (England) uses modern chess notation:

1. d4   Nf6
2. c4   g6
3. Nc3   Bg7

This means that the first pair of moves are white pawn to d4 (as only one piece can move to d4, the writer doesn't define which) and black knight to f6 (as more than one piece can move to f6, the writer has to say which – N stands for knight!).

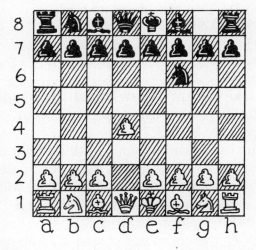

The next pair of moves, c4 g6, can only be pawn moves:

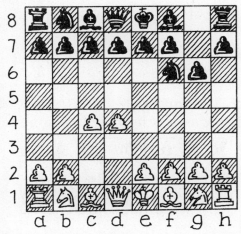

The third pair, Nc3 Bg7, means white knight to c3 and black bishop to g7:

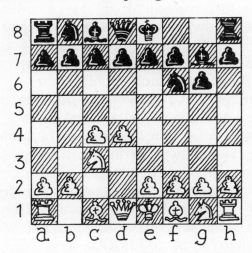

Karpov, playing white, eventually won this game. Children who play chess may like to set up the start of the match and see how the game might have progressed, recording their moves for others to follow and comment on later.

Formal co-ordinate representation

Only when children have had a good deal of experience of the two concepts of graphical representation – a position having a unique label and that we look along first – using squares as the 'information holders', should we introduce the idea that we can label the *lines* instead of the squares.

Convincing the children that they need to make this change is rather difficult. To claim it is necessary in order to be more accurate (as in trying to find buried treasure) is not entirely valid, as the children could be more accurate merely by making the squares smaller. Thus the following becomes more accurate simply by changing the size of squares:

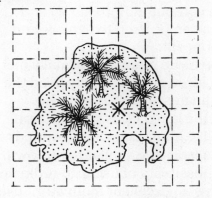

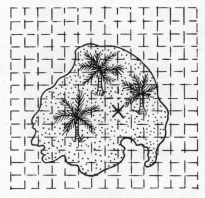

As, in neither case, is the treasure actually on a line, it is hard to see why moving on to lines is helpful!

However, you can explain to the children how it would be helpful to be able to draw a line which goes exactly through the treasure, but this requires, in the case above, using decimals. Perhaps if the children are not ready for decimals, then they are not ready for proper co-ordinates?

This argument is upheld by the National Curriculum, where the use of co-ordinates to represent a point (AT3 Level 4) coincides with the understanding of decimals (AT2 Level 4), excepting decimal money at Level 3. This certainly seems to be supported by common sense, if not by some of our older schemes of work.

It is proposed, therefore, that using the point or line definition of co-ordinates is delayed until the children are acquainted with decimals, at which time a viable and persuasive case can be made for their improved accuracy.

Co-ordinates on a computer

An excellent introduction to co-ordinates as representations of points is drawing using co-ordinates on a computer. Both LOGO and BASIC graphics can be used to explore and practise this concept.

In LOGO, the turtle graphics normally met by primary children do not usually need the input of co-ordinates. In fact, one of the advantages of the language is that the turtle moves rather like humans do and responds to commands in a language similar to our own. However, the possibility of using co-ordinates exists and forms an excellent motivator. Also, once a program is written and saved, exploration of the effect of changes to the co-ordinates becomes more accessible than the sometimes painstaking plotting of many points on paper.

The command to move the turtle to a position (x,y) is SETPOS [x y]. Try typing in a few co-ordinates:

```
SETPOS [200 0]
SETPOS [200 300]
SETPOS [0 300]
SETPOS [0 0]
```

If you want to save the drawing, you will first have to put the instructions in a procedure:

```
TO RECT
SETPOS [200 0]
SETPOS [200 300]
SETPOS [0 300]
SETPOS [0 0]
END
```

To make the turtle draw this shape, simply type: RECT. To save this procedure on to disc, type: SAVE "RECT.

If you are not sure of your position on the screen, type PRINT POS and the co-ordinates will be given. Don't forget that the turtle will always draw unless you type PENUP (and PENDOWN to restore drawing).

In LOGO, the computer screen is arranged with the origin (0,0) in the centre:

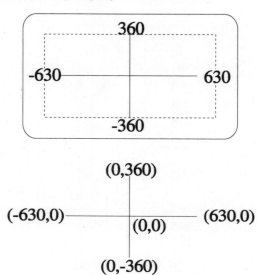

This is inconvenient for children who have not met negative numbers as only one quarter of the screen is available to them. Also, you will find that 200 does not go a long way in LOGO. Again, this is not helpful for the younger children. However, it is possible to use the function keys and a scaled down version of LOGO. The children will be limited slightly in what they can do, but the language is then accessible to Key Stage 1 children. (There are instructions in Appendix A under 'BabyLOGO' for making such changes. They do not specifically use co-ordinates, but will be of use to Key Stage 1 LOGO users.)

A simple concept keyboard is available which enables very young children to draw on screen using LOGO type commands (see Appendix A).

In BBC BASIC the origin is in the bottom left-hand corner of the screen. Before you begin you must prepare the screen for drawing by typing MODE 1. The two major commands required are MOVE and DRAW. Try the following:

```
MOVE 200,200
DRAW 200,500
DRAW 600,500
DRAW 600,200
DRAW 200,200
```

If you want to save a drawing, the program must be written with numbers at the beginning of each line:

```
10 MOVE 200,200
20 DRAW 200,500
30 DRAW 600,500
40 DRAW 600,200
50 DRAW 200,200
60 END
```

To make the turtle draw this shape, type: RUN. To save on to disc, type: SAVE "RECT".

A disadvantage of BASIC is that the text writes over the picture. This can be avoided by putting first:

```
VDU 24, 0; 0; 1100; 1100;
VDU 28, 0, 31, 39, 29
```

This defines the graphic window and the text window.

Basic can also be scaled down:

```
10 PRINT "Where do you want to go?"
20 INPUT X Y
30 PRINT "Do you want a line? Type Y or N"
40 INPUT A$
50 IF A$ = "Y" THEN DRAW X * 50, Y * 50
60 IF A$ = "N" THEN MOVE X * 50, Y * 50
70 GOTO 10
SAVE "SCALE
```

Children can now draw large pictures with small numbers (X and Y are multiplied by 50).

For further information on BASIC and LOGO see Appendix A at the end of the book (page 203).

Other activities to reinforce co-ordinates as representations of points are similar in style to the previous activities for 'block' representation. Very many of the activities already met are easily adapted.

Also to be introduced before pupils can represent mappings via co-ordinates (AT3 Level 6c) is the concept of co-ordinates in four quadrants (AT3 Level 5).

By this stage, children should have already met negative numbers horizontally (AT2 Level 3 PoS), for example, as a time-line:

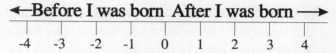

And vertically, for example, as a height/depth chart:

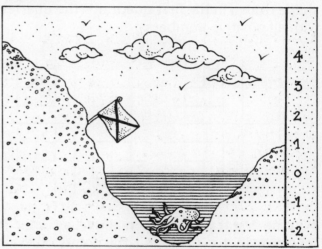

Therefore, it is a fairly simple procedure to combine the two. Ask the children how the points below could be labelled:

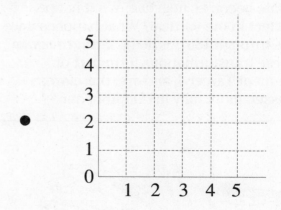

Help them, through questioning, to reach a solution.

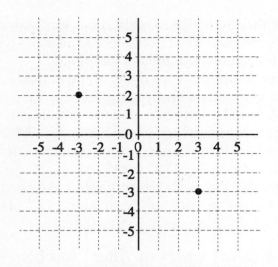

An excellent method of reinforcing the full co-ordinate system is through transformational geometry, that is through translating, enlarging, reflecting or rotating a shape drawn in the first quadrant (the quarter with all positive numbers).

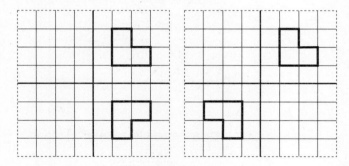

In the first transformation above, a reflection in the horizontal, the points on the shape have changed thus: $(1, 1) \rightarrow (1, -1)$; $(3, 1) \rightarrow (3, -1)$; $(2, 3) \rightarrow (2, -3)$. The 'x' co-ordinate does not change, but the 'y' co-ordinate becomes negative. What happens if we reflect in the vertical? What happens if we rotate through 180°, as in the second diagram?

These transformations form part of Attainment Target 4, and are, therefore, discussed more fully in Chapter Four.

Structured activities (Key Stage 2 only)

Co-ordinate pictures

What you need

Suggestions for co-ordinate pictures, squared paper, pencils.

What to do

Co-ordinate pictures are always a favourite activity! However, they can be a chore to devise, so you may welcome the ideas given below. The motivation to get the picture 'out' is a great concentrator of the mind on the rule 'along, then up'!

Tea-pot

A (5,9) (10,9)
B (12,7) (13,7) (14,6) (14,5) (13,4) (12,4) (12,7)
C (3,3) (3,8) (4,9) (5,9) (6,10) (7,10) (7,11) (8,11) (8,10) (9,10) (10,9) (11,9) (12,8) (14,8) (15,7) (15,4) (14,3) (12,3) (12,2) (9,0) (6,0) (3,1) (1,3) (1,6) (0,7) (1,8) (2,7) (2,4) (3,3)

Swan

A (3,8) (3,9)
B (7,2) (9,4) (8,4) (9,5) (6,5) (5,4)
C (4,10) (5,9) (5,6) (4,5) (4,4) (5,5) (7,6) (8,6) (10,5) (11,6) (11,5) (12,5) (11,4) (12,4) (10,2) (8,1) (3,1) (2,3) (3,5) (4,6) (4,8) (2,8) (4,10)

Explain to the children that the pictures are arranged in groups of co-ordinates. They should begin at the start of each group, marking and joining each point to the next. At the end of a group, they must abandon that line of dots, starting afresh with the next group.

Ask the children to make up their own pictures. Those who are ready for decimal work should include decimals in their co-ordinates. They will hence be able to produce much more detailed and more realistic pictures.

NC mapping

AT3 – Level 4 (c)

Line noughts and crosses/OXO/ Connect three: 2

What you need
Squared paper, pencils.

What to do
Adapt the game under the title 'Noughts and crosses' on page 61 to use line positions.

NC mapping
AT3 – Level 4 (c)

Symmetry

What you need
Squared paper, pencils.

What to do
Ask the children to draw a symmetrical shape on a grid, like the one below:

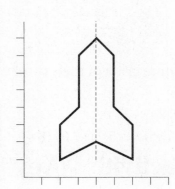

Left	Right
(3,7)	(5,7)
(3,4)	(5,4)
(2,3)	(6,3)
(2,1)	(6,1)

Using mirrors if required, the children should draw in the lines of symmetry. Next, ask them each to choose one point on their shape, write its co-ordinates and then write beside it the co-ordinates of its reflection point. They should repeat this several times. What do they notice? (If the mirror line is an 'x' line – as in the example above, which is $x = 4$ – then the x co-ordinates will be equally spaced on either side of it.)

What happens if the shape is inclined (for example, if the mirror line is a diagonal/ sloping line)?

NC mapping
AT3 – Level 4 (c)

Symmetry in four quadrants

Try this activity with children who are meeting negative co-ordinates for the first time, with the pictures drawn along the *x or* y axis:

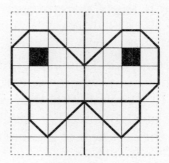

And along the *x and* y axes:

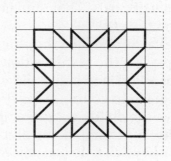

Snowflake pictures for a Christmas display come immediately to mind!

The line of symmetry may also be along a diagonal:

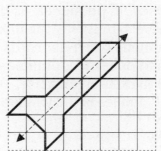

In each case, ask the children to choose points on one side of a mirror (symmetry) line and record where the reflection is. What do they notice?

NC mapping
AT3 – Level 5 PoS

Junior line families

A variation on 'Line families' (see page 58).

What you need

One blank 4×4 grid with x and y lines labelled 1 to 4 (the grid should be large enough to take playing cards at the line intersections); 48 blank playing cards on each of which is written (1, 1), or (1, 2), or (3, 2) and so on (there will be 16 kinds, three of each).

What to do

Sit the children around the blank grid and check that they know where the cards (2, 1), (2, 2), (2, 3), (2, 4) go and that they realise why we get a straight line. (For Level 6 children, do they know that the line is called $x = 2$?)

Explain that they are going to play a game similar to 'Happy families' where they have to collect a family of cards. Their families will make a line on the grid.

Shuffle the cards and deal the children four cards each, placing the rest face down in the centre. Choose who is to begin and which way you are going to go round the group. The first child asks the child next to her if he has any cards with, for example, the first number as a 3. (Or for Level 6, if he has any cards with x equal to 3.) If the other child has some, he must hand them over. If not, the first child must take a card from the top of the pile. Continue round the circle in this way until a child thinks she has a line family. At this point she must say so and put her cards on the grid to prove it (Level 6 must say the name of the line). She can then collect her cards up again and put them to one side. Continue playing in this way until there is an impasse. The child with the most families is the winner.

NC mapping

AT3 – Level 4 (c)

Negative line families

This activity can be adapted to use negative numbers. Use a 7×7 grid (–3 to 3 each way) and 98 cards (2×49). The children again need only find four in a line and these need not be consecutive.

NC mapping

AT3 – Level 5 PoS

68

Wobbly grids

This activity does not really introduce any new concept, but children enjoy it so much that it is well worth doing.

What you need

Blank plain grids, blank 'wobbly' grids (photocopiable page 189), pencils.

What to do

Ask the children to draw a simple shape on their blank grids and then choose a wobbly grid from photocopiable page 189. They must then copy the co-ordinates of their first pictures on to the wobbly grid and join them up to make the transformed shapes. Let the children compare results, choose another grid and repeat for a new picture.

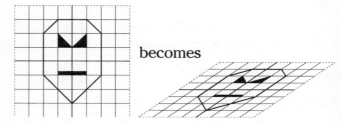

becomes

Can they make up some grids of their own?

NC mapping

AT3 – Level 4 (c)

Open-ended activities (Key Stage 2 only)

Computer drawing

What you need

Computers with either BASIC or LOGO; squared paper, pencils for planning.

What to do

Children can draw pictures using co-ordinates in both LOGO and BASIC. (See pages 64–66 for examples and instructions.) Set the children challenges such as the following:

• Draw a square and draw a smaller one inside it. Repeat this until there is no more room. These are called 'nested squares'. Draw some other nested shapes.

• Draw an equilateral triangle. Use another one to make a star.

• Draw a spiral, a maze and a frieze pattern.

Such activities reinforce the order and use of co-ordinates.

NC mapping

AT3 – Level 4 (c)

Computer drawing in four quadrants

In LOGO, children automatically find the need for negative co-ordinates. Hence they will naturally move into the four quadrants.

NC mapping

AT3 – Level 5 PoS

Curve stitching

What you need

Blank grids for the first quadrant, at least 0 to 6 on each axis.

What to do

Ask the children to join the following points: (5,0) to (0,0); (4,0) to (0,1); (3,0) to (0,2); (2,0) to (0,3); (1,0) to (0,4); (0,0) to (0,5). Can they see a pattern in the way the co-ordinates have been chosen? Ask them to make up some more patterns and plot them. If they are using a four-quadrant grid, ask them to predict the pairs, and then draw them.

NC mapping

AT3 – Level 5 PoS

Graphs of functions

For the more-able top juniors, we now enter an interesting world. Children at Level 6 should be: **'drawing and interpreting simple mappings in context, recognising their general features'** (AT3 Level 6 PoS). They should also: **'Use and plot Cartesian co-ordinates to represent mappings'** (AT3 Level 6c SoA).

'$x \rightarrow x + 1$ (or $y = x + 1$)
$x \rightarrow 2 - x$ (or $y = 2 - x$)
$x \rightarrow x^2$ (or $y = x^2$)' (AT3 Level 6 Examples).

The first step along this road, and one to be taken *before* Level 6 (at Level 4, say) is the concept of a co-ordinate system representing a mapping. For example, an 'Add 3' machine:

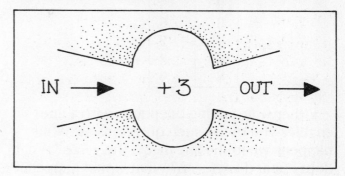

This gives a mapping:

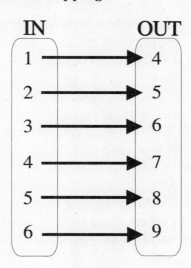

This can then be plotted:

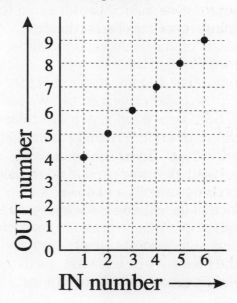

Alternatively, it can be written as a table. Now, however, in preparation for the graph, we call the 'IN' number 'x' and the 'OUT' number 'y':

x	y
1	4
2	5
3	6
4	7
5	8
6	9

Either way, joining the points with a line enables you to ask such questions as: What happens when the line meets the y axis? What does it stand for/mean? What would happen if we continued the line backwards or forwards? Will it ever end? If we fed in 4.5, what would come out? If 3.5 came out, what went in?

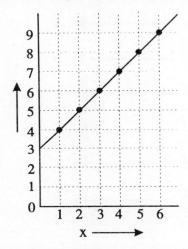

These last two questions are very important for establishing the idea that there are an infinite number of co-ordinates (decimals, of course) making up the line; in other words, seeing the function as continuous. Also, the questions give the children practice at *using* a graph. We have, in the past, been very good at getting children to draw graphs, but not at reading them and interpreting them. Given the amount of statistical evidence now used in advertising, television programmes and so on, it is important that the citizens of the future are able to analyse the information presented to them.

The next step towards Level 6 (at Level 5, say) is the concept of a line having a name. Let us look at some peculiar machines:

Co-ordinates in	Co-ordinates out
(5,2)	(3,2)
(6,9)	(3,9)
(4,7)	(3,7)
(2,6)	(3,6)

Whatever we feed in, the x co-ordinate will always become 3 (the first numbers 5, 6, 4, 2 have all changed to 3).

Plotting such a line will give the following:

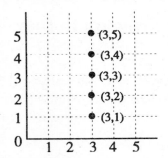

The line is called $x = 3$.

Similarly, if the second co-ordinate is always 4, and we call this number 'y', then the line these dots lie on is called $y = 4$:

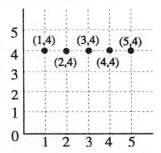

An activity for reinforcing this concept is 'Junior line families' (see page 67). Children collect playing cards, on which are written co-ordinate pairs, for example (1,1) or (1,2), or (3,2), until they have a set of four which form a straight line. This is a line 'family'. The child with the most line families at the end is the winner.

What is special about this line?

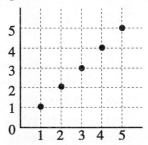

This could be the output from a 'do nothing' machine:

The co-ordinates are (1,1), (2,2), (3,3), (4,4) and so on, and therefore it is called, not surprisingly, y = x.

That we don't normally say x = y is purely a convention – 'y' is usually taken to be the 'unknown' which we are trying to find, with 'x' being the known value which we manipulate.

What about this set of points?

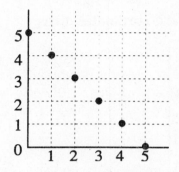

The co-ordinates are (0,5), (1,4), (2,3), (3,2), (4,1), (5,0) and the line is called y + x = 5. If we rewrite it as y = 5 – x, we have something very similar to the Level 6 example.

What sort of machine could produce these co-ordinates? Here is one:

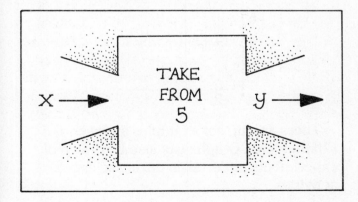

Children should be encouraged to plot relationships they know, such as the multiplication tables. For example, the two times table would have the following co-ordinates: (1,2), (2,4), (3,6), (4,8) and so on. It would be represented graphically as follows:

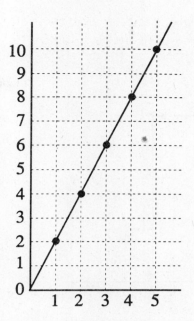

Drawing the line through the points helps us to see the 'slope'. Ask the children to compare this slope with the slope of the three times and four times tables:

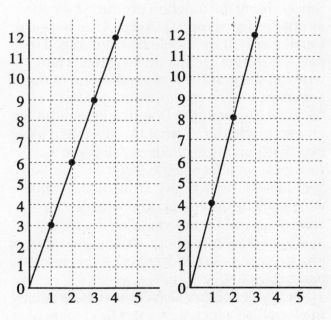

If the children have been working with inverse machines, ask them to try and work out how they can see both the machine and its inverse on the same graph. For example, on the graph above, if 8 came out of the machine, what went in? This encourages the children to read across and down to find the original number:

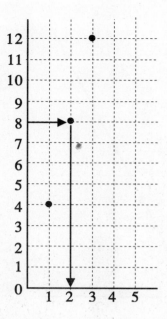

Graphing activities

Plotting sequences

Any sequence can be plotted and the line representing the function produced. As soon as children are ready (Level 6 of the National Curriculum), they should be encouraged to plot the results of their investigations and write on the graph the generalisation of the sequence (called the 'mapping' in the National Curriculum). Does the generalisation give some clue as to what the line might look like? With practice, children will come to recognise which sequences (or generalisations) will give straight lines and which will be curves. In other words, the children should try to visualise the function and then draw it to check. Only a good deal of practice can help children reach this level of understanding.

Such practice can also come from graphing the formulae which they meet in the rest of the mathematics curriculum. This gives the plotting of points more purpose, as well as improving their understanding of the relationship. Let us consider, as an example, plotting the area of a square.

What you need

Graph paper, the results of an investigation into the area of a square.

What to do

Explain to the children that the property we are changing is plotted along the x axis, while the results we obtain are plotted along the y axis.

Ask them to look at their table of results and identify the co-ordinates they will plot; for example, for the area of a square:

Length of side of square	Area of square	
1	1	(1,1)
2	4	(2,4)
3	9	➡ (3,9)
4	16	(4,16)
5	25	(5,25)

Plotting the co-ordinates gives:

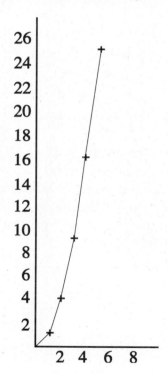

There are further examples at the end of Chapter Two. Graphs can also be drawn of experiments undertaken during science activities.

Chapter Two
Generalised arithmetic

Number structure and relationships

Children working at Level 2 of the National Curriculum will be heavily involved in the manipulation of number facts. They will be using addition and subtraction to solve simple number problems, beginning to work in 'tens' and learning to solve simple money and measurement problems. They are also required to 'know' number facts up to 10, rising to 20 by Level 3. By 'know' is meant the ability to recall answers without having to model them with fingers or bricks. In other words, the children should be able to manipulate these numbers mentally – a skill

which only develops slowly. The process can be greatly helped if children recognise both the structure of numbers and operations on those numbers.

NB: all the patterns and rules discussed in this chapter work for positive whole numbers. You may wish to explore for yourselves what happens for negative numbers, fractions and so on.

Some rules for addition

The simplest exploration of number structure is that of partitioning. Partitioning can be single (the splitting of a number into two smaller numbers) or multiple (a split into several numbers). Children often meet partitioning as the 'story' of a number, when they have to find all the ways of splitting that number. For example, the following is part of the story of 8, shown with counters:

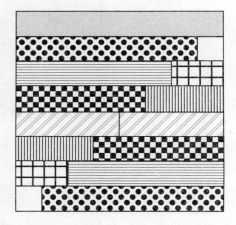

Using colour rods, the partitioning would look like this:

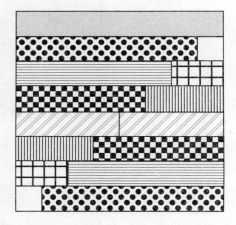

Single partitions of 5 can be shown with one hand:

1 and 4   2 and 3   3 and 2   4 and 1

Similarly, 10 can be shown with two hands:

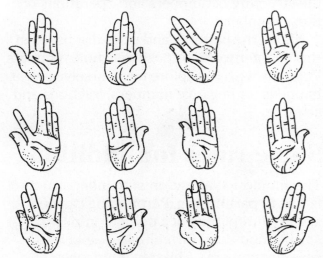

The children may see patterns in the rods and hands used in the above arrangements, for example the symmetry of the hand patterns for '3 and 7' and '7 and 3'. Formal recording of the results will help them to see the structure more clearly:

1 + 4 = 5	1 + 9 = 10
2 + 3 = 5	2 + 8 = 10
3 + 2 = 5	3 + 7 = 10
4 + 1 = 5	4 + 6 = 10
	5 + 5 = 10
	6 + 4 = 10
	7 + 3 = 10
	8 + 2 = 10
	9 + 1 = 10

The children may also notice – spontaneously or after a prompt – that:
• the numbers go down one way and up the other (although this may seem trivial to an adult, to a child this may be a revelation);
• there is symmetry about the table of results as a whole;
• 1 and 9 is at the top and 9 and 1 at the bottom, and so on.

Remembering that 1 + 9 is the same as 9 + 1 (the *commutative* property of addition) is very important as many mental methods of calculation depend upon this knowledge. Young children will, if asked to find 2 + 8 begin at the 2 and add on the 8 – usually on fingers. This is time consuming and there are many opportunities to go wrong. Only later will they realise that they can begin at the 8 and add 2 and get the same answer. Experimenting with partitions, as in the above examples, can help children to make these connections more quickly.

Older children, and adults, with quick and successful mental methods of calculation use such knowledge to find sophisticated short cuts. For example, in adding 27 and 45, one common method is to look for a 'complement' of 45, in other words a number which we can add to 45 to make a multiple of 10. Some will use 5, make 50 and then add on the remaining 22 (adding on to multiples of 10 being easier). Others will add 3 to the 27 to make 30: 27 + 45 = 30 + 42 = 72.

Many will begin with the 45, adding on 10, then 10, then 7, secure in the knowledge that it doesn't matter with which number you begin. Any group of numerate adults will produce further permutations of this theme.

Similarly, children will develop such transformations as: 7 + 8 = (7 − 2) + (8 + 2) = 5 + 10 = 15 while thinking: '7 + 8, add 2 to the 8 to make 10, so take 2 from the 7 to make 5, add 10 and 5'. By doing so, they exhibit the knowledge that subtraction is the inverse of addition.

We have all developed such methods independently of the way we were taught at school (some, however, do actually see the sum in their minds, as if written on paper, and carry out the formal method mentally) but it is now recognised that we can help children find their own methods by providing opportunities to make such pattern links.

Partitioning can also be multiple, for example:

$$5 = 1 + 1 + 1 + 1 + 1$$
$$5 = 2 + 1 + 1 + 1$$
$$5 = 2 + 2 + 1$$
$$5 = 3 + 1 + 1$$
$$5 = 3 + 2$$
$$5 = 4 + 1$$

This leads us on to another rule about the manipulation of numbers, the *associative* rule: if we take 5 = 3 + 1 + 1, from above, does it matter whether we add the 3 and 1 first and then the other 1, or if we add the two 1s and then add the 3? Children who realise that it *doesn't* matter can choose how to do the sum. For most of us, adding the two 1s first is easier, as doubling is one of the most natural of arithmetic processes.

Listing such partitions practises and reinforces number relationships, but there is also an important underlying process in striving to find them all. Younger children, and those with little experience of searching for pattern, tend to work erratically and impulsively. They will write down all the solutions which come to mind and will not realise if they have missed any. If they have some idea of the number of partitions there are – for example, if other more-able children become competitive about the number of solutions they have found – only then will they attempt to find others systematically. Some children will not manage this second step and can become frustrated and lose interest unless the teacher intervenes.

Helping children by showing them your own method of assuring you have all the partitions can be 'dangerous', as such a method may be seen as definitive. It is much better to collect the children together and ask them to explain, in turn, how they found their solutions. In this way, the children benefit from hearing several different ways of working, of seeing that these different ways are all acceptable and that they can then pick and choose methods for themselves. The communication skills of Attainment Target 1 (Using and applying mathematics) are also practised and the enthusiasm can be infectious!

Partitioning with money is interesting, as only *some* bonds are allowed. We are restricted by the coins we use. For example, in how many ways can we pay for a chocolate bar which costs 12p?

10p + 2p
10p + 1p + 1p
5p + 5p + 2p
5p + 5p + 1p + 1p
5p + 2p + 2p + 2p + 1p
5p + 2p + 2p + 1p + 1p + 1p
5p + 2p + 1p + 1p + 1p + 1p + 1p
5p + 1p + 1p + 1p + 1p + 1p + 1p + 1p
2p + 2p + 2p + 2p + 2p + 2p
2p + 2p + 2p + 2p + 2p + 1p + 1p
2p + 2p + 2p + 2p + 1p + 1p + 1p + 1p
2p + 2p + 2p + 1p + 1p + 1p + 1p + 1p + 1p
2p + 2p + 1p + 1p + 1p + 1p + 1p + 1p + 1p + 1p
2p + 1p + 1p + 1p + 1p + 1p + 1p + 1p + 1p + 1p + 1p
1p + 1p + 1p + 1p + 1p + 1p + 1p + 1p + 1p + 1p + 1p + 1p

Phew! It is not always necessary to find them all! The children will learn a valuable lesson by finding some of the combinations, and a group of children can combine their work. Even then, you may choose not to bother with all the possibilities. You must judge what is best for the particular group of children.

Some rules for subtraction

Through similar exercises to the previous partitioning ones, we can help children to discover that subtraction isn't commutative (the word is not important, only the idea); for example, while 7 equals $9 - 2$, it does not equal $2 - 9$.

Interestingly, if children try this on a calculator, they will get –7, which they will 'feel' is the same in some way, and we are brought into the world of negative numbers. Does this always work? Why? If we look at the length of the numbers on a two-way number line, and align this with colour rods, things may become clearer:

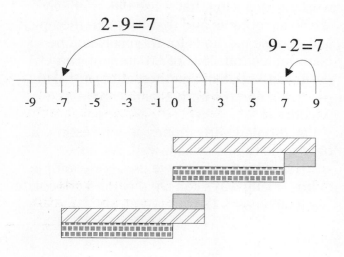

This is not easy to visualise, but the symmetry can be seen by the two 7 rods on either side of 0.

Subtraction is not associative either. If we take the sum $9 - 5 - 2$, the answer will depend upon which subtraction is done first; for example: $(9 - 5) - 2 = 2$ but $9 - (5 - 2) = 6$.

However, subtraction does follow some patterns. For example, $9 - 2 = 7$ and $9 - 7 = 2$. We shall call this the *swap* rule. The swap rule

is not one of the fundamental rules of arithmetic (like commutativity, associativity), but it is a consequence of them. Recognition of such patterns offers children a chance to check their answers mentally.

Some rules for multiplication

Multiplication often behaves like addition; for example, it is commutative: $3 \times 5 = 15$ and $5 \times 3 = 15$. It is also associative; for example, take the sum $2 \times 3 \times 4 = 24$. This is correct whether you first do 2×3 and then multiply by 4, or 3×4 and then multiply by 2.

Also multiplication *does not* obey the swap rule: $7 \times 8 = 56$ but 7×56 does not equal 8.

Some rules for division

Division often behaves in the same way as subtraction. It isn't commutative: $15 \div 3 = 5$ but $3 \div 15$ does not equal 5 (you may wish to look more closely at this with older juniors, as what we do get is '1 over' the number, or the reciprocal: $3 \div 15 = \frac{1}{5}$). Neither is division associative; for example, look at $20 \div 2 \div 5 = 2$. This is the solution if we do the divisions in the order in which they are written. However, if we do the $2 \div 5$ first and then divide 20 by this answer, we get 50! $20 \div (2 \div 5) = 20 \div 0.4 = 50$.

Division also obeys the swap rule: $15 \div 3 = 5$ and $15 \div 5 = 3$, giving a way of checking calculations.

A further rule for multiplication and division

The following rule provides an area of investigation for children who might just be learning about the concepts of multiplication and division.

Consider $8 \times 4 = 32$. The 8 can be split into $3 + 5$. If we then multiply the 3 and the 5 by 4, and add the answers together, we get the same final answer of 32.

Four lots of 8 makes 32:

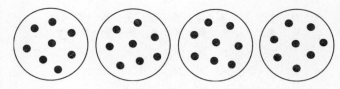

Split each 8 into a 5 and a 3:

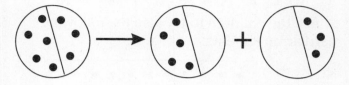

This gives four lots of 5 makes 20:

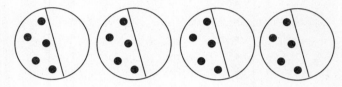

And four lots of 3 makes 12:

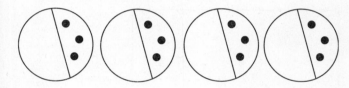

So, $8 \times 4 = (5 + 3) \times 4 = (5 \times 4) + (3 \times 4)$

This works for any partition of 8 and is called the *distributive* rule. It also holds for division:

$18 \div 3 = (12 + 6) \div 3 = (12 \div 3) + (6 \div 3) = 6$

Symbolic notation

The names for the various rules for addition, subtraction, multiplication and division are unimportant to the children. The concepts, though, are vital both for improving mental mathematics and for their future development in algebra.

These rules can all be represented symbolically and these are as follows:
• Commutative rule: a*b = b*a
(addition and multiplication)
• Associative rule: a*(b*c) = (a*b)*c
(addition and multiplication)
• Swap rule: if a*b = c, then a*c = b
(subtraction and division)
• Distributive rule: if a*b = c and a = d + e
then (d + e)*b = c, giving d*b + e*b = c
(multiplication and division)

Closure

Another interesting concept is that of *closure*. If whole positive numbers are added to whole positive numbers, we always get a whole positive number. We say addition is *closed* over the positive whole numbers. Multiplication is also closed – you can't multiply two positive whole numbers together and get a decimal (nor a negative number). Subtraction is not closed: 5 – 7 = –2, which isn't positive. Division is not closed either: 3 ÷ 4 = 0.75, which isn't a whole number. Juniors should be helped to find out these facts for themselves and also to investigate whether, for example, fractions are closed. (There is a closure exercise for young children on page 98. It is not difficult to set up others in the primary classroom.)

Structured activities for Key Stage 1

Curve stitching: 1

What you need

Cardboard squares with holes punched in them as shown below; needles and thread (alternatively, paper marked as below and coloured pencils).

What to do

Show the children how to sew a thread through to connect 9 and 1 as shown below.

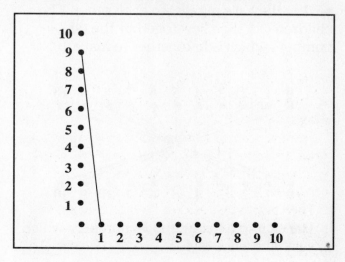

Ask them to continue sewing together numbers which add up to 10.

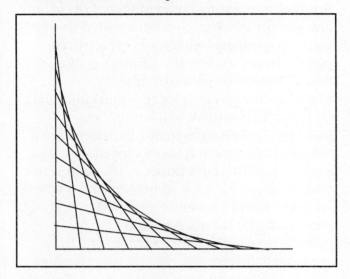

What would the pattern 'Join together numbers whose difference is 4' look like?

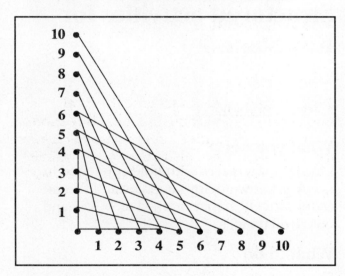

Alternatively, arrange the two number lines so that they are parallel to each other. The children can then sew together the two numbers which add together to make 10.

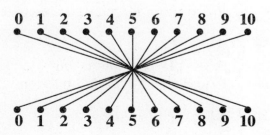

The example below shows numbers which have a difference of 4.

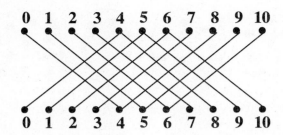

Ask the children to try also the following card arrangements:

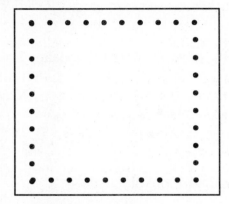

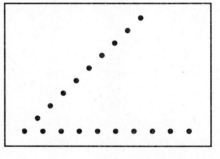

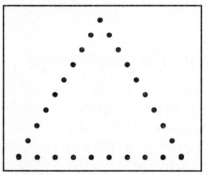

NC mapping

AT3 – Level 2 (a)
AT1 – Level 2 (a) (b)
AT2 – Level 2 (a)

Trios

What you need

A number of like objects, say six conkers; a box lid, set loop or tray.

What to do

Put the objects in a box lid, or on a tray, or in a set loop or in any other way that will emphasise that they are the only ones we are going to look at. Ask the children to count them, and then push two, say, to one side. Can the children think of a number connection to link the two separate piles? For example, they may say that 'two and four make six', or 'six take away two leaves four'.

As they find connections, write down their number sentences in words and symbols; for example 'Two and four make six' is written 2 + 4 = 6; 'six take away two leaves four' is written 6 – 2 = 4. Some number sentences will have the same symbolic notation (that is, the same *equation*); for example, 'The difference between six and two is four' is also written 6 – 2 = 4. Collect together all those number sentences which have the same equation for discussion.

For those which the children cannot think of, you can provide the language and ask the children to write down the symbolic forms; for example, 'Six is the same as two plus four': 6 = 2 + 4; 'Four is left behind if you have six and take two away': 4 = 6 – 2.

These activities prepare the way for turning equations around and reinforcing the link between addition and subtraction:

$$2 + 5 = 7$$
$$2 = 7 - 5$$
$$5 = 7 - 2$$

Ask the children to find trios and make up the expressions as above.

Also ask the children to fill in the gaps in cards such as:

7 =	2 +	5
7	2	5
7	5	2
7	5	2

NC mapping

AT3 – Level 3 (b)
AT1 – Level 2 (a) (b)
AT2 – Level 2 (a)

Domino triangle

What you need

Sets of dominoes, photocopiable page 190.

What to do

Show the children photocopiable page 190. Discuss with them what each row is doing and what each column is doing. Ask them to fill in the blank dominoes. They may need to use a real set of dominoes to help them.

NC mapping

AT3 – Level 2 (a)
AT1 – Level 2 (a) (b)
AT2 – Level 1 (a)

Dominoes

What you need

A set of dominoes.

What to do

Ask the children to investigate the total number of dots on each domino. They should then put together those dominoes which have the same total. How many dominoes make 0? How many make 1 or 2? Which numbers are made from double dominoes?

NC mapping

AT3 – Level 2 (a)
AT1 – Level 2 (a) (b)
AT2 – Level 2 (a)

Domino tens

What you need

A set of dominoes numbers up to nine.

What to do

Let the children play dominoes, but they should join dominoes that add up to ten.

NC mapping

AT3 – Level 2 (a)
AT1 – Level 2 (a) (b)
AT2 – Level 2 (a)

Baby kangaroo

What you need

Photocopiable page 191.

What to do

Baby kangaroo likes to show off his jumping by making all his jumps the same size. Ask the children to find a jump size which will get him exactly to the eighth stepping stone.

How many jumps will there be with this jump size? (Four jumps of 2 and two jumps of 4.) The children can then work through photocopiable page 191.

This activity prepares children for multiplication, and also demonstrates the commutative rule, that is 4×2 is the same as 2×4.

NC mapping

AT3 – Level 3 (a)
AT1 – Level 2 (a) (b) (c)
AT2 – working towards Level 3 (b)

Structured activities for Key Stage 2

Partition tens

What you need

Paper, pencils.

What to do

Ask the children to complete the following type of table:

$63 = 60 + 3$
$ = 50 + 13$
$ = 40 + 23$ and so on.

Follow this with isolated cases, for example:
$79 = 40 + \square$ and $56 = 20 + \square$

The children might also like to try partitioning hundreds.

Alternatively, ask them to look for patterns in the answers to such groups of sums as:

14 + 15	23 – 17
24 + 15	33 – 17
34 + 15...	43 – 17...

Can the children generalise to answer such questions as 74 + 15?

NC mapping

AT3 – Level 3 (a)
AT1 – Level 2 (a) (b) (c)
AT2 – Level 3 (b) (c)

Ancient numbers

What you need

No special requirements.

What to do

Children's understanding of the place value system we use can be enhanced by studying other, ancient place value systems.

Introduce the children to one of the number systems shown below. Ask them how that particular civilisation might have written, for example, the number 17.

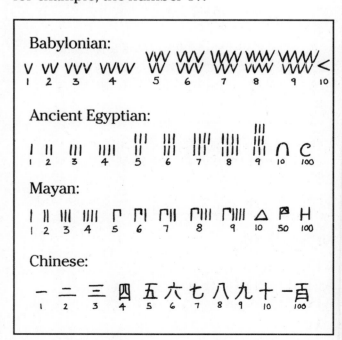

Repeat this process with other numbers until you think the children have grasped the concept. Ask them to make up some sums for a friend in that number system.

As an extension to this activity, see if the children can complete hundred squares for the ancient number systems.

NC mapping

AT3 – Level 4 (a)
AT1 – Level 4 (a) (b)
AT2 – working towards Level 4 (b)

The Chinese hundred square jigsaw

What you need

Photocopiable page 192.

What to do

Cut up the Chinese hundred square on photocopiable page 192 to make a jigsaw puzzle. Then ask the children to put it back together again. They may also like to have a go at this using jigsaw pieces they have made themselves.

NC mapping

AT3 – Level 4 (a)
AT1 – Level 4 (a) (b)
AT2 – working towards Level 4 (b)

A bigger table

What you need

Multiplication squares.

What to do

Children who are ready to extend their understanding and knowledge of multiplication bonds beyond 5 × 5, can use this knowledge to build upon. Give each child a multiplication square on which is written the facts to 5 × 5. (Alternatively, provide only the top row and side column numbers and ask the children to fill it in themselves.)

Ask the children if they can see any patterns. Can they continue the patterns to fill in the table?

NC mapping

AT3 – Level 4 (a)
AT1 – Level 3 (c) (d)
    – Level 4 (b) (c) (d)
AT2 – Level 3 (b) (c)

Curve stitching: 2

What you need

Circles which are marked on the circumference with 10° intervals.

What to do

Show the children how to start a 'multiples' pattern on one of the circles. For example, for the multiples of two they should join 1 to 2; 2 to 4; 3 to 6; 4 to 8 and so on. Ask the children to finish their own circles. What patterns do they get? Encourage them to try other multiples; for example:

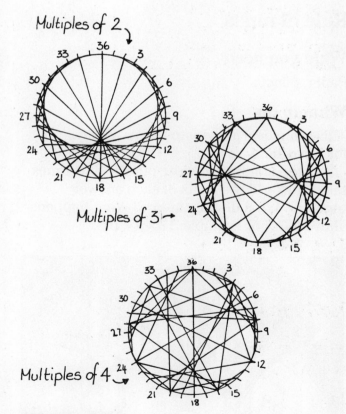

NC mapping

AT3 – Level 3 (a)
    – Level 4 (a)
AT1 – Level 3 (c) (d)
    – Level 4 (b)
AT2 – working towards Level 3 (b)

Divisibility rules

What you need

Paper, pencils, calculators (optional).

What to do

Ask the children to write out the two times table (they may need to go beyond 2×10) and look at the last digit in the answers. What do they notice? Through discussion, establish the pattern (2, 4, 6, 8, 0, 2, 4, 6, 8, 0...). How can they tell if a number can be divided by 2? Repeat this process for the five and ten times tables.

NC mapping

AT3 – Level 4 (a)
AT1 – Level 3 (c) (d)
      – Level 4 (b) (c) (d)
AT2 – Level 3 (b) (c)

Rule of nines

What you need

Paper, pencils.

What to do

This is an ideal activity to use as a follow-up for 'Divisibility rules'.

Ask the children to write out the nine times table, and add the digits of each answer together. What do they notice? What happens above 90? (For example: $12 \times 9 = 108$; $1 + 0 + 8 = 9$.)

The 'Rule of nines' is a famous test for divisibility by nine. Ask the children if they know of any other rules like this. For example, they may like to look at a pattern for eleven: 11, 22, 33 and so on. From 100 to 999 the two outer numbers add up to make the middle number: $11 \times 13 = 143$; $1 + 3 = 4$. From 1000 to 9999, the sum of the first and third number is the same as the sum of the second and fourth number: $11 \times 314 = 3454$; $3 + 5 = 4 + 4$. However, it is important that children look for rules themselves rather than just pointing them out to them.

NC mapping

AT3 – Level 3 (a)
AT1 – Level 3 (c) (d)
AT2 – working towards Level 3 (b)

Russian multiplication

What you need

Paper, pencils.

What to do

New light can be shed on the workings and structure of number by studying how different cultures calculate. The early Russians multiplied thus: if they had to solve 41×68 they would halve one number and double the other (rounding down if they got any halves). They would repeat this until they reached 1. They would then cross out any lines with an even number in the 'halved' column and add up the other column. Thus:

$$
\begin{array}{rl}
41 & \times\ 68 \\
\cancel{20} & \cancel{136} \\
\cancel{10} & \cancel{272} \\
5 & 544 \\
\cancel{2} & \cancel{1088} \\
1 & \underline{2176} \\
& 2788
\end{array}
$$

How does this work? It is based on the principle that if we halve one side of a multiplication, we must double the other side in order to keep the same answer: $32 \times 14 = 16 \times 28 = 8 \times 56 = 4 \times 112 = 2 \times 224 = 1 \times 448$.

In the above example, the problem can be reduced to 'one times something' and therefore the problem is solved purely through halving and doubling (a process which we find much easier than other number operations). However, problems will very rarely end as neatly as this. Many numbers do not divide equally in two. The Russians have got round this by rounding down whenever halving doesn't give a whole number, but this means that part of the answer would be lost. Consider the original example, 41×68:

$$41 \times 68$$
$$\overline{20} \quad \overline{136}$$

When the 41 is halved and rounded to 20, we lose one lot of 68. Therefore 68 must be added on at the end.

$$5 \quad 544$$
$$\overline{2} \quad \overline{1088}$$

When the 5 is halved and rounded to 2, we lose one lot of 544. Therefore 544 must be added on at the end. Hence, adding all the right-handed numbers next to an odd left hand number will give the final answer.

This activity – besides its fascination – encourages doubling and halving skills and an improved understanding of place value.

NC mapping

AT3 – Level 3 (a)
     – Level 4 (a)
AT1 – Level 3 (c) (d)
AT2 – Level 4 (a) (b)

Ancient Egyptian multiplication

What you need

Paper, pencils.

What to do

The way that the Ancient Egyptians multiplied was discovered when the Rhind Papyrus (found by Henry Rhind in 1858) was translated. It was discovered that the Egyptians would solve a problem like 7×15 by repeated doubling and final addition:

$$1 \times 15 = 15$$
$$2 \times 15 = 30$$
$$\underline{4 \times 15 = 60}$$
$$7 \times 15 = 105$$

Similarly for 25×25:

$$1 \times 25 = 25$$
$$2 \times 25 = 50$$
$$4 \times 25 = 100$$
$$\underline{8 \times 25 = 200}$$
$$15 \times 25 = 375$$
$$8 \times 25 = 200 \text{ (already worked out above)}$$
$$\underline{2 \times 25 = 50}$$
$$25 \times 25 = 625$$

Show these examples to the children and ask them to make up some multiplication sums of their own to try.

NC mapping

AT3 – Level 3 (a)
     – Level 4 (a)
AT1 – Level 3 (c) (d)
AT2 – Level 4 (a) (b)

Vedic multiplication

What you need

Paper, pencils.

What to do

Vedic mathematics is an ancient Indian form of mathematics, rediscovered earlier this century by Sri Bharati Krsna Tirthaji. Vedic multiplication, like modern vertical multiplication, depends heavily on the understanding of place value and is hence a reinforcement of place value for older juniors.

Explain the method to the children.

● **Example 1: 54×42**

Write the numbers one below the other:

$$5\,4$$
$$\underline{4\,2}$$

Multiply the right-hand digits together and write the answer on the right-hand side:

$$\begin{array}{r} 5\,4 \\ \underline{4\,2} \\ 8 \end{array}$$

Cross multiply the digits diagonally opposite each other and add, that is $(5 \times 2) + (4 \times 4) = 26$. Put down the 6 and carry the 2.

$$\begin{array}{r} 5\,4 \\ \underline{4\,2} \\ 6\,8 \end{array}$$

Multiply the left-hand digits together and add the carried 2, that is $(5 \times 4) + 2 = 22$.

$$\begin{array}{r} 5\,4 \\ \underline{4\,2} \\ 2\,2\,6\,8 \end{array}$$

This method can be modelled on a dot system (the dots representing digits):

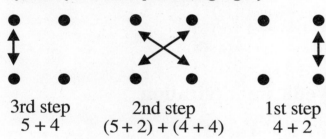

3rd step   2nd step   1st step
5 + 4   (5 + 2) + (4 + 4)   4 + 2

• Example 2: 123 × 456

First, do the right-hand multiplication: $3 \times 6 = 18$, put down the 8 and carry the 1:

$$\begin{array}{r} 1\,2\,3 \\ \underline{4\,5\,6} \\ 8 \end{array}$$

Now there are three possible crossings. Taking the right-hand cross multiplication first: $(2 \times 6) + (5 \times 3) = 27$, plus the carried 1 makes 28. Put down the 8 and carry the 2:

$$\begin{array}{r} 1\,2\,3 \\ \underline{4\,5\,6} \\ 8\,8 \end{array}$$

Now take the crossing from the far right to the far left, and add the middle multiplication:

$(1 \times 6) + (4 \times 3) + (2 \times 5) = 28$, plus the carried 2 makes 30. Put down the 0 and carry the 3:

$$\begin{array}{r} 1\,2\,3 \\ \underline{4\,5\,6} \\ 0\,8\,8 \end{array}$$

Now take the left-hand cross multiplication: $(1 \times 5) + (4 \times 2) = 13$, plus the carried 3 makes 16. Put down the 6 and carry the 1:

$$\begin{array}{r} 1\,2\,3 \\ \underline{4\,5\,6} \\ 6\,0\,8\,8 \end{array}$$

Finally, do the left-hand multiplication: $1 \times 4 = 4$, plus the carried 1 makes 5:

$$\begin{array}{r} 1\,2\,3 \\ \underline{4\,5\,6} \\ 5\,6\,0\,8\,8 \end{array}$$

The modelling would be:

• Example 3: 123 × 45

If the numbers do not have the same number of digits, just put in zeros until they do.

$$\begin{array}{r} 1\,2\,3 \\ \underline{0\,4\,5} \\ 5\,5\,3\,5 \end{array}$$

This comes from: $3 \times 5 = 15$
$(2 \times 5) + (4 \times 3) = 22$, plus 1 makes 23
$(1 \times 5) + (0 \times 3) + (2 \times 4) = 13$, plus 2 makes 15
$(1 \times 4) + (0 \times 2) = 4$, plus 1 makes 5
$1 \times 0 = 0$

The modelling for two four-digit numbers would be:

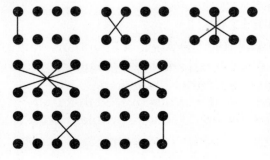

84

To see how Vedic multiplication works, let us return to the first example:

$$\begin{array}{r} 54 \\ \underline{42} \\ 2268 \end{array}$$

We can divide the answer into three sections: number of units; number of tens and number of hundreds. Ask the children where the number of units will come from (two lots of 4 – that is units by units), where the tens will come from (two lots of 50 and four lots of 40 – that is units by tens), and finally where the hundreds will come from (forty lots of 50 – that is tens by tens). For the second example: the hundreds come from the units by hundreds, as well as the tens by tens:

$$\begin{array}{r} 123 \\ \underline{456} \\ 56088 \end{array}$$

Finally, for a four-digit by a four-digit number, the thousands will come from the units by thousands and the tens by hundreds and so on.

Ask the children to make up some multiplication sums and solve them using the Vedic algorithm.

NC mapping

AT3 – Level 4 (a)
AT1 – Level 4 (b)(d)
     – Level 5 (a)
AT2 – Level 5 (a)

Open-ended activities for Key Stage 1

Multipartitions

What you need

Multilink or other number-modelling apparatus, paper, pencils.

What to do

Show the children how a stick of ten Multilink

can be split into two numbers, or three numbers and so on. In how many different ways can they break up 10 into smaller numbers? Can they find five ways or ten ways?

There are 29 answers, but you should not expect the children to find them all! (This is a good opportunity for group work.) However, they should be encouraged to be systematic about the way they find more answers, rather than letting them conduct a random search. For example, having found a way with all 2s (2 + 2 + 2 + 2 + 2), they should try leaving three of these 2s alone while they think what to do with the other two (giving 2 + 2 + 2 + 2 + 1 + 1 or 2 + 2 + 2 + 3 + 1).

NC mapping

AT3 – Level 2 (a)
AT1 – Level 2 (a) (b) (c)
AT2 – Level 2 (a)

Difference pairs

What you need

A set of cards labelled 0 to 10.

What to do

Ask the children to show you a pair of cards which have a difference of 1. Can they show you a different pair, also with a difference of 1? Ask them to find as many pairs as they can, and write them down.

In how many ways can the children pick up pairs of cards with a difference of 2 or 3?

NC mapping

AT3 – Level 2 (a)
AT1 – Level 2 (a) (b) (c)
AT2 – Level 2 (a)

5p, 10p

What you need

A set of plastic coins.

What to do

Show the children these coins:

The coins add together to make 5p. Can the children find other ways of making 5p? Repeat for 10p and, for children working towards Level 3, 20p.

NC mapping

AT3 – Level 2 (a)
AT1 – Level 2 (a) (b) (c)
AT2 – Level 2 (a) (b)

5 rod, 10 rod

What you need

Colour rods.

What to do

Ask the children to find different ways of making a rod the same length as a 5 rod. Then ask them to repeat the task for a 10 rod.

NC mapping

AT3 – Level 2 (a)
AT1 – Level 2 (a) (b) (c)
AT2 – Level 2 (a)

Three dice

What you need

Three dice per child or pair of children; paper, pencils.

What to do

Show the children how three dice can be put in a line so that the numbers on the top add up to a total of 11.

Ask the children to see how many other ways they can put the dice to make 11. Can they find some different totals and investigate them?

NC mapping

AT3 – Level 2 (a)
AT1 – Level 2 (a) (b) (c)
    – Level 3 (c)
AT2 – Level 2 (a)

Shuffle four

What you need

Four cards labelled 1 to 4.

What to do

Shuffle the cards, turn over the top two cards and add the numbers shown together. Turn over the other two cards and add them together. Finally add the two answers together. Ask the children to shuffle the cards and to repeat this process a few times. Do they always get the same answers? What happens if they use four different numbers?

This activity demonstrates the distributive rule.

NC mapping

AT3 – working towards Level 3 (a)
AT1 – Level 2 (a) (b) (c)
    – Level 3 (c)
AT2 – Level 2 (a)

Abacus

What you need

A two- and three-pronged peg abacus (the ones with removable prongs are best).

What to do

Show the children a two-pronged peg abacus and one bead. Ask them which numbers they can make with this bead. (They can make 1 or

10.) Now introduce another bead. With two prongs and two beads which numbers can they make? (This gives 2, 11 or 20.)

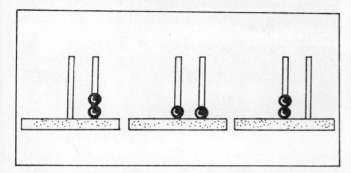

What if the children use three beads or four beads? As well as recording all the numbers they can make, they should count how many different combinations are possible. This gives the pattern: 2, 3, 4, 5 and so on.

This activity reinforces place value, as well as systematic searching for combinations, recording skills and pattern recognition. If there are children in the class who are beginning to use hundreds, the activity can be extended to using three prongs. How many numbers can they make with three prongs and one bead? (They can make 1, 10, 100.)

With two beads we find: 2, 11, 101, 110, 20, 200.

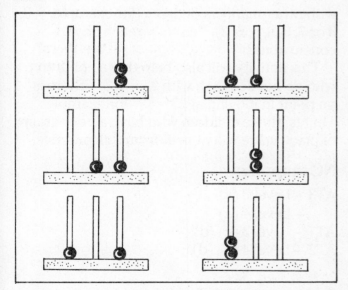

What if we use three beads or four beads? These combinations will give a number pattern: 3, 6, 10, 15 and so on.

These are the triangle numbers, though at this level it is sufficient that the children recognise the pattern goes up by 3, then by 4, then by 5 and so on.

NC mapping
AT3 – Level 2 (a)
AT1 – Level 2 (b) (c)
– Level 3 (c)
AT2 – working towards Level 3 (a)

Open-ended activities for Key Stage 2

Calculator bracelets

What you need
Calculators.

What to do
This activity is an extension of 'Bracelets' (on page 33).

Show the children how to use the calculator constant function. Then, show them the following doubling sequence: $2 \times 2 = = =$ gives 4, 8, 16, 32... (If this does not work for your calculator, refer to the manufacturer's instructions).

Ask the children to write down the last digit of each number and then look at the numbers together. What do they notice? Ask them to draw the 'bracelet for 2s'. Can they find some other bracelets?

NC mapping
AT3 – Level 4 (a)
AT1 – Level 3 (c)

Brackets

What you need
Paper, pencils.

What to do
Ask the children to give you three numbers that are less than 20. Write two subtraction sums, with brackets, using the numbers in descending order. For example, if the children give you 15, 17 and 9 you could write the sums: $17 - (15 - 9)$ or $(17 - 15) - 9$.

Explain to the children that when you calculate sums which include brackets you always work out the sum inside the brackets first:

$$17 - (15 - 9) = 17 - 6 = 11$$
$$(17 - 15) - 9 = 2 - 9 = -7$$

Ask the children to try several of these types of sums themselves. What do they notice? (The difference between the two answers is double the smallest number. In the above sum the two answers are 11 and –7. The difference between them is 18, which is double 9 – the smallest number in the original sum.) Children may need a number line to work out the differences when their numbers result in a negative answer.

NC mapping

AT3 – Level 4 (a)
AT1 – Level 4 (d)
AT2 – Level 3 PoS

Constant zeros

What you need

Calculators.

What to do

Ask the children to choose any number and put it in the calculator. Using the constant function (see page 20), ask them to keep adding any number ending with zero and record the results. How about two zeros on the end? How about subtracting? Which digits change each time?

NC mapping

AT3 – Level 3 (a)
    – Level 4 (a)
AT1 – Level 3 (c) (d)
AT2 – Level 4 (b)

Largest sum

What you need

Paper, pencils, calculator (optional).

What to do

Write down five digits and ask the children to

find the largest addition sum they can make with them. For example, with the numbers 2, 5, 4, 3 and 7 which will be largest: 542 + 73 or 54 + 732 or 532 + 74? Let the children check their guesses with a calculator.

Leave the children to experiment with other digits (for example, 9, 8, 7, 6, 5), and/or with other *numbers* of digits (for example, 6, 3, 8 or 7, 3, 9, 5, 6, 2). Can they reach any conclusions?

This activity will also help those children who do not see that, with 2, 5, 4, 3, 7 there is no point in looking at 25 + 437 for example. That is, those children who have a poor grasp of place value will benefit from this practice.

NC mapping

AT3 – Level 3 (a)
    – Level 4 (a)
AT1 – Level 3 (c) (d)
AT2 – Level 4 (b) (d)

Largest multiple

What you need

Paper, pencils, calculators.

What to do

This activity is similar to the previous one,

but uses multiplication. Write down five digits and ask the children to find the largest multiplication sum they can with them. For example, with 2, 5, 4, 3 and 7, which will be the largest: 542×73 or 54×732 or 532×74? Let the children check their guesses with a calculator.

Leave the children to experiment with other digits (for example, 9, 8, 7, 6, 5), and/or with other *numbers* of digits (for example, 6, 3, 8 or 7, 3, 9, 5, 6, 2). Can they reach any conclusions?

NC mapping

AT3 – Level 3 (a)
– Level 4 (a)
AT1 – Level 3 (c) (d)
AT2 – Level 4 (b) (d)

Multiple sums

What you need

Paper, pencils, calculators, ten cards labelled 1 to 10.

What to do

Ask the children to put the cards into five pairs, multiply the pairs of numbers together and add the answers. What totals do they get?

For example, if they paired the numbers as follows: 2 and 7; 4 and 1; 10 and 6; 9 and 3; 8 and 5; they would get the following:

$$2 \times 7 = 14$$
$$4 \times 1 = 4$$
$$10 \times 6 = 60$$
$$9 \times 3 = 27$$
$$8 \times 5 = 40$$
$$\text{Total} = 145$$

The children will probably all get different totals. Who has got the largest? What do they think is the largest possible number they can get? Ask them to experiment and see what is the biggest total they can make.

NC mapping

AT3 – Level 4 (a)
AT1 – Level 3 (c) (d)
AT2 – Level 4 PoS

Steady multiples

What you need

Paper, pencils, calculators.

What to do

Ask the children to take any number and multiply it by 9, then write down the last two digits. For example, $7 \times 9 = 63$, so they should write down 63.

Now ask them to multiply the new answer by 9 and write down its last two digits. This would give, for the above example, $63 \times 9 = 567$. If they continue this process what happens? ($67 \times 9 = 603$; $3 \times 9 = 27$; $27 \times 9 = 243$; $43 \times 9 = 387$; $87 \times 9 = 783$; $83 \times 9 = 747$; $47 \times 9 = 423$; $23 \times 9 = 207$ which brings us back to the beginning.)

Ask the children to try other numbers multiplied by 9. Do they always get back to the beginning. How long does it take? What about using a number other than 9?

NC mapping

AT3 – Level 3 (a)
– Level 4 (a)
AT1 – Level 3 (c) (d)

Swap and take

What you need

Paper, pencils, calculators (optional).

What to do

Ask the children to take a two digit number, swap over the tens and units to make a different number, then find the difference between these two. They should repeat this several times with the new numbers. For example: $26 \rightarrow 62$; $62 - 26 = 36$; $36 \rightarrow 63$; $63 - 36 = 27$; $27 \rightarrow 72$; $72 - 27 = 45$; $45 \rightarrow 54$; $54 - 45 = 9$. What did they all find? Will this always happen? Leave the children to investigate and try to explain.

NC mapping

AT3 – Level 4 (a)
AT1 – Level 3 (d)
AT2 – Level 4 (b)

Properties of numbers

Odd and even numbers

The first number property that children are expected to recognise is that of odd or even (AT3 Level 2 PoS). Children need to carry out quite a few activities to reinforce the definitions that even numbers can be divided exactly by two (that is, to put this at the children's level, a tower of an even number of Multilink can be split into two equal towers). Odd numbers can't. Even numbers can be recognised by their 'endings', that is, 2, 4, 6, 8 and 0, and children should also recognise numbers which can be divided by 5 or 10 from *their* endings (AT3 Level 3 PoS).

There are other rules for divisibility, which Key Stage 2 children enjoy using and telling others about. An example of this is the 'rule of nines'. To see if a number can be divided by 9, add the digits together. If the answer (the digital root) is nine then the number can be divided by nine, for example:

81 the digital root is 8 + 1 = 9
126 the digital root is 1 + 2 + 6 = 9
675 the digital root is 6 + 7 + 5 = 18 → 1 + 8 = 9

Children should be encouraged to find other rules for divisibility for themselves, or tell the rest of the class of any they hear about.

Multiples, factors and squares

By the time they reach Level 4, children should understand the correct mathematical language used to connect numbers: **'generalising, mainly in words, patterns which arise in various situations, e.g. symmetry of results, "multiple", "factor", "square" '** (AT3 Level 4 Programme of Study).

Multiples

If we take a particular number – say 4 – then a multiple of that number is any number that it can divide into exactly; for example:
4, 8, 12, 16...

Multiples can be modelled using growing rectangles:

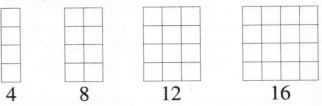

4   8   12   16

Activities requiring the children to find particular multiples of more than one number are more challenging than simple repetition. For example, which numbers are multiples of three *and* four? A rectangle three one way and four the other must give a multiple of both (as in the diagram for 12 above).

Factors

If we take a particular number – such as 12 – then a factor of that number is any number which can divide exactly into it; for example 1, 2, 3, 4, 6 and 12. So if we take 12 square counters, we can arrange them in the following rectangles:

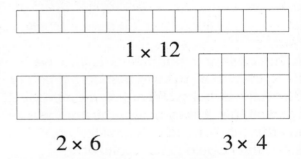

1 × 12

2 × 6   3 × 4

Notice that when you have a list of factors, they pair off from either end to make the possible rectangles. Therefore, if there are an odd number of factors the number must be a square number. For example: 36 → 1, 2, 3, 4, 6, 9, 12, 18, 36. This will give rectangles of 1 × 36; 2 × 18; 3 × 12; 4 × 9; leaving 6 over to make a square 6 × 6.

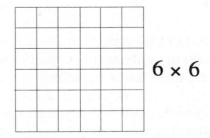

6 × 6

This fact is the clue to the investigation 'Lockers' on page 99.

Games using both the concepts factor and multiple are an excellent method of reinforcement. Computer games such as 'Define' on *MicroSMILE the Next 17* (London: ILECC) require children to combine their knowledge of number properties (see Appendix A).

Work on factors and multiples will obviously practise mental recall of multiplication facts (AT2 Levels 3 and 4).

Fractions

Factors and multiples deal with positive whole numbers, but children working at this level (Levels 5 and 6 of the National Curriculum) are also becoming acquainted with fractions. Recognising equivalent fractions spatially is discussed under 'Spatial arrangements' (see page 102).

The structure of fractions and their manipulation can be explored by looking at some ancient number systems. For example, the Ancient Egyptians only used fractions which had a numerator (the top number) of one: $\frac{1}{2}$, $\frac{1}{3}$, $\frac{1}{4}$ and so on. They could make any fraction by repeated addition: $\frac{3}{4} = \frac{1}{4} + \frac{1}{4} + \frac{1}{4}$, but can the children find quicker ways? ($\frac{1}{2} + \frac{1}{4}$ is the obvious way here).

The Ancient Babylonians worked in base 60, and all their fractions were written as 'something over 60'. If children are asked how the Ancient Babylonians would write $\frac{1}{2}$ or $\frac{2}{3}$, then they are automatically moving towards equivalent fractions; $\frac{1}{2} = \frac{30}{60}$ and $\frac{2}{3} = \frac{40}{60}$.

Prime numbers, cubes, square roots and cube roots

Although children may find out all sorts of properties of numbers (for example, which numbers can be made by adding their factors together), the only others mentioned in the National Curriculum at the primary level are: **'understanding and using terms such as "prime", "cube", "square root" and "cube root"'** (AT3 Level 5 Programme of Study).

Prime numbers

A prime number is any whole number which cannot be made by multiplying together other whole numbers, except for multiplying itself by 1. For example, 7 is a prime number because only $1 \times 7 = 7$, but 6 is not prime because $2 \times 3 = 6$. Using the rectangle model, prime numbers can *only* make the long thin rectangles which are 'one by something'.

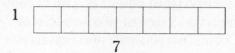

Prime numbers can also be identified through activities such as the 'Sieve of Eratosthenes' (see page 96). They can also be reinforced by drawing factor trees. A factor tree shows how a number can be split again and again into factors until you reach a prime. This will be the end of a branch (the prime factors are like apples on the end of branches). For example:

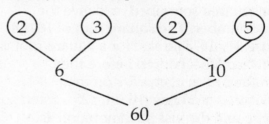

Hence, $60 = 2 \times 3 \times 2 \times 5$. The children can check this with a calculator: 2, 3 and 5 are all prime numbers.

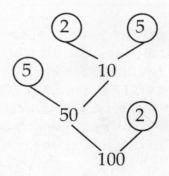

$100 = 5 \times 2 \times 5 \times 2$

Such answers can be simplified by putting together the 'like' terms, that is, putting together all the 2s, all the 5s, and so on:

91

$$60 = 2 \times 2 \times 3 \times 5 = 2^2 \times 3 \times 5$$
$$100 = 2 \times 2 \times 5 \times 5 = 2^2 \times 5^2$$
$$360 = 2 \times 2 \times 2 \times 3 \times 3 \times 5 = 2^3 \times 3^2 \times 5$$

Squared and cubed numbers

Squared and cubed numbers like those above can be reinforced through measurement activities. For example, the area of a square which has sides of three squares is 3×3 or 3^2 (three squared) and equals 9. The volume of a cube which has sides of two squares is $2 \times 2 \times 2$ or 2^3 (two cubed) and equals 8.

As we have seen, the National Curriculum expects knowledge of squares and cubes for children working at Level 5. However, the introduction of the correct symbol, as above, is not needed until Level 7, but able top juniors cope easily with the concept.

Square and cube roots

A square root (or cube root) is the number which squared (or cubed) will give the original number. The square root of 16 is 4 because $4^2 = 16$. The sign for a square root is known to many children before they understand it, as it appears on their calculator as $\sqrt{}$. Thus, $\sqrt{16} = 4$; $\sqrt{25} = 5$ and so on. We could dismiss such notation as unnecessary to the primary-aged child if it were not for the fact that often they *ask* us what the $\sqrt{}$ sign means! The best approach is to ask them to see if they can find out themselves.

A cube root is written: $\sqrt[3]{}$, and does not appear on most calculators.

These number properties (square, square root, cube, cube root) are often best met originally as spatial arrangements (as discussed on page 102) and through measurement activities.

Structured activities for Key Stage 1

Bagging evens

What you need

Small bags labelled 1 to 20, or a similarly labelled sorting tray; counters, a bag of pairs of socks (optional), washing line (optional).

What to do

Ask the children to count the correct number of counters into each bag, but they are only allowed to pick up two counters at a time. Which numbers can they *not* make? Why not? What do we call these numbers? (You will probably need to demonstrate one number that works and one that doesn't.)

To help explain to the children why they can't make certain numbers it is helpful to arrange the numbers like this:

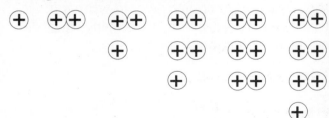

Alternatively, give the children a bag of socks, or picture cut-outs of socks, which are all jumbled up. Ask them to sort out the socks into pairs and hang each pair on a washing line. Ask them to count the number of socks on the lines. What do they notice? What do we call these numbers?

NC mapping

AT3 – Level 2 (a)
AT1 – Level 1 (a) (b) (c)
AT2 – Level 1 (a) (b)

2 rods

What you need

Colour rods.

What to do

Ask the children which rod lengths can be made with 2 rods only. What do we call these numbers?

NC mapping

AT3 – Level 2 (a)
AT1 – Level 1 (a) (b) (c)
AT2 – Level 1 (a) (b)

Two by two

What you need

No special requirements.

What to do

When the children line up in twos say, for example, 'We've got 28 children in class today. Have you all got a partner? What sort of number is 28?' This will provide an occasional – though repeating – reinforcement of odds and evens.

NC mapping

AT3 – Level 2 (a)
AT1 – Level 1 (a) (b) (c)
AT2 – Level 1 (a) (b)

Odds and evens: 1

What you need

Hundred squares, blank addition squares, coloured pencils.

What to do

Ask the children to colour in all the even numbers on the number square up to 100. (They will need to realise that you count in twos to get the next even number.) Can they continue the pattern? What do they notice? For children who are not yet ready for such large numbers, use only part of the square, up to 30 say.

Are there the same number of evens as odds? Why are there five columns? What do we add each time we go down a column (for example: 2, 12, 22, 32...)?

1	2	3	4	5	6	7	8	9	10
11	12	13	14	15	16	17	18	19	20
21	22	23	24	25	26	27	28	29	30
31	32	33	34	35	36	37	38	39	49
41	42	43	44	45	46	47	48	49	50
51	52	53	54	55	56	57	58	59	60
61	62	63	64	65	66	67	68	69	70
71	72	73	74	75	76	77	78	79	80
81	82	83	84	85	86	87	88	89	90
91	92	93	94	95	96	97	98	99	100

What if the children colour in all the evens on an addition square? Do they get the same number of evens as odds? Why do some diagonals have the same numbers in them (for example, 5, 5, 5, 5 – which comes from 4 + 1, 3 + 2, 2 + 3, 1 + 4)? Why do other diagonals have the odd numbers in order (3, 5, 7, 9...)?

+	1	2	3	4	5	6	7	8	9	10
1	2	3	4	5	6	7	8	9	10	11
2	3	4	5	6	7	8	9	10	11	12
3	4	5	6	7	8	9	10	11	12	13
4	5	6	7	8	9	10	11	12	13	14
5	6	7	8	9	10	11	12	13	14	15
6	7	8	9	10	11	12	13	14	15	16
7	8	9	10	11	12	13	14	15	16	17
8	9	10	11	12	13	14	15	16	17	18
9	10	11	12	13	14	15	16	17	18	19
10	11	12	13	14	15	16	17	18	19	20

NC mapping
AT3 – Level 2 (a)
– towards Level 3 (b)
AT1 – Level 2 (a) (b)
AT2 – Level 2 (a)

Pairs of cards

What you need

Two sets (one yellow, one green) of eight cards each labelled from 1 to 8.

What to do

Ask the children to find pairs of cards, one yellow, one green, so that:
• each pair adds up to make an even number;
• each pair adds up to make an odd number;
• the difference between the numbers is even;
• the difference between the numbers is odd.

NC mapping

AT3 – Level 2 (a)
AT1 – Level 2 (a) (b)
AT2 – Level 2 (a)

Structured activities for Key Stage 2

Factors and primes

What you need

Square counters, cardboard squares or square dotted paper.

What to do

Show the children how 12 squares can be made into a rectangle. Ask them what other rectangles they can make with 12 squares (see page 90). Ask them to find rectangles for other numbers between 1 and 30. Some numbers can only make a straight line (for example, 7 can only make 1×7). What do we call these numbers (primes)?

Introduce the word 'factor'; for example, as twelve can make rectangles of 3×4, 2×6 and 1×12, then 3, 4, 2, 6, 1 and 12 are all factors of 12. Twelve can be split into these number of

groups, or twelve can be divided exactly by these numbers. Can the children now tell you *all* the factors of all the numbers from 1 to 30?

NC mapping

AT3 – Level 4 (a)
AT1 – Level 3 (d)
– Level 4 (b)
AT2 – working towards Level 3 (b)
AT4 – Level 4 (d)

Factors on the table

What you need

Multiplication squares.

What to do

Building on the work from the previous activity, show the children how the rectangles they found for 12 can be found on a multiplication square. Here are the rectangles for 12, not including the 1×12:

x	2	3	4	5	6	7	8	9	10
2	4	6	8	10	12	14	16	18	20
3	6	9	12	15	18	21	24	27	30
4	8	12	16	20	24	28	32	36	40
5	10	15	20	25	30	35	40	45	50
6	12	18	24	30	36	42	48	54	60
7	14	21	28	35	42	49	56	63	70
8	16	24	32	40	48	56	64	72	80
9	18	27	36	45	54	63	72	81	90
10	20	30	40	50	60	70	80	90	100

x	2	3	4	5	6	7	8	9	10
2	4	6	8	10	12	14	16	18	20
3	6	9	12	15	18	21	24	27	30
4	8	12	16	20	24	28	32	36	40
5	10	15	20	25	30	35	40	45	50
6	12	18	24	30	36	42	48	54	60
7	14	21	28	35	42	49	56	63	70
8	16	24	32	40	48	56	64	72	80
9	18	27	36	45	54	63	72	81	90
10	20	30	40	50	60	70	80	90	100

x	2	3	4	5	6	7	8	9	10
2	4	6	8	10	12	14	16	18	20
3	6	9	12	15	18	21	24	27	30
4	8	12	16	20	24	28	32	36	40
5	10	15	20	25	30	35	40	45	50
6	12	18	24	30	36	42	48	54	60
7	14	21	28	35	42	49	56	63	70
8	16	24	32	40	48	56	64	72	80
9	18	27	36	45	54	63	72	81	90
10	20	30	40	50	60	70	80	90	100

x	2	3	4	5	6	7	8	9	10
2	4	6	8	10	12	14	16	18	20
3	6	9	12	15	18	21	24	27	30
4	8	12	16	20	24	28	32	36	40
5	10	15	20	25	30	35	40	45	50
6	12	18	24	30	36	42	48	54	60
7	14	21	28	35	42	49	56	63	70
8	16	24	32	40	48	56	64	72	80
9	18	27	36	45	54	63	72	81	90
10	20	30	40	50	60	70	80	90	100

Twelve appears on the multiplication table in four places, so we can draw four rectangles. Ask the children to find all the places for 20, and draw all the rectangles for 20. What are the factors of 20?

What happens with these numbers: 4, 9, 16, 25...? (These numbers will all give squares on the table.)

Finally, ask the children to look at numbers beyond 30.

NC mapping

AT3 – Level 4 (a)
AT1 – Level 3 (d)
    – Level 4 (b)
AT2 – working towards Level 3 (b)
AT4 – Level 4 (d)

Multiples

What you need

Multiplication squares.

What to do

Following on from the activities above, show the children how *multiples* can be found from the multiplication square. Where are the multiples of 6? Which number is a multiple of 6 and 4? Is 48 a multiple of 6 and 4?

NC mapping

AT3 – Level 4 (a)
AT1 – Level 3 (d)
    – Level 4 (b)
AT2 – working towards Level 3 (b)
AT4 – Level 4 (d)

Odds and evens: 2

What you need

Multiplication square.

What to do

Ask each child to shade in all the odd numbers on a multiplication square. What do they notice?

x	2	3	4	5	6	7	8	9	10
2	4	6	8	10	12	14	16	18	20
3	6	9	12	15	18	21	24	27	30
4	8	12	16	20	24	28	32	36	40
5	10	15	20	25	30	35	40	45	50
6	12	18	24	30	36	42	48	54	60
7	14	21	28	35	42	49	56	63	70
8	16	24	32	40	48	56	64	72	80
9	18	27	36	45	54	63	72	81	90
10	20	30	40	50	60	70	80	90	100

Why are some rows and columns empty? Ask the children the following:
• What do you get if you multiply an odd number by an odd number?
• What do you get if you multiply an odd number by an even number?
• What do you get if you multiply an even number by an even number?
• Why are there so few odds on the multiplication square?

NC mapping
AT3 – Level 4 (a)
AT1 – Level 2 (a) (b) (c)
AT2 – Level 4 (b) (d)

Fraction lines

What you need

Paper, pencils, squared or graph paper.

What to do

Ask the children to work out some equivalent fractions. (This should not be their first meeting with the concept, but a reinforcement exercise.) Explain that they are going to graph the fractions, making the numerator (the top number) the 'x' value of the co-ordinate and the denominator (the bottom number) the 'y' value of the co-ordinate. For example, for the fractions: $^1/_2 = {}^2/_4 = {}^3/_6 = {}^4/_8 = {}^5/_{10} = {}^6/_{12}$, they should plot the points: (1, 2) (2, 4) (3, 6) (4, 8) (5, 10) (6, 12). What do the children think this graph might look like?

It is better at this stage not to show the children a mapped example, as this would spoil their own discovery of a straight line. All sets of equivalent fractions will give straight lines, the example above giving:

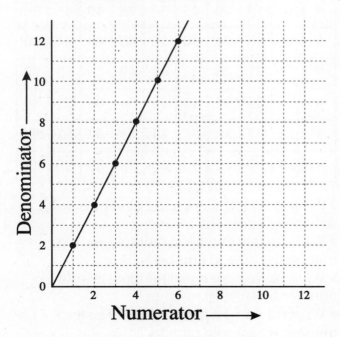

Can the children explain why they get a straight line? If they find the missing ratios of

the lengths of the sides of the rectangles made by the numbers (for example: $^4/_8 \rightarrow$ (4, 8) $\rightarrow$ a 4 by 8 rectangle), then they will all be the same and hence the vertices will line up.

NC mapping

AT3 – Level 4 (a) (c)
AT1 – Level 2 (b) (c) (d)
AT2 – Level 4 PoS

Sieve of Eratosthenes

What you need

Hundred squares.

What to do

Eratosthenes was an Ancient Greek mathematician, who devised the following activity to show all the prime numbers from 1 to 100. Talk the children through the first stages of the activity, leaving them to continue when you think they have understood the principle.
• Cross out the number 1 (1 is not defined as a prime number).
• Put a ring around the number 2, and then shade in every number which is a multiple of 2 (which 2 goes into exactly).
• Put a ring around the number 3, and then shade in every number which is a multiple of 3. Some will already have been shaded (they are, therefore, multiples of 2 *and* 3).
• Look for the next unshaded number (in this case 5). Put a ring round it, and shade in every number which is a multiple of it.
• Look for the next unshaded number (in this case 7). Put a ring round it, and shade in every number which is a multiple of it.
• Continue until all the numbers are either ringed or shaded.

The ringed numbers are the prime numbers. The illustration below shows the finished sieve.

NC mapping

AT3 – Level 5 PoS
AT1 – Level 4 (b)
AT2 – Level 3 (b)

Prime factor trees

What you need

Paper, pencils.

What to do

Show the children how to make a prime factor tree, as in the example shown below:

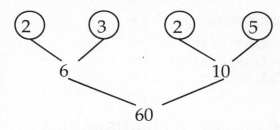

$60 = 6 \times 10$ and therefore the tree can be split into 6 and 10. $6 = 2 \times 3$ and therefore the tree can be split into 2 and 3. However, 2 and 3 cannot be split, so we put a ring round each of them. $10 = 2 \times 5$ and therefore the tree can be split into 2 and 5. As 2 and 5 cannot be split, we put a ring round each of them.

We call 2, 3 and 5 the prime factors of 60. Ask the children to find the prime factors of 60. Then ask them to find the prime factors of other numbers.

This activity leads nicely into the need for index notation. For example, $48 = 2 \times 2 \times 2 \times 2 \times 3$ which can be written more succinctly as $2^4 \times 3$. This is a Level 7 concept in the National Curriculum but, as the children are using 2^2 and 2^3 at Level 5, and in their measurement activities, there is no need to hold them back in this respect.

As an extension, consider the following:
• Which numbers only contain 2s or 3s?
• Which numbers have the most varied prime factors (for example, they contain a 2, 3, 5 and so on)?

NC mapping

AT3 – Level 5 PoS, Level 7 PoS
AT1 – Level 5 (a)
AT2 – Level 5 PoS

Indices snap

What you need

A set of playing cards on which are written, for example, 2^3 on one, $2 \times 2 \times 2$ on another and 8 on a third; 4^2 on one, 4×4 on another and 16 on a third and so on.

What to do

Shuffle the pack and play snap.

NC mapping

AT3 – Level 5 PoS, Level 7 PoS
AT2 – Level 5 PoS

Lift off!

What you need

Photocopiable page 193, three dice, counters.

What to do

Give the children photocopiable page 193. They must take turns to throw the dice. When the dice are thrown, the children must try to make a prime number by adding, subtracting, multiplying or dividing the numbers on the dice. For example, if the dice show: 2, 3, 5, they can make 17 ($5 \times 3 + 2$) or 13 ($5 \times 3 - 2$) or 11 ($3 \times 2 + 5$). If they *can* make a prime number and explain it to their opponents, then their fuel level goes up by one. When the fuel level reaches the top, we have lift off and that child is the winner.

NC mapping

AT3 – Level 4 PoS
AT1 – Level 4 (c)
AT2 – Level 3 (c)

What's my number?

What you need

Cards which describe the properties of a particular number (there is an example below).

What to do

Give the children a card similar to the one shown below and ask them to identify the number.

```
It's between 50 and 100.
It's even.
It's in the eight times table.
It's a multiple of 10.
The number is ___ ?
```

In the case of the above example the number is 80.

This can be made into a game using the hot seat principle (see page 25).

Include on the cards terms such as 'square', 'prime', 'factor' and so on.

Ask the children to make up and play with their own cards for particular numbers.

NC mapping

AT3 – Level 4 PoS, Level 5 PoS
AT1 – Level 3 (b)
– Level 4 (a)
AT2 – various

Open-ended activities for Key Stage 1

Towers

What you need

Multilink.

What to do

Ask the children to take a pile of Multilink, count them and write down how many they have. Can they make two towers of the same height with their Multilink? Ask them to try again. What do they notice?

NC mapping

AT3 – Level 2 PoS
AT1 – Level 1 (a) (b) (c)
AT2 – Level 2 (c)

Necklaces

What you need

Beads of two colours, thread.

What to do

Ask the children to give you a number that is less than 20. They must then string that number of beads on to a thread, alternating the colours and counting as they go. Once they have finished they should tie the thread to make a necklace. Did the number they gave you make a complete pattern, that is alternating all the way round, or were there two colours the same at the end? Can the children explain why?

Ask the children to pick other numbers and experiment.

NC mapping

AT3 – Level 2 PoS
AT1 – Level 2 (a) (b) (c)
AT2 – Level 1 (a)

Odd and even combinations

What you need

A bag containing red and yellow counters.

What to do

Write odd numbers on the red counters and even numbers on the yellow. Ask the children to feel in the bag and pull out two counters. Do they have two even counters, two odd counters, or an odd and an even counter? Ask them to add the numbers on the two counters together and record them as below:

Even + Even	Even + Odd	Odd + Odd
6	9	4
8	7	6

What do the children notice?

NC mapping
AT3 – Level 2 PoS
AT1 – Level 1 (a) (b) (c)
AT2 – Level 2 (a)

Equal rods

What you need

Pencils, paper, colour rods.

What to do

Show the children a brown rod (an 8 rod). Can they make the same length as a brown rod, but only using one colour?

Possible responses are:

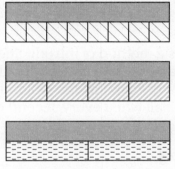

Ask the children to find similar combinations for other rods.

This activity provides a good preparation for multiplication and for factor/multiple work.

NC mapping

AT3 – Level 2 (a)
AT1 – Level 2 (a) (b) (c)
AT2 – working towards Level 3 (b)

Open-ended activities for Key Stage 2

Prime patterns

What you need

Pencils, paper, counters.

What to do

If the children have worked with prime factors and primes in the activities in the 'structured activities' section they will already know that prime numbers cannot be arranged into rectangles other than 'one by something'. Ask them to find out what shapes *can* be made with primes. Can they make any symmetrical shapes? Illustrate the question with an example made with counters. For example, using seven counters, we can make the following patterns:

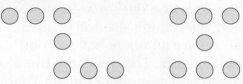

Both have rotational symmetry, the second also has reflectional symmetry. Can the children find some more patterns for 7? What about other prime numbers?

This activity helps children see the structure of prime numbers, and provides links with Attainment Target 4 (Shape and space).

NC mapping

AT3 – Level 5 PoS
AT1 – Level 4 (b)
AT4 – Level 3 (b)
    – Level 4 (c)

Lockers

What you need

Pencils, paper, counters (optional).

What to do

Explain the following problem to the children:

There are 100 school lockers in a row. All of them are open. A child walks through the locker room, closing every locker. A second child walks through, and opens every *other* locker. A third child walks through and *changes the state* of every third locker; that is if a locker is open, she closes it, if it is closed, she opens it. The sequence continues with each child changing the state of the lockers which are multiples of his or her number. For example, the tenth child will change the tenth, twentieth, thirtieth, lockers and so on. If the locker is open, he will close it, if it is closed, he will open it.

Which lockers are open and which lockers are closed after the hundredth child has been through the locker room? Can the children explain the results?

(All the doors on the squared numbers will be closed, everything else will be open, because square numbers have an odd number of factors. The doors are therefore changed an odd number of times.) There is a hint on page 90.

NC mapping

AT3 – Level 4 (a)
AT1 – Level 3 (c) (d)
    – Level 4 (c)

Passaola

What you need

Balls or bean bags.

What to do

Divide the children into groups of eight and ask each group to make a circle (this is best done outside, or in the hall). Give each group a ball or bean bag and ask them to throw it to one another in order around the circle (the first child to the second, the second to the third and so on) until it returns to the first child. Check that everyone touched the ball. Now ask the children to start again, but pass the ball to the next but one child to them, that is missing a child out. When the ball returns to the beginning, ask the children who touched the ball to put up their hands. Repeat this again, but this time they should miss out two children, then three and so on.

Move back to the classroom and record the results on paper as shown below.

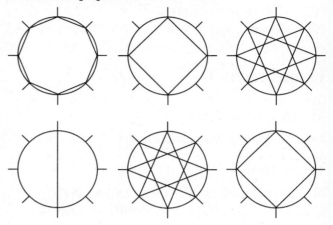

Ask the children to try passing the ball again but with different-sized groups. Can they predict what will happen before they start?

Passaola is a method of introducing children to factors. Two and four are factors of eight, and hence not all the children will get to touch the ball when every second or fourth child are thrown to.

NC mapping

AT3 – Level 4 (a)
AT1 – Level 3 (c) (d)
    – Level 4(b) (c) (d)
AT2 – Level 3 (c)

Three-dimensional multiplication square

What you need

Multilink and a Multilink pegboard or cubes and a large hundred square.

What to do

Explain to the children that they are going to build up towers of multiples, but that they should leave out the number 1. They should first look at the square for 2 and choose a colour to stand for the number 2. Ask the children to put that colour cube on every number into which two divides.

They should then look at the square for 3. Has it got a cube on it? As 3 is not divisible by 2 it won't have a cube on it and so they should choose another colour to stand for the number 3 and put that colour cube on every number into which three divides. Next they should look at number 4. This will have a cube on it already, so they should leave it and look at the next number and so on. Which numbers have only one cube? Ask the children to look at those numbers which have two cubes on them. Can they use the numbers the colours stand for to make the number? Ask them to look at those numbers with three cubes on and so on.

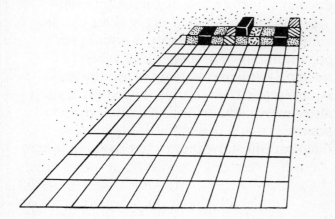

NC mapping

AT3 – Level 4 PoS
    – Level 5 PoS
AT1 – Level 3 (c) (d)
AT2 – Level 3 (c)

Egyptian fractions

What you need

Paper, pencils.

What to do

Explain to the children that the Ancient Egyptians only used fractions which had a numerator (the top number) of one: $\frac{1}{2}$, $\frac{1}{3}$, $\frac{1}{4}$ and so on. They could make any fraction by repeated addition: $\frac{3}{4} = \frac{1}{4} + \frac{1}{4} + \frac{1}{4}$, but can the children find quicker ways to make fractions?

Show them how $\frac{3}{4}$ can also be written as $\frac{1}{2} + \frac{1}{4}$. Ask them to find the following fractions using only Ancient Egyptian fractions: $\frac{2}{12}$, $\frac{3}{12}$, $\frac{4}{12}$, $\frac{5}{12}$, $\frac{6}{12}$, $\frac{7}{12}$, $\frac{8}{12}$, $\frac{9}{12}$, $\frac{10}{12}$, $\frac{11}{12}$. For example: $\frac{2}{12} = \frac{1}{6}$ and $\frac{5}{12} = \frac{1}{6} + \frac{1}{4}$.

Ask them to investigate other ordinary fractions.

NC mapping

AT3 – Level 5 PoS
AT1 – Level 5 (a)
AT2 – Level 5 PoS
    – Level 6 (a)

Babylonian fractions

What you need

Paper, pencils.

What to do

Explain to the children that the Ancient Babylonians worked in base 60, and all their fractions were written as 'something over 60'. How would the Ancient Babylonians have written $\frac{1}{2}$ or $\frac{2}{3}$? Show the children the equivalent fractions: $\frac{1}{2} = \frac{30}{60}$ and $\frac{2}{3} = \frac{40}{60}$.

Ask the children to find the Babylonian fractions equivalent to: $\frac{1}{4}$, $\frac{3}{4}$, $\frac{1}{5}$, $\frac{2}{5}$, $\frac{3}{5}$, $\frac{4}{5}$, $\frac{1}{6}$, $\frac{5}{6}$. How will they deal with $\frac{1}{7}$? (They will not be able to find a Babylonian fraction for $\frac{1}{7}$ just as we can't write $\frac{1}{7}$ in our decimal system in an exact way.)

NC mapping

AT3 – Level 5 PoS
AT1 – Level 5 (a)
AT2 – Level 5 PoS
    – Level 6 (a)

Primes from squares

What you need

Paper, pencils, calculators.

What to do

Show the children the following:
$5 = 1^2 + 2^2$ and 5 is a prime number.
$13 = 2^2 + 3^2$ and 13 is a prime number.

Can the children find any other primes which are made from the addition of squares?

NC mapping

AT3 – Level 5 PoS
AT1 – Level 3 (c) (d)
AT2 – Level 3 (c)

Spatial arrangements

As has already been seen, spatial arrangements can help a child to understand addition and subtraction bonds, odds and evens, and rules for simple arithmetic. Children will be used to seeing multiplication described spatially:

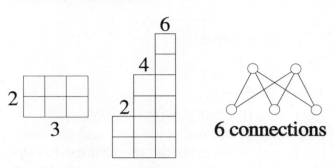

Their first meeting with a square number will often be in the form:

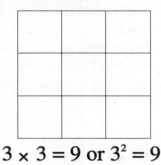

$$3 \times 3 = 9 \text{ or } 3^2 = 9$$

Less usual is to set a problem where the area of the square is known but the children have to find out its length. This is an interesting exercise for beginning 'trial and improvement' exercises. For example, if we know that the area of a square is 10cm², what is the length of one side?

Similarly, a cube number will be met as:

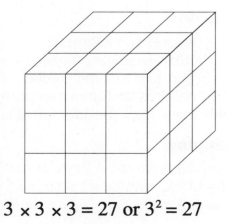

$$3 \times 3 \times 3 = 27 \text{ or } 3^2 = 27$$

Children should be asked, for example, if they lock together 1000 little cubes to make one big cube how many little cubes long will one side be? That it is as small as 10 comes as a great surprise to most children.

Again, trial and improvement methods can be used to find the size of a cube which holds half a litre of water (a litre occupies 1000cm³, so we are in fact asking for the $^3\sqrt{500}$). This is an excellent sort of exercise for children who are coming to terms with the meaning of decimals (using a calculator, of course!)

Making shapes twice as big gives children some insight into the scale of square and cube numbers. For example, if asked to imagine a square made up of four little squares, and then double the length of each side, many children will think that the new square is made of eight little squares. A diagram will show them what really happens:

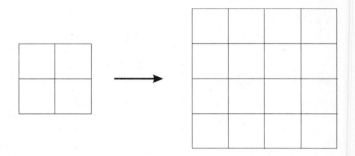

The four little squares become sixteen (the area is multiplied by a factor of 4).

Similarly, for a $2 \times 2 \times 2$ cube (that is eight little cubes):

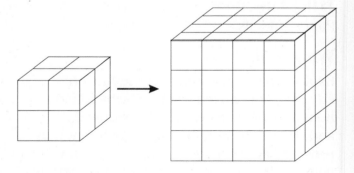

The eight little cubes become 64 ($4 \times 4 \times 4$).

Spatial arrangements can also often help children to understand why they get a certain result. For example, why does the addition of three consecutive numbers always give a number in the three times table?

102

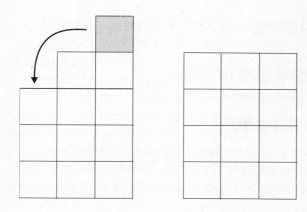

A spatial arrangement can also help children to understand why squares grow in odd numbers. To make a 'one square' into a 'four square', you have to add three. To make a 'four square' into a 'nine square', you have to add five. The need for three or five can be seen from the 'L' shapes added below:

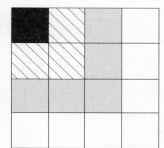

$$1 + 3 = 4$$
$$1 + 3 + 5 = 9$$
$$1 + 3 + 5 + 7 = 16$$

Hence, it is important to encourage children to model their work (by drawing, by building with cubes and so on) whenever possible.

Fraction boards are well established in junior classrooms and are a good use of spatial arrangements.

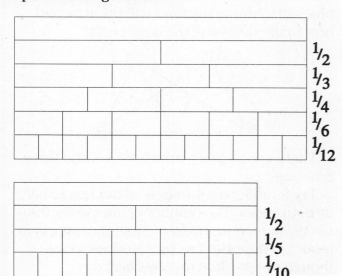

There are also spatial arrangements which help children to understand and find equivalent fractions. For example, if we need to find fractions that are equivalent to $^2/_5$, we begin by drawing a rectangle divided into fifths and shading two sections:

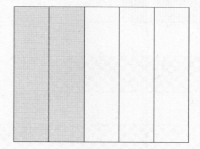

To find an equivalent fraction, we divide the rectangle once more to give 10 equal sections, of which four will be shaded, and follow this by a further subdivision, using two new lines, to make 20 equal sections, of which eight will be shaded:

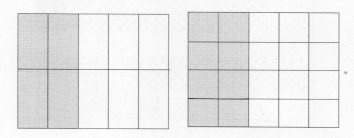

Therefore, $^2/_5 = {}^4/_{10} = {}^8/_{20}$

Structured and open-ended activities for Key Stage 1

Staircases

What you need
Multilink.

What to do
Ask the children to build staircases of 9 steps using Multilink, where each step is a different colour from the others.

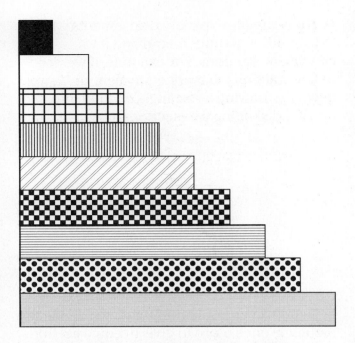

Can the children combine their staircases to make a rectangle?

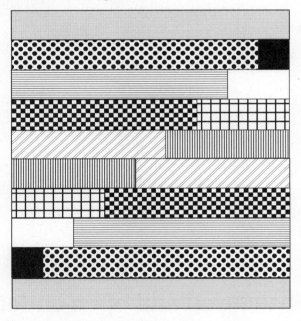

Discuss with the children what has happened. They have made a 10×9 rectangle which shows all the simple partitions (that is, into two numbers) of 10: $9 + 1 = 1 + 9 = 3 + 7 = 7 + 3$ and so on.

If preferred, begin with 4 steps, if partitions of 5 need reinforcing, 5 steps for 6 and so on, leading to 9 steps.

NC mapping

AT3 – Level 2 (a)
AT1 – Level 1 (a) (b) (c)
AT2 – Level 1 (a) (b)

Zigzag

What you need

Paper, pencils.

What to do

Draw a zigzag line on paper. Show the children how they can travel down the line writing the counting numbers at each corner.

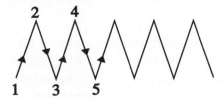

Ask the children to draw their own zigzags and continue the pattern. What is special about the numbers on the top? What is special about the numbers at the bottom?

NC mapping

AT3 – Level 2 (a)
AT1 – Level 1 (a) (b) (c)
AT2 – Level 1 (a)

Dots and crossings

What you need

Paper, pencils.

What to do

Ask the children to draw two red dots next to each other. Opposite, they should draw three blue dots. If they join all the red dots to all the blue dots, how many lines will there be and how many times will the lines cross?

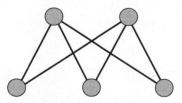

There are six lines, from $2 \times 3 = 6$ and three crossings.

Try for different numbers of dots on either, or both, sides. The number of lines gives the *Cartesian product model* of multiplication, a model as important as repeated addition, though not so often met by children.

The number of crossings provides a number pattern (2×2 gives one crossing, 2×3 gives three, 2×4 gives five and so on).

NC mapping
AT3 – Level 2 (a)
      – working towards Level 3 (a)
AT1 – Level 2 (a) b) (c)
AT2 – working towards Level 3 (b) (c)

Dressing bears

What you need
Photocopiable page 194, coloured pencils.

What to do
Tell the children that, when dressing, the bear on photocopiable page 194 has certain choices to make; for example, he may have a red hat or a blue hat, red boots or blue boots. How many different outfits can the bear wear? Ask the children to find out by colouring the bear's outfits on the worksheet. The answer can be reinforced by a Cartesian mapping:

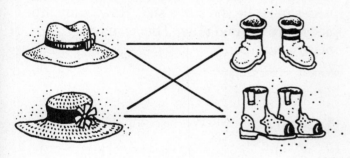

NC mapping
AT3 – Level 2 (a)
      – working towards Level 3 (a)
AT1 – Level 2 (a) (b) (c)
AT2 – working towards Level 3 (b) (c)

Structured and open-ended activities for Key Stage 2

Twice as big

What you need
Squared paper, pencils, Multilink.

What to do

Activity 1
Ask the children to draw a small shape made up from three, four or five squares on squared paper, and then draw a shape twice as big in all directions (you may wish to establish that there are two directions, along and up).

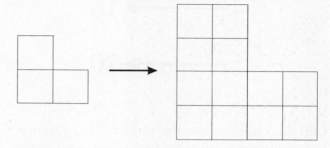

How many squares do their new, larger shapes need? Ask the children to draw mapping diagrams of their results.

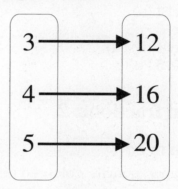

Can the children see the pattern? How many little squares would a 'twice as big' shape need if the first shape was made from six little squares?

Activity 2
Ask the children to make a small shape with three, four or five Multilink and then make another one twice as big in all directions (make sure that the children realise that there are now three directions).

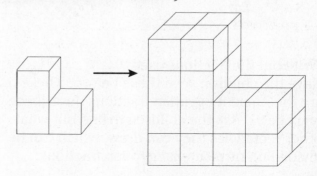

105

How many cubes do their new, larger shapes need? Ask them to draw mapping diagrams of their results.

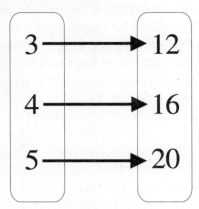

Can the children see the pattern? How many cubes would a 'twice as big' shape need if the first shape was made from six cubes?

NC mapping

AT3 – Level 4 (a)
   – Level 5 PoS
AT1 – Level 4 (b) (d)
AT2 – Level 5 PoS

Egyptian fractions: 2

What you need

Squared paper, pencils, coloured pencils.

What to do

Draw for the children a rectangle made up of 12 squares. Ask them how many squares should be coloured if they wanted to colour half the rectangle. They can then colour these squares and repeat the question for one quarter, one sixth and one twelfth. The whole rectangle will now be coloured:

 or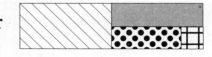

Write out the fractions used: $\frac{1}{2}$, $\frac{1}{4}$, $\frac{1}{6}$, $\frac{1}{12}$. Have the children seen these before? These are the Ancient Egyptian fractions described on page 91. Ask the children to find out what other rectangles they can draw, which can be divided up by *different* Egyptian fractions.

106

NC mapping

AT3 – Level 5 PoS
AT1 – Level 5 (b)
AT2 – Level 5 PoS

Equivalent fractions

What you need

Squared paper, pencils, coloured pencils.

What to do

Show the children the equivalent fraction example explained on page 103 or alternatively show them a problem of the following type:

Find the missing number: $\frac{3}{4} = \frac{\square}{12}$

To solve this problem, tell the children to draw a rectangle and divide it into four parts and shade in three of them. Check that the children understand that $\frac{3}{4}$ of the shape has been shaded. Next, ask them to draw lines to divide the shape into 12 – stress that all the pieces must be the same size. How many little pieces are shaded now? This gives our missing number, 9.

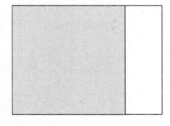

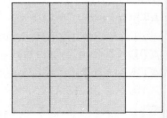

Ask the children to find their own sets of equivalent fractions, or to set missing number fraction problems for their friends.

NC mapping

AT3 – Level 5 PoS
AT1 – Level 5 (b)
AT2 – Level 5 PoS

Formulae, equations and inequalities

It is important at the start of this section to differentiate between a *formula* and an *equation*. An *equation* represents the balance between two combinations of objects or numbers:

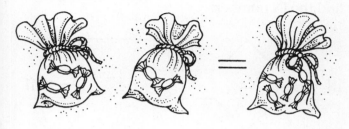

Three sweets and two sweets are the same as five sweets (3 + 2 = 5) or:

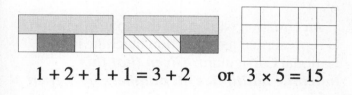

$$1 + 2 + 1 + 1 = 3 + 2 \quad \text{or} \quad 3 \times 5 = 15$$

A *formula* is a specific case of an equation which involves a relationship that never changes. For example, the perimeter of a rectangle is found by adding its length to its width and doubling, so we can write:
$p = 2(a + b)$.

Each letter has a specific meaning, and the relationship between them is set for all time. The property we are trying to find is usually written first, on one side of the equals sign, and the manipulation of the other properties which is necessary to find it, is written on the other side. Like all equations, it balances, but unlike other equations, the letters stand for something specific, often a scientific or economic relationship; for example, for $s = ut$ for constant motion in a straight line (no acceleration), s = distance, u = speed and t = time.

Equations and function machines

The need to balance an equation is met as soon as children begin to use them. Adding 3 to 5 is purely an arithmetic process, but recognising the symbols in an equation such as $5 + 3 = \square$ is an algebraic concept. Children may meet the need to solve the above through weighing, using an equaliser (see activities page 114) and so on, as well as the standard examples of 'If I had five sweets and you gave me three...'.

As soon as they can cope with the arithmetic process, however, it is also time to try turning the question around: 'I had five sweets, but then you gave me some more. Now I've got eight. How many did you give me?', or 'I had a handful of sweets, but then you gave me three. Now I've got eight. How many did I start with?'

Such machinations are not easy, and have to be modelled with bricks or counters for young children to understand the language. Once they have grasped the concept, the use of symbols can be introduced:
$$5 + \square = 8$$
$$\square + 3 = 8$$
In order to solve such problems, the children need to know that addition and subtraction are inverses of each other. However, the word 'inverse' need not be used and often children talk of one being the 'opposite' of the other. The National Curriculum gives several examples of inverses: ***'Use doubling and halving, adding and subtracting, and FORWARD and BACKWARD (in LOGO) etc., as inverse operations'*** (AT3 Level 3 Examples).

FORWARD and BACKWARD in LOGO has a slight disadvantage in that the natural way to get back to a spot is to turn round and go forward in the opposite direction. For example: FD 100. To get back: RT 180 FD 100 rather than: BK 100.

Children are more likely to choose the former for their turtles, roamers, pips and so on. However, when they draw on the screen and wish to erase a line, then children *do* tend to use BACKWARDS: FD 100. To erase: PE BK 100 rather than: FD 100 RT 180 PE FD 100.

LOGO inverses are always present, however, for turns. For example, take the robot for a walk: FD 100 RT 90 FD 50 LT 90 FD 50 RT 90 FD 100.

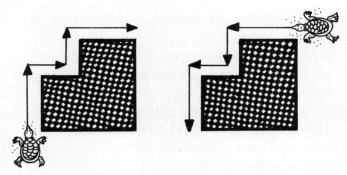

To get back (having turned round): FD 100 LT 90 FD 50 RT 90 FD 50 LT 90 FD 100.

To reinforce the idea, the children can write the initial instructions on paper to pin on a 'washing line':

When trying to get the turtle back, ask the children to look and see what needs to be changed. They will have to begin at the right-hand side and work backwards and will quickly catch on to the fact that only the RTs and LTs change.

Not only does this show how right and left are opposites, but it introduces the children to the concept of working back *from right to left* – which is an important idea for solving equations in which more than one operation is taking place.

Function machines

An excellent way to help children to visualise the idea of an inverse is to use a function machine (function machines were first introduced in Chapter One, see page 50).

We have already seen function machines used to represent a simple attribute change or to produce a number sequence, but they are even more useful for finding unknowns in other positions:

The model this provides of the unknowns: $5 + \square = 8$ and $\square + 3 = 8$, gives the children a focus for *where* the change happens and *what* causes the change.

When an equation contains more than one operation, for example $2n + 3 = 11$, children need to be able to break it down. Modelling each operation as a separate function machine is helpful, where children need to find the IN number:

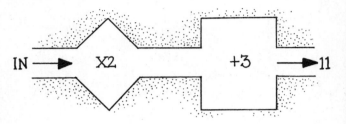

If the children work backwards through the machine they get: $4 \leftarrow \div 2 \leftarrow -3 \leftarrow 11$. So $p = 4$.

An equation with more than one operation is represented as a function machine in the National Curriculum: ***'Given that this machine multiplies all numbers by 5, then adds 2,***

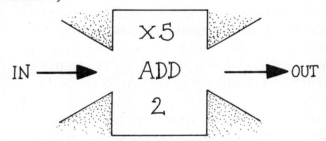

complete the table':

IN	OUT
2	12
3	?
?	37

(AT3 Level 4 Examples).

In order to solve the last line of the table, children need to break this machine down into separate parts:

$\text{IN} \rightarrow \times 5 \rightarrow +2 \rightarrow \text{OUT}$

To get back to the starting number, they should begin from the right and work left. What is the inverse (or opposite) of adding 2? What is the inverse of multiplying by 5?

$\text{IN} \leftarrow \div 5 \leftarrow -2 \leftarrow \text{OUT}$

So, taking our answer, 37:

$7 \leftarrow 35 \leftarrow 37$

Similarly, for the second example: *'Solve a problem such as: "If I double a number then add 1, and the result is 49, what is the number?"'* (AT3 Level 4 Examples)

The problem states:

number $\rightarrow \times 2 \rightarrow + 1 \rightarrow 49$.

Therefore, if you work backwards you get:

IN $\leftarrow \div 2 \leftarrow - 1 \leftarrow 49$

This gives:

$24 \leftarrow 48 \leftarrow 49$

As children love puzzles, this type of activity is popular. A similar type of problem is one in which either the answer is always the same, or you can very easily work out the number your friend was thinking of ('THOANS' on page 122 is an example of such an activity).

By Levels 5 and 6 of the National Curriculum, the children should have been introduced to the symbolic representation of the relationships discussed above. Many readers may remember their own first introduction to 'letters for numbers'. A common method was to talk about 'apples and bananas', leading on to 'a and b'. Perhaps you were told: 'You can't add an apple and a banana, so you can't add an "a" and a "b"'. This was fine for addition and subtraction, but the cause of many problems when moving on to multiplication: What does an apple times a banana mean? We can write ab for a × b, so apple times banana must mean something!

Avoid all talk about fruit! The function machine activities listed in this chapter provide an excellent model for change, and IN and OUT for variables. A letter to stand for a variable can be introduced through repeated questioning; for example, look at this table of a function machine:

IN	OUT
1	4
2	8
3	12
4	16

- What will you get out if you feed in 100 (400)?
- How did you get 400 (4 × 100)?

- How would you get the answer if 1000 is fed in (4 × 1000)?
- What if a million is fed in?

So, what if we don't know the IN number, but call it 'n' (4 × **n**)?

If the children can't reach this point, you can always *tell* them that this is a way of writing the answer! If we can give the IN number a letter, why not the OUT? How about using the letter 'm' to represent the OUT number? Can they see that now **n** = 4 × **m**?

To reinforce this idea, previous work on functions and on equations, which was successfully attempted, should be revisited and the children asked for suggestions for letters to take the place of the things which changed. For example, the earlier mental puzzle: *'Solve a problem such as: "If I double a number then add 1, and the result is 49, what is the number?"'* (AT3 Level 4 Examples).

If we call **n** the number and **r** the result, we get: **n** × 2 + 1 = **r**. If we know **n**, we can look for **r** or if we know **r** (here we were told it was 49), we can look for **n**.

By Level 6, children should be using correct algebraic notation, that is, not **n** × 2 but 2**n**. Again, this is something they will need to be *told*.

NB: in preparing photocopiable worksheets on equations and function machines, this symbolic notation has been purposely omitted. Children will vary as to when they can take this notation on board and the rate will not directly match their ability to cope with the concepts of functions and equations. If the symbols were to appear on the same sheets, children may be denied appropriate material for fear they cannot cope with *all* of the sheet. Teachers are, therefore, asked to add the symbolic notation to the sheets themselves for individual children when required.

More difficult equations

The 'weighing' model

Sometimes, before an equation can be solved by 'working back' it is necessary to get it into the form where we can initially 'see' the answer. For example, using x instead of **n** for the unknown: '$3x + 4 = 10 - x$' (AT3 Level 6 Examples).

Where is the OUT number? In order to solve this we need to have the OUT number worked out and we need to have the INs all together (the 'x' represents the IN number).

Many readers will remember from school the need to 'get x on its own', and mnemonics such as 'take across the equals and change the sign'. Many pupils have learned to do this without ever understanding why. Others have never managed to apply it simply *because* they didn't understand what was happening.

Modelling the equation as objects in the weighing pans of balancing scales can help children to understand this concept.

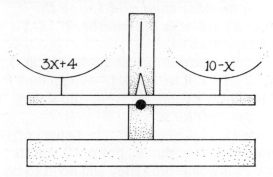

As the two sides are equal, they balance the scales. To find the answer, that is, what is x (our IN number from the function machine analogy), we need to find a balance with an x in one pan and numbers (our OUT number from function machines) in the other. How could we get rid of the '$-x$' on the right hand side? Guide the children through questioning to the fact that adding an 'x' will make a '$-x$' disappear. However, if the scales are going to stay balanced, then we'll have to add an x to *both* sides of the scales.

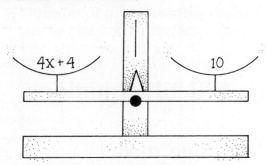

There is now a choice of method. If we use the 'working back' method we get:

$$IN \rightarrow \times 4 \rightarrow + 4 \rightarrow 10$$
$$IN \leftarrow \div 4 \leftarrow -4 \leftarrow 10$$
$$1.5 \leftarrow 6 \leftarrow 10$$

If we continue with the balancing method we still don't know the OUT number, as some of it is attached to the xs and to remove it, we need to subtract the 4 from the left-hand side. To do this, though, would unbalance the scales unless we also subtract 4 from the right-hand side.

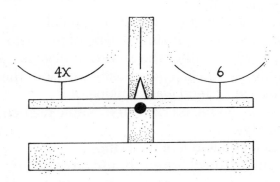

Again, there is a choice of method, but children working at this level – Level 6 of the National Curriculum – should be able to see how to find the x if $4x$ is 6. If you wish to continue the balancing, to remove the 4 from the left-hand side, we need to divide by 4, and hence must divide both sides by four. This will then give a balance with x on one side and 1.5 on the other. So, $x = 1.5$.

There is need for a word of warning here. Children are often made to follow through such methods to the point of absurdity. When they reach the point where they can *see* the answer, then this is the time to stop. The method is only there to help them, not to inhibit their mental calculations.

Trial and improvement

Sometimes, equations cannot be solved by the modelling method used above. It may be impossible to 'get x on its own', for example if you had to find two consecutive numbers which multiply to give 506. Symbolically, this could be written as: $x(x + 1) = 506$ or, if we multiply it out: $x^2 + x = 506$. This cannot be simplified on a weighing picture to get a single 'x' in one pan. Neither can it be simplified by using the function machine model.

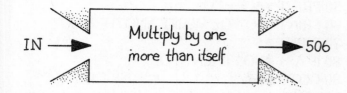

IN ⟶ Multiply by one more than itself ⟶ 506

Trying to work backwards, we get:
IN ← divide by one more than the IN number ← 506. But as we don't know the IN number yet (in fact, it's what we're trying to find), this cannot be done.

Sometimes, trying to work backwards may give the children a function beyond their understanding, for example from the National Curriculum: '*Solve equations such as $x^2 = 5$ and $x^3 = 20$...*' (AT3 Level 6 Examples).

Children may well be aware of the square root button on their calculators, but very few will know how to find the cube root.

To solve equations of either type, it is necessary to use the 'trial and improvement' method, previously known as trial and error. The spreadsheet is an excellent tool for this, but initially it is better for children to try the method using a calculator so that they can appreciate the process.

Taking the first problem of the consecutive numbers – our target is 506. The trial and improvement method might look like this:

lst number	2nd number	Answer	Comments
30	31	930	Too big
20	21	420	Too small
25	26	650	Too big
22	23	506	Just right!

For the problem of finding the cube root of 20, our record might look like this:

x	x^3	Comments
3	27	Too big
2	8	Much too small
2.7	19.683	A good guess
2.75	20.796875	Too big
2.73	20.346417	Better
2.72	20.123648	Better
2.71	19.902511	Too small
2.715	20.012876	Better, but too big
2.714	19.99077	Very close
2.7145	20.001821	Close enough!

There comes a point where such calculation, even with a calculator, will become tedious. Also, there may be several functions to manipulate. For example, a problem such as: 'Three consecutive square numbers multiply together to make 2184; what were the numbers?', will need three columns for the three square numbers plus a column for the multiplication. Using a spreadsheet (see Chapter One) this calculation will be less repetitive and faster.

The computer is programmed so that Column B will be Column A plus one, and Column C will be Column B plus one. Then, putting any number in Column A will automatically enter the three consecutive numbers, for example:

	A	B	C	D	E	F	G
1	3	4	5				
2	10	11	12				
3							
4							
5							
6							
7							
8							
9							
10							

These figures are only added to illustrate the function. They are not to solve the problem. While programming, the spreadsheet will either be blank or will come up with zeros (reading a blank as a zero).

Column D is then programmed to be Column A times Column B times Column C, and the answers will be entered automatically, for example:

	A	B	C	D	E	F	G
1	3	4	5	60			
2	10	11	12	1320			
3							
4							
5							
6							
7							
8							
9							
10							

The spreadsheet is then ready to use. Here is a possible run. Remember that the child only needs to put numbers in Column A.

	A	B	C	D	E	F	G
1	20	21	22	9240			
2	15	16	17	4080			
3	10	11	12	1320			
4	11	12	13	1716			
5	12	13	14	2184			
6							
7							
8							
9							
10							

Besides taking the tedium out of the trial and improvement method, the use of the spreadsheet requires formalised thinking from the children. They must be able to break up the problem into a series of simpler processes, understand the order in which they can be done, and enter the processes as symbols. That is, they must separate the three consecutive numbers into x, $x + 1$ and $x + 2$ and then multiply them. This is an excellent forerunner to symbolic equation work and formulae.

We can also use short LOGO programs to help us with trial and improvement activities; for example, to find which number multiplied by one more than the number makes 100 you can write a program as follows:

```
TO GUESS :NUM
PRINT :NUM
PRINT :NUM + 1
PRINT :NUM* (:NUM + 1)
PRINT [DO YOU WANT TO TRY AGAIN?]
MAKE "ANS RL
IF :ANS = [NO] [PRINT [OK]] [PRINT [TYPE:
GUESS (NEW NUMBER)]]
END
```

To use BASIC for the trial and improvement calculation:

```
10 PRINT "TYPE IN YOUR GUESS"
20 INPUT Y
30 PRINT Y
40 PRINT Y + 1
```

```
50 PRINT Y*(Y + 1)
60 PRINT "DO YOU WANT ANOTHER GO?"
70 INPUT A$
80 IF A$ = "NO" THEN STOP
90 GOTO 10
100 END
```

However, despite these programs, spreadsheets, once set up, allow much speedier exploration.

Structured activities for Key Stage 1

Beginnings

What you need

Examples of change from everyday life, for example time sequence pictures such as the ones shown below:

What to do

Introduce the idea of change to the children by discussing changes which happen in everyday life, for example:

Hungry puppy	→	Feed the puppy	→	Not-hungry puppy

Or from the time sequence above:

Dry pavement	→	Rain	→	Wet pavement

Time sequence pictures are useful for discussing cause and effect, and also tie in with measurement activities.

112

Magic curtain

What you need

A curtain or screen big enough for a child to hide behind.

What to do

Pin up a curtain and tell the children that this is a magic curtain that will make small changes as you walk behind it. Pick one child to stay behind the curtain and who gives an instruction, which you have devised, to the other children as they walk behind the curtain. Choose children one at a time to walk behind the curtain. As each child goes through, they are told the simple instruction such as: swap your shoes over; walk with one arm on your hip; sit down cross-legged when you reach your place, and so on.

The first child to guess the instruction is the next to stay behind the curtain to give instructions.

After a while, the children may like to make up their own changes.

NC mapping

AT3 – working towards Level 3 (b)
AT1 – Level 1 (c)

LOGIC machines

What you need

A function machine, made perhaps from a soap powder carton; a set of logic shapes, function signs such as the ones shown below:

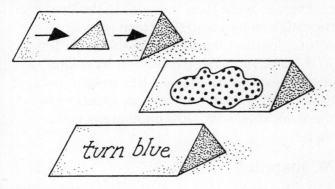

What to do

Put a sign showing a rule (the function) on top of the machine box, explaining that this is what the machine will do. Feed in a logic shape and ask the children to choose what should come out. Repeat this until you are sure they have all understood what has occurred. Let a child choose another rule and feed logic shapes in and out while the others check or provide the answer.

Next, tell the child to feed in logic shapes but to keep the rule secret. The first child to guess the rule can then operate the machine and, with help from an adult, feeds pieces in and out while others try to guess.

Finally, choose a rule and place it on top of the box. Feed out a piece and ask the children to tell you what piece must have gone in.

NC mapping

AT3 – working towards Level 3 (b)
AT1 – Level 2 (a) (c)

Money machine

What you need

A function machine box; money, real or plastic.

What to do

Explain to the children that this function machine changes coins into the number of pennies they are worth. For example, if they fed in a coin such as a 5p, it would feed out five pennies. Ask the children to repeat this process for a different coin. Let the children take turns until you are sure they have understood the function.

This can be adapted for simple addition (feed in several coins, feed out the total in pennies) and for grouping (feed in the pennies, how many 2ps or 5ps come out?)

NC mapping

AT3 – working towards Level 3 (b)
AT1 – Level 2 (a) (c)
AT2 – Level 1 (a) (b)

Adding machines

What you need

A function machine box, number cards,

function signs for addition or subtraction (as shown below).

What to do

Put a sign on top of the function machine and explain what the machine will do. Proceed as in previous function machine activities. Vary this activity – by changing the size of the number or type of number bond – according to the abilities of the group.

NC mapping

AT3 – working towards Level 3 (b)
AT1 – Level 2 (a) (c)
AT2 – Level 1 (a) (b)

Equal weights

What you need

A set of scales with weights (such as Multilink), photocopiable pages 195 and 196.

What to do

This activity can be used to introduce the children to equations and finding missing parts. Put six Multilink in the left-hand side of the weighing scales and nine in the right. Ask the children to say where they will have to add Multilink so that the scales will balance and let them count in the Multilink they need.

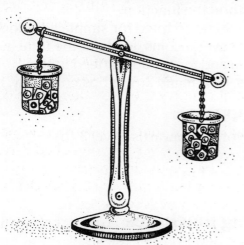

Explain that the problem can be written thus: 6 + ❑ = 9 and check that the children

understand where the 6 and the 9 come from and that the ❑ is what they have to find. Repeat this process several times, asking the children to write their answers in the box. Let the children make up their own problems and then distribute photocopiable page 195.

This activity can be taken further by asking such questions as: 'What would happen if I take two Multilink out of this side?' and so on, establishing the need to balance the numbers.

An alternative method, introducing the same concepts, is to use an equaliser instead of weighing scales.

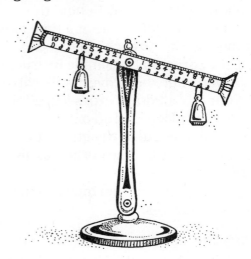

Place one weight on 6, say, on the left-hand side and one weight on 9 on the right-hand side. Ask the children where a weight must be put to balance the equaliser.

Explain that the problem can be written thus: 6 + ❑ = 9 and check that the children understand where the 6 and the 9 come from and that the ❑ is what they have to find. Repeat this process several times, asking the children to write their answers in the box. Let the children make up their own problems before distributing photocopiable page 196.

This activity can be extended by asking such questions as: 'If I take this weight away, how could I make the equaliser balance? Is there another way? How many ways are there?'

NC mapping

AT3 – Level 2 (b)
AT1 – Level 1 (a) (b) (c)
    – Level 2 (c)
AT2 – Level 1 (a) (b)

Shy machines

What you need

A function machine box, number cards, plus a card labelled with a question mark, function signs labelled as shown below.

What to do

After simple function machine work and equation work similar to the activities above, the children should be ready for this activity.

Explain that this function machine is shy and it won't tell us what it can do.

With a rule in mind, feed in and out a pair of numbers. Can anyone guess what the rule is? When a child guesses correctly, let her have a go at feeding in and out a pair of numbers.

Tell the children that another machine won't tell them what number was fed in.

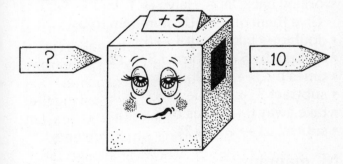

This is harder to solve, and introduces children to inverses (or opposites).

NC mapping

AT3 – Level 2 (b)
    – Level 3 (b)
AT1 – Level 1 (c)
    – Level 2 (c)
AT2 – Level 1 (a) (b)
or – Level 2 (a) (b)

Structured activities for Key Stage 2

Sweet bagging machines

What you need

Function machine box on which you can write the 'bagging' number, that is, you can write the number of sweets which the machine puts in each bag.

What to do

Draw the function machine on the board and explain that this machine puts sweets into bags of 8 (for example). If there are any left over, the machine saves them to add to the next batch.

How many bags will come out if 32 sweets go in? How many bags will be made from 42 sweets or 22 sweets followed by 10, or 34 sweets followed by 26 followed by 10?

Repeat this activity with a different bagging number.

Using a function machine box, ask what number of sweets this machine is putting in each bag:

IN	OUT
35	5
84	12
161	23

Obviously, this exercise introduces, or reinforces, division. Any arithmetic skill can be practised in this way, for example a machine which takes the sweets out of the bags would practise multiplication.

Remember to try the two other forms of this type of work:
• not knowing the function – have a sweet bagging machine where we don't know the number of sweets put in a bag;
• not knowing the input – that is, we don't know how many sweets are fed in.

Also, let the children make up their own machines and list their results.

These activities reinforce the link between multiplication and division:

$$7 \times 8 = 56$$
$$56 \div 7 = 8$$
$$56 \div 8 = 7$$

Finding the inverses prepares the way for solving equations.

NC mapping

AT3 – Level 3 (b)
AT1 – Level 2 (c)
    – Level 3 (d)
AT2 – Level 3 (c)

Clever machines: 2

What you need

Double machine blanks on which you can write the functions.

What to do

By Level 4, children should be combining machines, in preparation for solving more difficult equations:

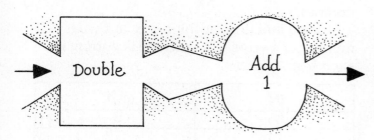

Explain to them that some machines can do more than one function at a time. Ask the children if they can see what this 'clever' machine is doing:

IN	OUT
3	7
7	15
4	9
1	3
11	23

Show the children the above example and explain that this machine can be split into simpler machines. Ask them what the OUT number would be for several IN numbers.

116

Let the children make up their own clever machines and list their results.

Can they work out the INs if they know the OUTs?

NC mapping

AT3 – Level 4 (b)
AT1 – Level 3 (c)
AT2 – Level 3 (c)
    – Level 4 (a)

Reversing doubles

What you need

Double machine on which you can write the functions and the out numbers.

What to do

This activity is generated by the final question of 'Clever machines: 2', 'Is it possible to work out the INs if the OUTs are known?'.

Show the children an example of a double machine. If we know what comes out, how can we find out what went in?

Ask the children to record what the machine does. Can they use their own recording to work back? Help them to find a method of recording which is useful, otherwise you may wish to show them the following: IN → Double → Add 1 → OUT. Working back: IN ← Halve ← Take 1 ← OUT.

Give them other OUT numbers to try:
• double → take away 4 → 6;
• multiply by 5 → subtract 8 → 12;
• times by 3 → add 2 → 14;
• subtract 3 → double → 8;
• take away 6 → times by 3 → 15;
• subtract 1 → × 3 → 24.

NC mapping

AT3 – Level 4 (b)
AT1 – Level 3 (c)
AT2 – Level 3 (c)
    – Level 4 (a)

Bagging/unbagging

What you need

Blank double machines.

What to do

If the children are having trouble understanding the concepts involved in 'Reversing doubles', and yet you feel they are ready for them, try looking at the sweet bagging machines again.

Show the children the following sweet bagging machine, which puts two bags on one side for the machine inspector to check every time the machine is used.

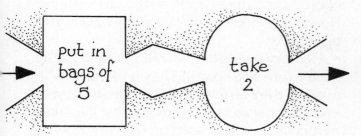

Talk about what is happening, for example: 'Loose sweets go into the machine and are bagged in bags of 5. The machine then sets aside two bags for the inspector and sends the rest to the packers. Can a packer work out how many sweets went into the machine by looking at the number of bags he received?'

In trying to solve this problem, the children must keep in mind the 'units' with which they are dealing. They must take the number of bags and add two *bags*. Only then can the bags be turned into sweets.

Many children working on inverses for the first time will work from left to right, but will put in the inverse functions, for example: IN → Divide by 5 (to bag in 5s) → Take 2 (for the inspector) → OUT. The *correct* inverse is: IN ← multiply by 5 (to take the sweets out of the bags) ← Add 2 (from the inspector) ← OUT. But many will write: OUT → multiply by 5 (to debag) → Add 2 (from the inspector) → IN.

This error has to be challenged by looking at the 'real' situation. What is the inspector adding – sweets or bags?

NC mapping

AT3 – Level 4 (b)
AT1 – Level 3 (c)
AT2 – Level 3 (c)
     – Level 4 (a)

'Stay the same' machines

What you need

Photocopiable page 197.

What to do

Hand out copies of photocopiable page 197. Can the children find numbers which remain unchanged by these machines, in other words where the IN number and the OUT number are the same?

NC mapping

AT3 – Level 4 (b)
AT1 – Level 3 (c)
AT2 – Level 3 (c)
     – Level 4 (a)

Word puzzles

What you need

No special requirements.

What to do

The listed puzzles in this activity are for children who have experience of inverse machines. Most require inversing 'clever' machines.

Read the children a problem. For example: 'I had a bag of sweets. I gave half to Jane and I ate three. I've now got six left. How many did I start off with? How many did I give to Jane?'

Discuss with them how this problem might be solved. One way would be to write the story as: IN → Halve (half to Jane) → Take away 3 (eaten) → 6. Working backwards: IN ← Double ← Add 3 ← 6 which gives: 18 ← 9 ← 6.

So, I started with 18 sweets. Ask the children to check that the answer is correct by working through the question again using the solution.

Distribute the following problems. Choose problems appropriate for the individual children. The problems are listed in order of difficulty.

• Mary bought a bunch of flowers. She gave six to her gran, kept one for herself and gave her mum the rest. If she gave her mum 12 flowers, how many were there in the bunch?

• My father made some biscuits. He put half of them away to store, and shared the rest between my sister and me. I got 4 biscuits. How many did Dad make?

• A squirrel collected a pile of chestnuts. He dropped three. He put an equal number of nuts in each of his three hiding places. If each hiding place got two more nuts, how many had the squirrel collected?

• Jane is equally good at four sports events. She needs to get 20 points to go through to the next round. The judge takes four points off her for wearing the wrong trainers. She just manages to qualify for the next round. How many points did she get in each event?

• Mrs Brown borrows a set of books from the School Mobile library. Half of them are for Mr Jones in the next-door classroom. Two are for the headteacher. Mrs Brown has five books for her own class. How many did she borrow?

• On average, the police in Sharptown catch the criminal in one quarter of reported crimes. They have estimated that there are twice as many crimes committed as there are crimes reported. In one week, they catch 21 criminals. How many crimes were committed that week?

• A group of friends go on holiday together. Half of the friends are married and everyone's wife or husband is on the trip. Of the rest, one third of them are women. If there are two unmarried women on the trip, how many people are there altogether in the group?

• The local bakery makes exceedingly good cherry buns. They put three glacé cherries on the top of each one. The apprentice baker is a greedy girl who eats the glacé cherries when no one is looking. One day, she ate ten glacé cherries and made three dozen cherry buns. How many glacé cherries did the bakers use up that day?

• A factory needs five wheels for each car it makes (one is a spare). They find that on average they have to throw away eight tyres each day because they have faults. If on one particular day they used up 68 tyres, how many cars did they make?

NC mapping

AT3 – Level 4 (b)
AT1 – Level 3 (a) (b) (c)
    – Level 4 (b)
AT2 – Level 3 (c)
    – Level 4 (a)

Infinite and infinitesimal

What you need

Machine blank.

What to do

Show the children a simple function machine, which may be adding or multiplying. The machine becomes perpetual if we add a feedback tube and only use the IN tube to start the machine off; for example:

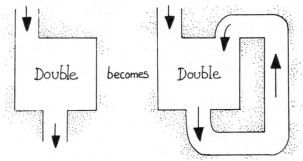

Discuss what will happen with this machine, which will take the IN number, double it, double again, and again... *ad infinitum*. The children may notice the patterns of the end digits, generating a repeated sequence. Alternatively, they may become interested in the way their calculators cope with very large numbers. Calculators vary, but most use a standard form in some way, for example: 134217728 (a number reached quite quickly by doubling) is too big for most calculators, which may therefore write: 1.3422 08 or perhaps give a slightly longer answer if the children have fairly sophisticated calculators. The 08 represents eight place value places (eight decimals or eight zeros) which have been removed. To get back to the number, it is necessary to move eight places:

$$1.3422 \ 08 =$$
$$13.422 \ 07 =$$
$$134.22 \ 06 =$$
$$1342.2 \ 05 =$$
$$13422 \ 04 =$$

Now we are in trouble, as we don't know the rest of the digits. Instead we must add the zeros, and accept that our answer is only an approximation:

$$13422 \ 04 =$$
$$134220 \ 03 =$$
$$1342200 \ 02 =$$
$$13422000 \ 01 =$$
134220000 which is as close as we can get to 134217728 using a calculator.

Try the activity again with a halving machine, or any multiplying or dividing machine. What if we add a negative number? Will this be the same as using a subtracting machine? What if we began with a number between 0 and 1 or between −1 and 0?

Through such exercises, children can come to have a greater understanding of number structure.

A piece of software which will interest teachers of top juniors is *Numerator*, by Longman/Logotron. With this, the children can build their own function machines on the computer screen, and the machine will then operate according to the children's rules. It is an excellent extension to the visualisation provided by machine boxes. (See Appendix A for details.)

NC mapping

AT3 – Level 4 (a)
     – Level 5 (a)
AT1 – Level 3 (c)
     – Level 4 (b)
AT2 – Level 4 (b)

Try and try again

What you need

Puzzle cards (see below), calculators or a computer spreadsheet program.

What to do

These activities practise the 'trial and improvement' method of solving equations and can be undertaken using either calculators or computers.

Activity 1

Make up puzzle cards of the form:
- $\square^2 = 289$, for whole numbers (this could be the area of an unknown square);
- $\square^2 = 280$, for decimals.

You and the children will need to decide how long the decimal should be before it is considered 'close' enough to the true answer.

Encourage the children to be systematic about their recording:

Try	Answer	Comment
15	225	Too small
16	256	Too small
17	289	Too big
16.5	272.25	Too small
16.75	280.5624	Too big
16.7	278.89	Too small
16.72	279.5584	Too small
16.74	280.2276	Too big
16.73	279.8929	Too small
16.735	280.060225	Close enough

Activity 2

Prepare cards on which you have written large whole numbers which you know to be the product of two other consecutive whole

119

numbers such as 6162 (78 × 79). The children should then select a card and try to find the two whole numbers.

Try	Answer	Comment
100 × 101	10100	Too big
60 × 61	3660	Too small
80 × 81	6480	Too big
75 × 76	5700	Too small
77 × 78	6006	Better
78 × 79	6162	Just right!

Activity 3

Ask the children to find the length of the side of a cube which has a volume of 500 cubic centimetres. (A spreadsheet such as *Datacalc*, *Primary Spreadsheet* or *Grasshopper: an introductory spreadsheet* [Birmingham: Newman Software] will speed up the calculation [see Appendix A]. Also, the children must formalise their thinking in order to program the sheet, encouraging the writing of processes as equations or formulae.)

NC mapping

AT3 – Level 6 (b)
AT2 – Level 4 (a)
      – Level 5 (a) (spreadsheets)

Open-ended activities for Key Stage 1

Simple Simon

What you need

A mask made to look like a function machine box.

What to do

Play the usual game of 'Simple Simon says...', but now Simple Simon is a machine who will make the children do what he says. If he doesn't say 'Simple Simon says' then the machine is not switched on!

NC mapping

AT3 – working towards Level 3 (b)

Sticky calculators

What you need

Calculators for which you are familiar with the constant function.

What to do

Work with a small group of children, pre-program their calculators to carry out constant functions (see page 20). Can the children find out what their calculators are 'stuck' on? For example, if you press +3 = = = 0 (different calculators may vary), then the calculator is programmed always to add three when a number and the equals sign are pressed; that is, if 7 = is pressed then the calculator will give 10.

Show the children how to get stuck on something else, such as × 3 = = = 0, and then let them set each other problems to solve.

NC mapping

AT3 – working towards Level 3 (a)
AT1 – Level 1 (c)
AT2 – Level 1 (b)

Back and forth

What you need

Mazes, made with school furniture or PE equipment, for LOGOing children (that is giving the children LOGO commands to follow); or a Roamer, or other programmable toy, and a maze made with junk material on the classroom floor.

What to do

Using the children themselves, or a programmable toy such as Roamer, ask the children to find ways of getting from a to b around a maze. What would the instructions be to get back from b to a? Let the children make up other outward and return journeys. (It can help to pin instructions on a number line, with the inverse underneath.)

NC mapping

AT3 – working towards Level 3 (b)
AT4 – Level 1 (b)

Join machines/split machines

What you need

Photocopiable pages 198 and 199 .

What to do

Explain to the children that some machines can be joined together, for example:

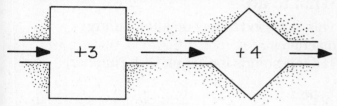

This is the same as:

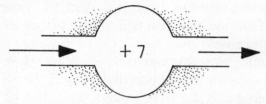

Let them practise using joined machines (see photocopiable page 198) until you are happy that they have grasped the concept. Now, provide them with a machine such as:

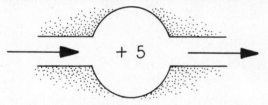

Can they suggest two machines which would do the same job as this one? Once you are sure they understand, distribute photocopiable page 199.

NC mapping

AT3 – Level 3 PoS
AT1 – Level 2 (c)
AT2 – Level 2 (b)

Equalisers

What you need

Equalisers, weights.

What to do

Ask the children to find as many ways as they can to balance an equaliser:

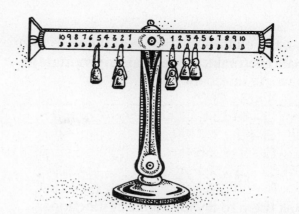

Encourage them to record their findings thus:

$$7 = 2 + 5$$
$$4 + 7 = 2 + 9$$
$$3 + 3 + 5 = 2 + 2 + 7 \quad \text{and so on.}$$

This is an excellent introduction to the idea of 'balance' in equations, which should be reinforced at every stage up to solving equations (Level 6).

NC mapping

AT3 – Level 2 (a)
AT1 – Level 1 (a) (b) (c)
　　 – Level 2 (c)

'Can't decide' machines

What you need

A function machine box.

What to do

Set up the box or sheet to show the following machines.

This machine can't decide what to subtract:

$10 - \square = \square$

Sometimes it might subtract 2: $10 - 2 = \square$ and sometimes 5: $10 - 5 = \square$.

What else might it decide to subtract, and what would the answer be? This activity will lead to the children generating their own bonds, which will help them to improve their mental work.

Let the children try some of these variations (make as many as appropriate):

$$8 - \square = \square$$
$$\square - 4 = \square$$
$$\square - \square = 3$$
$$\square = 9 - \square$$
$$\square = \square - 5$$

Ask them to try for different functions:
$3 + \square = \square$

Older pupils might like to look at the following:

$$\square \times 4 = \square$$
$$\square = \square \div 5$$

NC mapping

AT3 – Level 2 (a) (b)
     – Level 3 (a) (b)
AT1 – Level 2 (c)
     – Level 3 (c)
AT2 – Level 2 (a)

Open-ended activities for Key Stage 2

Funny machines

What you need

No special requirements.

What to do

Funny machines behave rather oddly. Ask the children to find the functions that these funny machines are carrying out:
• whatever you put in, the machine always gives you back your IN number;
• whatever you put in, the machine always gives you the number 1;
• whatever you put in, the machine always gives you zero.

Ask the children to make up their own 'funny' machines.

NC mapping

AT3 – Level 4 (a) (b)
     – Level 5 (a)

AT1 – Level 5 (a) (c)
AT2 – various, depending on outcomes

Thoans

What you need

No special requirements.

What to do

This is a good follow-up after 'Funny machines'.
THOAN stands for **TH**ink **O**f **A** **N**umber.

Type 1

Tell the children the following puzzle:
'Think of a number. Double it. Add 4. Divide by 2. Take away 2. You will now get back to your number!'

Discuss why this works: $n \rightarrow \times 2 \rightarrow + 4 \rightarrow \div 2 \rightarrow - 2 \rightarrow n$. When you divide by 2, the ×2 is cancelled and the +4 is halved to +2. The –2 then cancels the +2.

Another way of looking at it, if the children are working with symbolic notation, is:

$$\frac{2n + 4}{2} - 2 = n$$

This gives: $\dfrac{2n + 4}{2} = n + 2$

This gives: $n + 2 = n + 2$ (though this is beyond the vast majority of primary children).

Ask the children to try making up their own puzzles which behave like this.

Type 2

Tell the children the following puzzle:
'Think of a number. Double it. Add 4. Divide by 2. Take away the number you first thought of. The answer is 2!'

Follow the same process as above to discuss why this works.

NC mapping

AT3 – Level 4 (a) (b)
     – Level 5 (a)
AT1 – Level 5 (a) (c)
AT2 – various, depending on outcomes

Calendar capers

What you need

A calendar.

What to do

As calendars are made of two functions (the numbers go in ones along and sevens down), identifying and explaining patterns on a calendar grid models going through functions several times and in different orders.

Show the children a calendar month:

Mon	Tues	Wed	Thur	Fri	Sat	Sun
				1	2	3
4	5	6	7	8	9	10
11	12	13	14	15	16	17
18	19	20	21	22	23	24
25	26	27	28	29	30	

Can they see any patterns in the diagonals on this table (4, 12, 20, 28 or 2, 8, 14, 20, 26)? Why do they go up in this way? What about 'knight's moves' (as on a chessboard – for example from 25 to 20 to 15 to 10)? What other patterns can the children find? What if they take a small square off the grid, for example:

6	7
13	14

Tell the children to add the diagonally opposite numbers, for example, 6 + 14 and 7 + 13. What do they notice? Ask them to multiply the numbers, 6 × 14 and 7 × 13. What do they see? Let them try again for two other small squares. What do the children notice? What about other sizes of square?

Take out a cross shape:

	5	
11	12	13
	19	

What patterns/rules can the children find here? For example, 5 + 19 = 24 and 11 + 13 = 24, both of which are double the number in the middle. Can the children work out why? The difference between 11 and 5 is 6, and the difference between 19 and 13 is also 6. Why does this happen?

Let the children try other sizes and shapes. If they need further experience of explaining moves of different meaning, try 'Machine table' on page 54, which links this work with sequences.

NC mapping

AT3 – Level 4 (a) (b)
AT1 – Level 4 (a) (b) (c) (d)
 – Level 5 (a) (d)
 – Level 6 (a) (c)

Formulae

Specific mention of formulae does not appear in the National Curriculum until Level 4 of Attainment Target 3: **'b) Use simple formulae expressed in words'** (Statements of Attainment).

However, the examples that are given for Attainment Target 3 Level 4 are of equations, not formulae. It could be inferred that children at Level 4 should be able to express, in words, physical relationships, for example, 'If you multiply the three sides of a box together, you get the volume', but this is a matter of personal interpretation. Formulae expressed symbolically are introduced at Level 5, and there is no ambiguity about the understanding required: *__Use the fact that the perimeter p of a rectangle is given by p = 2 (a + b) where a and b are the dimensions__* (Level 5 Examples).

Children learn to cope with such abstraction through their work with functions and equations.

There are many cross-curricular opportunities for working with formulae, some of which are discussed in Chapter Five. Here are three which are purely mathematical; the first two common situations for primary children, the third uncommon, but interesting and with repercussions for later mathematics.

Perimeters

What you need

Shape templates of regular (equal-sided) shapes.

What to do

Explain to the children that an equilateral triangle has each side equal to length, l. If we call the perimeter p, we can write $p = 3l$.

How could we write the perimeters of other regular (equal-sided) shapes? Use this question to stimulate discussion of the templates shown below. What is the perimeter of these shapes?

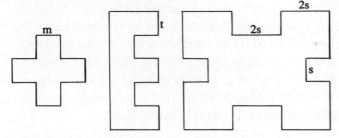

Ask the children to make up shapes with other perimeters.

NC mapping

AT3 – Level 5 (b)
AT4 – Level 4 (d)

Colour rod connections

What you need

Colour rods.

What to do

Show the children how, for example, two red rods equal a pink rod. If we call the red rods r and the pink rods p, we can write: $2r = p$. A red rod and a green rod equal a yellow rod, so we can write: $r + g = y$.

How many different formulae can the children find by connecting the different rod pieces?

Ask such questions as:
• If $2r = p$ and $2p = b$ (a brown) then how many reds make a brown?
• If $r + w$ (a white) $= g$ and $3g = B$ (a blue), then what is the formula linking r, w, and B (this will be $3r + 3w = B$).

NC mapping

AT3 – Level 4 (a)
   – Level 5 (b)
AT1 – Level 4 (b) (d)

Euler's rule

What you need

Clixi, Polydron or other construction material.

What to do

Make a three-dimensional shape such as a pyramid. Explain to the children which parts of the shape are the faces, the edges and the vertices (corners).

Ask the children to make three-dimensional shapes with no holes. They must then count the faces, edges and vertices of their shapes. What do they notice? They may need to combine all their results on a table.

The result: Faces + Vertices = Edges + 2 or F + V = E + 2 is known as Euler's Rule, after a famous eighteenth-century Swiss mathematician. Euler worked on many such relationships, adding greatly to the fields of topology and graph theory.

NC mapping

AT3 – Level 5 (b)
AT4 – Level 5 (b)

Inequalities

An inequality is a statement which, instead of showing arrangements which are equal (as in an equation), shows which of the elements is the larger. For example, 5 is greater than 2, is written 5 > 2, or 3 is less than 7, is written 3 < 7.

Inequalities are not mentioned in the National Curriculum until Level 7: *'List the values of n where n is a whole number such that: –9 < n £ 20'* (AT3 Level 7 Examples).

However, children should, and do, meet the concept much earlier. Many Key Stage 1 schemes contain the standard notation, < and >, and the children cope well with the material. At this stage, only positive whole numbers are normally used, but as soon as children meet a new concept, for example, negative numbers or fractions, then there is no reason not to introduce inequalities into the work.

When looking at negative numbers, it is important to be aware of a common misconception among children that –7 is bigger than 4 because the digit is bigger. Such children should be shown a number line to help them see why this is not true:

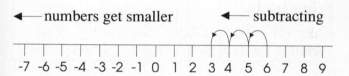

We 'take away' as we go to the left, so the numbers get smaller as we go to the left. Therefore, 1 < 4; –1 < 1; –4 < –1; and –7 < 4.

When looking at fractions, children often find it more difficult to see which of two fractions is the smaller, until they have been changed to equivalent fractions. For example, $^3/_5 \square \, ^7/_{12}$, what should go in the square, < or >? Therefore, change each to fractions which have the same denominator (that is, what number is a multiple of 5 and 12) so that $^3/_5 = \, ^{36}/_{60}$ and $^7/_{12} = \, ^{35}/_{60}$ and now we can see that $^3/_5$ is bigger, so we can write: $^3/_5 > \, ^7/_{12}$.

a half ½   a quarter ¼

Structured and open-ended activities for Key Stage 1

Towers

What you need

Multilink, cards labelled as below:

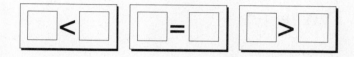

What to do

Make towers of Multilink so that their heights go up in the stages 1, 2, 3, 4 and 5 – repeat some if you like. Show the children one of the cards and ask if they know what it means. If they do know, ask them which towers could go in the squares. If they do not understand the cards, explain the symbols and show them one or two examples. Ask them to find as many tower pairs as they can and record them on paper: 3 < 4; 2 = 2; 5 > 2 and so on.

As an alternative, provide half of the pair, and ask the children to find how many ways there are to complete it, still using the original towers; for example: 1 < ❑ or ❑ > 3.

NC mapping

AT3 – working towards Level 7 (b)
AT1 – Level 1 (a) (b)
AT2 – Level 1 (a)

Activities for Key Stage 2

Equal adds

What you need

Counters or Multilink, paper, pencils.

What to do

Ask the children to make two Multilink towers, and to place them on paper with an inequality between them. What happens if they add the same number of Multilink to each tower? What happens if they subtract?

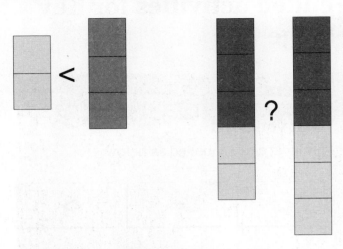

Ask the children to experiment. Can they provide a rule?

NC mapping

AT1

Adding and subtracting inequalities

What you need

Counters or Multilink, paper, pencils.

What to do

Make the following arrangements from counters or Multilink and discuss them with the children:

What happens if we add the larger rectangle from each pair?

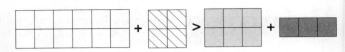

Completing the following table will help reinforce the idea:

a	b	c	d	a + c	b + d	(a + c) ? (b + d)
8	1	5	4	13	5	>
7	4	6	2			
3	−1	−3	−5			
−4	−5	−6	−8			
87	84	11	−2			

Notice that a > b and c > d in each case. What happens with subtraction?

Again, the children will be helped by the completion of a table:

a	b	c	d	a − c	b − d	(a − c) ? (b − d)
8	6	5	4	3	2	>
7	4	6	2			
3	−1	3	−5			
7	6	5	4			
87	34	11	2			

Is there a rule for subtraction? (No!)

NC mapping

AT3 – Level 5 (b)
  – working towards Level 7 (b)
AT1 – Level 4 (d)
AT2 – Level 5 PoS

Chapter Three
Bringing it all together

Many areas of human endeavour and many methods we use to express ourselves can be appreciated at several levels. For example, a child learning to read concentrates initially on recognising individual words. She pays little attention to the meaning of the sentence and her reading is atonal, lacking any expression. A little later, she learns to build up from letters or parts of words those words she cannot recognise, or she may look for clues in the pictures beside the text. In doing so, she exhibits a growing understanding of the meaning behind the words. As reading becomes easier, she will stress certain words in a sentence, come to appreciate emotions expressed in the text and start to have a feel for syntax.

Older readers learn that the story can have a tale to tell and also a moral to teach; that people have motives behind what they do which often aren't plainly written on the page. Adults learn to appreciate the many layers of meaning within a piece of writing. All these different stages can be met in one single piece of writing.

Similarly, a young child's understanding of the geography of his immediate environment will be simple facts such as the way to school, where it is safe to cross the road, or which is the closest playground to home. Older children will appreciate the layout of the area and answer questions such as, 'Why do you think they chose to put the pelican crossing here instead of there?' or 'Where do you think it would be best to build a new swimming pool?' Adults, looking at the same surroundings will see even more, appreciating the socio-economic profile of the area, the need for traffic regulation and so on.

Mathematics is no different. What might seem like a simple piece of arithmetic, or geometric pattern, will have different meanings for an infant and a junior child, for a secondary pupil and a student of mathematics at university.

This chapter takes three starting points – Pascal's triangle, magic squares and the Fibonacci sequence – and shows how they are accessible to different ability levels. Initially, each area is described for the 'not-so-mathematical' adult. However, because the mathematical progression of such topics does not proceed in neat, equal bundles of knowledge, mappings to the National Curriculum will not proceed simply, level by level. Teachers can best judge the appropriateness of an activity by reading through the instructions or looking at the possible results, though the National Curriculum mappings will provide some guidance. Algebraic skills, numerical skills, spatial skills and data handling skills do not usually all map to the same level for a particular activity. Looking at the 'average' mapping may provide teachers with some guidance.

Pascal's or the Chinese triangle

The origins of this number pattern are uncertain. It was known to Omar Khayyám in the twelfth century and an account of it was published in China about AD1300. However, as Pascal brought it to the attention of the Western world, and did so much research into it, it is usually known as Pascal's triangle.

Blaise Pascal (1623–1662) was an exceptional French mathematician. At the age of sixteen, he was writing definitive essays on geometry. At the age of 18 he invented the first calculating machine. However, he is most famous for his contributions to the study of

probability, and it is here – as we shall see – that the 'triangle' pattern of numbers plays an important part.

The triangle is an arrangement of numbers:

```
              1
            1   1
          1   2   1
        1   3   3   1
      1   4   6   4   1
    1   5  10  10   5   1
  1   6  15  20  15   6   1
```

This arrangement has many properties and uses which will be developed in this section. For example, new numbers are made by adding the two numbers above it:

Rows within the triangle follow specific rules, that is, they form a sequence; for example: 1, 3, 6, 10, 15 are the triangle numbers.

Activity progression across Key Stages 1 and 2

Let us see how the pattern develops by first looking at an activity for younger children.

The mouse and the cheese

What you need

A portable whiteboard or large sheets of paper, string, objects to represent a mouse and a piece of cheese.

What to do

Tell the following story to the children, in a small group, and help them reach their conclusions:

> A mouse lives in a maze of underground tunnels under a house. The maze leads to a hole in the wall of a kitchen. The cook in this kitchen is very clumsy and is always dropping his favourite food, cheese, on the floor. Cheese is also the mouse's favourite food and so she

spends a lot of time trying to find the quickest way to the hole.

Ask the children then to work out how many ways the mouse can get to the hole, if the maze looks like the one below.

The children should identify that there are two ways. Can they say which is the shorter way? (They are both the same.)

In how many ways can the mouse get to the hole, if the maze looks like this?

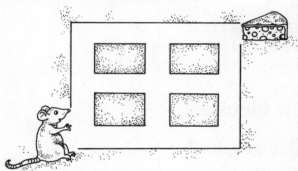

There are six ways now. It is important to explain here that the mouse is trying to find *quick* ways, and therefore she will not want to go 'backwards'. As the cheese is to the right and up from the mouse, anything to the left or down will be 'backwards'. For example, the following two routes are not acceptable:

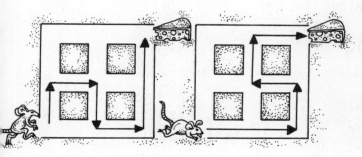

Can the children see why these routes are not the fastest? Can they show you what the mouse could have done instead? Below are

shown the six fastest routes. The children should draw and measure them with string to show that they are all the same distance.

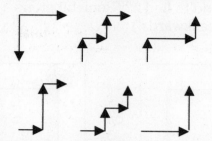

The children will not be so systematic, and may need help seeing some of the ways. This is a concept only slowly developed, and has important links across the curriculum: **'giving and understanding instructions for movement along a route'** (AT4 Level 1 PoS), **'recording with objects or drawing and commenting on the results'** and **'recognising possible outcomes of random events'** (AT5 Level 1 PoS).

If the children are coping well with this and enjoying the challenge, try them with the next size of grid (3×3) where there are 20 different routes!

NC mapping

AT1 – Level 1 (a) (b) (c)
AT2 – Level 2 PoS (measurement)
AT4 – Level 1 PoS (movement)
AT5 – Level 1 PoS (probability)

The previous activity helps children to find their way to the end of the maze. However, to find all the numbers in the triangle, they will need to look at all the junctions within the maze.

The dropped cheese puzzle

What you need

Photocopiable page 200.

What to do

Explain the following to the children, with the help of a drawing:

> The mouse has a friend who also likes to take cheese from the kitchen. However, he is as clumsy as the cook,

and keeps dropping the cheese in the maze. If he drops the cheese at a corner, how many ways are there for his friend to find it? (Remember, no going backwards!)

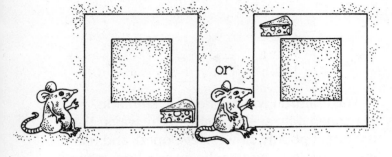

Distribute photocopiable page 200 to the children, checking that they understand where the corners are in the mazes. They should be encouraged to draw a cheese in one of the corners each time they begin to look for routes. For example, they will need to draw a cheese in the middle top corner on three different mazes to find all the routes to that corner:

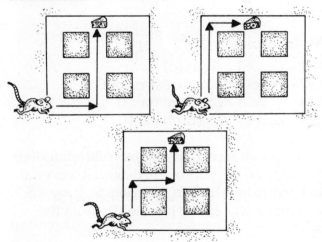

The numbers of routes to all the corners are shown below.

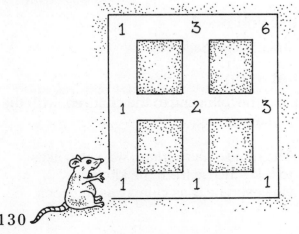

Can the children see any patterns? Two lines are all 1s; two are the counting numbers; two lines go 1, 3, 6, which is 'add 1 then add 2'. There is therefore symmetry in the picture.

Seeing the next grid size up (or by working it out if they are able) may help the children to see the patterns more clearly.

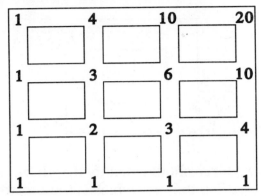

NC mapping

AT3 – Level 3 PoS
AT1 – Level 2 (a)(b)(c)
AT2 – Level 1 (b)
AT4 – Level 1 PoS (movement)
AT5 – Level 1 PoS (probability)

The binostat

What you need

A binostat (these are sold by several school suppliers, often as part of a probability kit).

What to do

A binostat is like a pin-ball machine. Balls are fed in at the top, fall through a triangular grid, and collect in a series of slots:

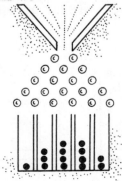

The children may be used to such arrangements from stalls on fairgrounds and so on. The routes that a ball can take through the binostat follow the same rule as the mouse in the maze. For example, there is one way of getting to the far right slot.

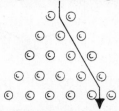

However, there are four ways of getting to the next slot:

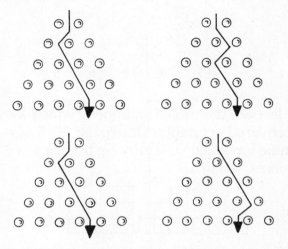

These two numbers (1 and 4) are the two numbers on the end of row five of Pascal's triangle. Ask the children which slots they think are most likely to fill up if lots of balls are fed in at the top of the grid. They can then carry out an experiment to check. (Allocating numbers of balls which would collect in each of the slots, if we fed in 100 balls, say, is beyond most juniors, but the idea of the slots *not* being equally likely to fill up is very important.)

NC mapping
AT3 – Level 4 (a)
AT1 – Level 4 (b) (c)
AT5 – Level 3 (c)

Coins

What you need
Coins, paper, pencils.

What to do
This is an alternative investigation to the binostat activity, which also leads to Pascal's triangle.

Show the children a coin and ask what the outcome might be if you tossed it. What if you threw two coins? There might be two heads, the first could be a head and the second a tail, the first could be a tail and the second a head, or there could be two tails. Therefore there are four outcomes: two heads in one way, a head and a tail in two ways, two tails in one way. What about if you tossed three coins or four coins and so on? Ask the children to work on the problem together.

The results are shown below:

1 coin: **1**H (head), **1**T (tail)

2 coins: **1**(HH) **2**(HT, TH) **1**(TT)

3 coins: **1**(HHH) **3**(HHT, HTH, THH) **3**(TTH, THT, HTT) **1**(TTT)

4 coins: **1**(HHHH) **4**(HHHT, HHTH, HTHH, THHH) **6**(HHTT, HTHT, HTTH, THHT, THTH, TTHH) **4**(TTTH, TTHT, THTT, HTTT) **1**(TTTT)

Can the children see Pascal's triangle in their results?

NC mapping
AT3 – Level 4 PoS
AT5 – Level 4 PoS

Whatever the level of the children, and whichever method you use to introduce the triangle to children, they ought next to explore the numbers inside it.

Patterns in Pascal

What you need
Photocopiable page 201.

What to do
Show Pascal's triangle to the children soon after they have met the numbers through any of the above activities. Do they recognise the numbers? Have they seen them somewhere before? Can they see any patterns in this triangle of numbers? Everyone will be able to see the '1s' lines:

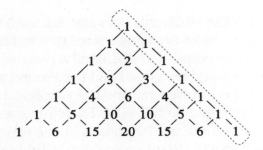

They should also recognise the counting numbers:

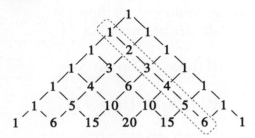

But can the younger children also find the way the numbers are made? For example:

Recognising this pattern enables the children to find subsequent numbers in the triangle themselves. Let them try completing photocopiable page 201. Do the children have to work out *all* the numbers in this way? What do they notice about the pattern lines? Can they see the symmetry?

Through such an activity, the children experience a repeating pattern (1, 1, 1...), a number sequence (1, 2, 3...), a repeating rule (the two numbers above added together give the below number) and a pattern/relationship shown as a spatial arrangement. The repeating rule can be modelled using a function machine, providing an appropriate introduction to the idea of a machine with two inputs:

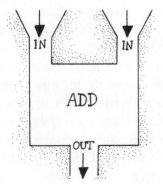

Missing parts of an equation can then be introduced:

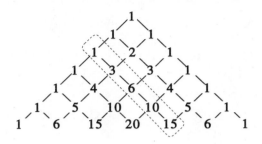

Can the children find any other patterns?

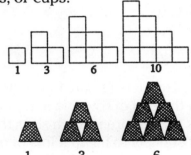

Here are the triangle numbers, which were discovered in Chapter One (page 42). They can be modelled with growing triangles of squares, or cups.

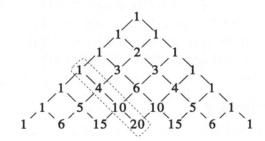

What about the next diagonal?

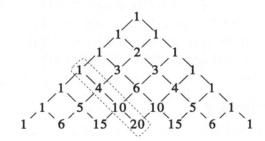

This doesn't look so easy.

Encourage the children to look at the differences between the numbers (AT3 Level 6), and we find the triangle numbers again! Why do the children think this is the case? (Because we added the triangle numbers to get these numbers!) Interestingly, this sequence can be modelled with growing tetrahedra (triangular-based pyramids) of cans. Try it!

Other diagonals are harder to explore, as at the moment we can see so little of them. However, once the children have the pattern of how the numbers are made, they can make larger triangles themselves.

NC mapping

This activity has been mapped at several levels because different children will be able to work to different levels within the activity.
AT3 – Level 3 PoS
    – Level 4 (a)
    – Level 5 (a)
AT1 – Level 3 (b) (c) (d)
    – Level 4 (b) (d)
    – Level 5 (a) (b) (c)

Teachers may also choose this work with Pascal's triangle as an appropriate time to introduce generalisation to the older juniors.

Generalising Pascal

What you need

No special requirements.

What to do

Children will, by Level 5 or 6, have already had a good deal of experience of explaining patterns *iteratively*, for example: 1, 3, 6, 10, 15, 21, 28 might be explained as, 'You add two, then you add three, then four, and so on'; or the pattern might be explained as, 'If you're looking for the fourth number, you add 4 to the number before, for the fifth number add 5 to the last one, and so on.'

However, children at this stage need to be able to access the hundredth term or the 'nth' term, without finding all the others. They need to find a *generalisation*:

$$1 \rightarrow 1$$
$$2 \rightarrow 3$$
$$3 \rightarrow 6$$
$$4 \rightarrow 10$$
$$5 \rightarrow 15$$

Ask the children what they could do to 3 to get 6. Two possible answers are: 'Double' or 'Add 3', but these don't work for the other numbers: 4 doubled isn't 10 and so on.

We have to find a rule which works for *all* the numbers. Some children may notice: 3×4 gives 12, and half of 12 is 6 or 4×5 gives 20, and half of 20 is 10.

But many will need help with the aid of a table:

Term	Add 1	Number in pattern
1	2	1
2	3	3
3	4	6
4	5	10
5	6	15

Can they see it yet?

Term	Add 1	× together	Number in pattern
1	2	2	1
2	3	6	3
3	4	12	6
4	5	20	10
5	6	30	15

Now? The rule is 'the term number times (term number + 1), then halve'.

Looking at the spatial arrangement can also help the children understand the generalisation:

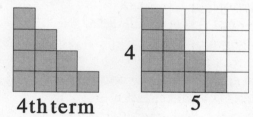

4th term   4   5

Half of the rectangle on the right gives the number we want, and the rectangle's sides are the term number (4) and one more (5).

Children able to cope with symbolic notation can then record the result as: nth term $= \dfrac{n(n + 1)}{2}$

Ask the children to generalise the other patterns in Pascal's triangle.

NC mapping

AT3 – Level 6 PoS
    – Level 7 (a)

Plotting Pascal

What you need

Graph paper, pencils.

What to do

Ask the children to take each of the diagonals from Pascal's triangle and plot them. First it will be necessary to draw up the table for each sequence; for example:

Term	Value of function
1	1
2	3
3	6
4	10
5	15

This gives the co-ordinates: (1,1) (2,3) (3,6) (4,10) (5,15) which plotted gives:

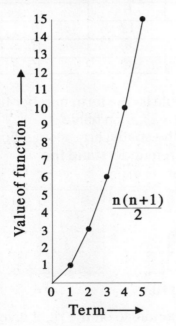

Ask the children to plot other diagonals. They may need first to work out further terms from Pascal's triangle. Which sequences are the steepest?

NC mapping

AT3 – Level 6 (c)

AT1 – Level 6 (b)

Finally, both to make the point that the triangle was known long before Pascal, and also for a bit of fun, here is an activity on the Chinese triangle.

The Chinese triangle

What you need

No special requirements.

What to do

Explain to the children that the triangle we call Pascal's triangle was known to the Chinese long before the Western world.

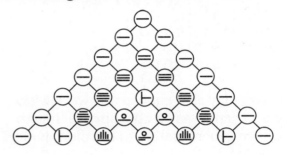

Can the children work out what the Chinese number for 20 is? Ask them to draw their own Chinese triangle.

NC mapping

AT3 – Level 4, Examples

Magic squares

Magic squares are numbers which have been arranged on a square grid in such a way that the sum of the numbers in each row, column, or main diagonals is the same. They have fascinated mathematicians for thousands of years. The earliest known magic square is the *lo-shu* from China, where numbers are represented as dots:

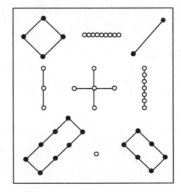

The *lo-shu* was known in 1000 BC, perhaps even earlier (legend states that a divine tortoise appeared to the Chinese Emperor Yu in about 2200 BC with this pattern inscribed upon its back). The *lo-shu* was thought to be lucky (it was considered a protection against the plague in the Middle Ages) and is still found engraved on charms and amulets today in several countries. The square above can be drawn with our own (Arabic) numerals to give:

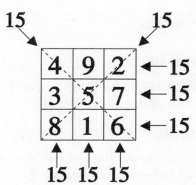

As can be seen every row, column and major diagonal adds up to 15.

As soon as children can count to 15, and understand what addition means, they can begin to work with magic squares. If they can't yet add numbers such as those above, they should be given structured apparatus (Unifix, Multilink, Multibase) to model the numbers and they should have access to calculators. Children should not be deprived of the chance to explore numbers simply because their arithmetic skills are not yet well developed.

Activity progression across Key Stages 1 and 2

Complete the square

What you need
Photocopiable page 202.

What to do
Show the children a copy of a magic square. Can they add the numbers in a line? Ask them to add the numbers in a different line. What

do they notice? Explain to the children what a magic square is and distribute photocopiable page 202, on which there are magic squares which have numbers missing. Do the first one or two questions together and then ask the children to complete the other squares.

This activity practises partitions of 15, the use of inverses (as they know the answer but not all of the question) and addition, as well as general problem-solving skills.

Some children will realise quite quickly that they are dealing with the same numbers over and over. Why is this? The squares are basically the same, only 'flipped over' (reflected) or turned around (rotated). The symmetries should be discussed with children who discover this short cut. For example:

Original square	Reflected horizontally	Reflected vertically
4 9 2	2 9 4	8 1 6
3 5 7	7 5 3	3 5 7
8 1 6	6 1 8	4 9 2

Original square	Reflected in one diagonal	Reflected in other diagonals
4 9 2	6 7 2	4 3 8
3 5 7	1 5 9	9 5 1
8 1 6	8 3 4	2 7 6

Original square	Rotated square
4 9 2	2 7 6
3 5 7	9 5 1
8 1 6	4 3 8

Rotated again	and again
6 1 8	8 3 4
7 5 3	1 5 9
2 9 4	6 7 2

Do these changes make any difference to the totals of the lines?

Can the children see any number patterns in the magic squares? For example, one diagonal goes 4, 5, 6, the other goes 2, 5, 8; one line goes 3, 5, 7 and another goes 1, 5, 9. These can be written in a 'difference' order:

4, 5, 6	difference of 1
3, 5, 7	difference of 2
2, 5, 8	difference of 3
1, 5, 9	difference of 4

Also, the corner numbers are always 4, 6, 2 or 8. What sort of numbers are these? The side numbers are always 1, 9, 3 or 7. What sort of numbers are these?

NC mapping

AT3 – Level 2 (a) and PoS
– Level 3 (b) and PoS
AT1 – Level 1 (a) (b) (c)
– Level 2 (c)
AT2 – Level 1 (b)
AT4 – working towards Level 3 (b) and Level 4 (c), though accessible much earlier

Add to the square

What you need

A selection of the completed magic squares from the first activity, squared paper, pencils, calculators (optional).

What to do

Ask the children to choose a magic square and to add any number they like to every number in the square. They should record their answers on a 3 × 3 square on squared paper. For example:

4	3	8
9	5	1
2	7	6

If we add three to each number we get:

7	6	11
12	8	4
5	10	9

What are the totals in each line now? Why? What would happen if we added a different number?

Ask the children to look at the diagonal patterns. Why do the diagonals still only change by 1 or 3? (That is: 4, 5, 6 has become

7, 8, 9, with a difference still of 1; 2, 5, 8 has become 5, 8, 11 still with a difference of 3.)

NC mapping

AT3 – Level 2 (a)
– working towards Level 4 (a)
AT1 – Level 2 (c)
– Level 3 (d)
– Level 4 (c)
AT2 – Level 2 (b)

Magic sums

What you need

A copy of the original magic square, paper, pencils, calculators (optional).

What to do

Ask the children to look at the sum of the corners of the original square: 2 + 4 + 6 + 8 = 20. Why is it 20? (With a five in the middle and a total of 15, the corners of each diagonal must be 15 − 5 = 10; there are two diagonals giving the four corners, so we get 20.)

When a number is added to every member of the square, what happens to this corner total? For example, adding three, 5 + 7 + 9 + 11 = 32. How does this connect with our total for the original square (20)?

What do *all* the numbers in the original magic square add up to? Is there any connection between this and the total of a line? (1 + 2 + 3 + 4 + 5 + 6 + 7 + 8 + 9 = 45; a row = 15.) What about those squares which the children have changed by adding to them?

NC mapping

AT3 – Level 3 (b)
– Level 4 (a)
AT1 – Level 2 (a) (b) (c)
– Level 3 (d)
AT2 – Level 2 (b)

Patterns on the square

What you need

A selection of the completed magic squares from the first activity, coloured pens.

What to do

Ask the children to draw lines connecting the number patterns they have found. For example, on the original square, join together: 1, 2, 3, 4, 5, 6, 7, 8, 9.

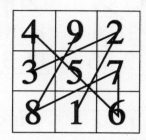

Or join 1, 3, 5, 7, 9, and then 2, 4, 6, 8.

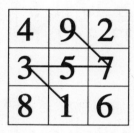

Do all the squares give the same patterns? Is there any symmetry in the patterns? It is interesting to compare these to the patterns provided by 4 × 4 or 5 × 5 magic squares. Try the same activity also on the squares generated by the following activity.

NC mapping

AT3 – Level 3 PoS
AT1 – Level 3 (d)
AT4 – Level 3 (b)
    – Level 4 (c)

Growing magic

What you need

Requirements depend upon the activity being undertaken.

What to do

Take a 4 × 4 magic square.
• Ask the children to check that this is a magic square.
• Make worksheets with missing numbers for the children to calculate.
• Ask the children to find number patterns in the lines.

• Ask the children to make other magic squares using this one, either by rotating, reflecting, or adding a constant.
• Ask the children to join up number sequences, for example 1, 2, 3, 4, 5, 6, 7, 8, 9 or 1, 3, 5, 7, 9 or 2, 4, 6, 8, with coloured pens.

The National Curriculum mapping will be the same as for the first of these activities, only the arithmetic skills have increased.

The five activities are traced out below with a 4 × 4 magic square.
• Ask the children to check that this is a magic square (all lines add up to 34).

1	15	14	4
12	6	7	9
8	10	11	5
13	3	2	16

• Make worksheets with missing numbers for the children to calculate, for example:

1			
12		7	9
8		11	5
	3	2	

• Can the children find number sequences?

4, 7, 10, 13	difference of 3
1, 6, 11, 16	difference of 5

• Ask the children to make other magic squares using this one, either by rotating, reflecting, or adding a constant.

A rotation followed by a horizontal reflection:

16	5	9	4
2	11	7	14
3	10	6	15
13	8	12	1

Adding four:

5	19	18	8
16	10	11	13
12	14	15	9
17	7	6	20

• Ask the children to join up any number sequences using coloured pens.

The counting numbers:

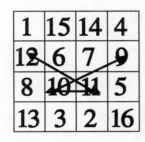

Adding in twos:

Adding in threes:

Adding in fours:

Adding in fives:

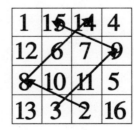 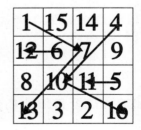

Adding in sixes:

Adding in sevens:

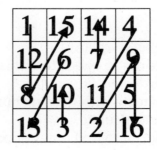

138

Adding in eights:

NC mapping

AT3 – Level 3 (b) and PoS
AT1 – Level 3 (c) (d)
AT2 – Level 2 (a)
AT4 – Level 3 (b)
    – Level 4 (c)

Magic variations

What you need

Squared paper, pencils.

What to do

Negative squares

A square with negative numbers can be easily constructed by subtracting a large number from a magic square. For example:

4	9	2
3	5	7
8	1	6

If we subtract 6 we get:

-2	3	-4
-3	-1	1
2	-5	0

Explain to the children how you made the square and ask them what the sum of each row, column or main diagonal is now. Ask the children to make their own negative squares, including some squares where *every* number is negative. Can they find any connection between the number they subtract and the new total?

This activity is a good reinforcement exercise for negative numbers, as the children are fairly sure what the answer should be.

NC mapping

AT3 – Level 4 (a)
AT1 – Level 4 (a) (c) (d)
AT2 – working towards Level 5 PoS

Multiplying squares

Ask the children to find out what happens if the numbers in a magic square are multiplied by a small number.

4	9	2
3	5	7
8	1	6

If we multiply by 2 we get:

8	18	4
6	10	14
16	2	12

What effect does this have on the totals and the patterns?

NC mapping

AT3 – Level 4 (a)
AT1 – Level 4 (a) (c) (d)
AT2 – Level 3 (c)

Generalising magic squares

What you need

A selection of magic squares.

What to do

The generalisation for magic squares is fairly complicated, and it is unlikely that any but the most-able top juniors will find it for themselves. However, children working at Level 5 should at least have the rule explained for them to check, and at Level 6 some children may be able to cope with the formal symbolisation.

Let us look at magic squares where the numbers used begin with 1 and progress by adding 1 (that is, only 1, 2, 3, 4... are used).

4	9	2
3	5	7
8	1	6

The total given by each line is 15 (called the magic constant for this square). The length of the square is 3. If we square the length – which incidentally gives the largest number on the magic square (9) – and add 1 (giving 10), multiply by the length (giving 30) and halve this answer (15), then we get the magic constant.

Again, for a 4 × 4 square:

1	15	14	4
12	6	7	9
8	10	11	5
13	3	2	16

The length is 4. Square the length (16), add 1 (17), multiply by the length (68), and halve the answer (34). Therefore, the magic constant is 34. Ask the children to check by adding, for example, the top line:
1 + 15 + 14 + 4 = 34.

The process can be represented by a flowchart:

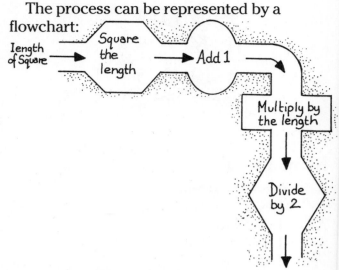

Some children may be able to cope with the symbolic notation:

Magic constant, $m = \dfrac{n(n^2 + 1)}{2}$

Ask the children to work out the magic constants for a 5 × 5, a 6 × 6 magic square and so on.

NC mapping

AT3 – Level 5 (a)
    – Level 7 (a)
AT1 – Level 5 (a) (b) (c)

Creating magic squares

What you need

Squared paper, pencils, a spreadsheet program.

What to do

There is only one basic 3 × 3 magic square, all others being transformations (reflections and/or rotations) or additions, subtractions, multiplications and so on to the basic square. However, there are 880 possible 4 × 4 magic squares and more than 13,000,000 5 × 5s! (The exact number is not known.) There are complicated instructions to produce these squares, which will not be reproduced here as they are deemed too difficult for primary school. However, children who have access to a spreadsheet can find magic squares by 'trial and improvement' methods.

Set up a spreadsheet, or ask the children to, using the instructions below, to produce a 4×4 magic square. The instruction may change slightly, depending on the spreadsheet used.

• Make the cell E2 equal to the sum of the cells A2, B2, C2 and D2.
• Copy this formula into cells E3 to E5.
• Make the cell A6 equal to the sum of the cells A2, A3, A4 and A5.
• Copy this formula into the cells B6 to D6.
• Program cell E1 to be the sum of cells A5, B4, C3 and D2.
• Program cell E6 to be the sum of cells A2, B3, C4 and D5.

The program is now ready to manipulate the numbers which the children feed into the grid. All the totals will appear automatically, saving a lot of time and drudgery. The children may need reminding that they can only use each number from 1 to 16 once. Here is a possible progression:

	A	B	C	D	E	F	G
1					23		
2	7	4	10	1	22		
3	3	15	4	9	31		
4	11	2	6	13	32		
5	16	5	12	8	41		
6	37	26	32	31	36		
7							
8							
9							
10							

From the generalisation, the children should be aiming for a total of 34. The first row and one of the main diagonals are far from this total, and the children should therefore

swap larger numbers for some numbers in these lines. Looking at the totals produced by these changes, they need to continue swapping numbers until all lines give 34.

NC mapping

AT3 – Level 6 (a)
AT1 – Level 5 (a) (b)
    – Level 6 (b)

The Fibonacci sequence

Leonardo Fibonacci was perhaps the greatest Western mathematician of the Middle Ages. Born in Pisa, he travelled around the eastern Mediterranean with the merchant vessels, learning the mathematical traditions of the Middle East.

Fibonacci is most famous for his sequence: 1, 1, 2, 3, 5, 8, 13, 21...

In this sequence each new number is made from the addition of the previous two numbers:

$$0 + 1 = 1$$
$$1 + 1 = 2$$
$$1 + 2 = 3$$
$$2 + 3 = 5 \text{ and so on}$$

This result in itself is remarkable because of its occurrence in the natural world (rabbit and bee populations, the numbers of petals on flowers, the growth of spirals in nature, such as snail shells and so on).

Children can find the pattern through investigations such as Stamps (page 34), through spatial arrangements such as Dominoes (page 43), and through the St Paul's staircase investigation (page 40).

With children of *all* ages, the method of working – looking for all the answers in a systematic way so that you are sure you haven't missed any – is as important as finding the pattern. If they manage to find the correct numbers of the sequence, however, there are more relationships to be found, and more patterns, as we found with Pascal's triangle.

Activity progression across Key Stages 1 and 2

The children can find the first few Fibonacci numbers through working on 'Stamps' (see page 34). They will need to discuss the numbers with you to establish how they grow. Can they, using a calculator, find the first 12 numbers? Having done this, they will be ready to try the following activities.

Odds and evens in Fibonacci

What you need

Paper, pencils.

What to do

Show the children the first 12 of the Fibonacci numbers: 1, 1, 2, 3, 5, 8, 13, 21, 34, 55, 89, 144. Ask them which numbers are odd and which are even. Can they predict whether the next number in the sequence will be odd or even?

The children should find that they get the repeating pattern: O O E O O E O O E O O E....

NC mapping

AT3 – Level 1 (a)
– Level 2 (a)

Subtracting Fibonacci

What you need

Paper, pencils, calculators.

What to do

Look at the first 12 of the Fibonacci numbers with the children. Ask them to find the difference between pairs of numbers:

$$1 - 1 = 0$$
$$2 - 1 = 1$$
$$3 - 2 = 1$$
$$5 - 3 = 2$$
$$8 - 5 = 3$$
$$13 - 8 = 5$$

The children will see that they get the same sequence once again!

If the children have not already discovered that adding pairs of numbers gives the sequence, this would be an appropriate time to ask them to do this too.

$$1 + 1 =$$
$$2 + 1 =$$
$$3 + 2 =$$
$$5 + 3 =$$
$$8 + 5 =$$

NC mapping

AT3 – Level 2 (a)
AT2 – Level 2 (a)

For juniors, you may wish to use an application of the Fibonacci sequence to biology, rather than the investigations in Chapter One. Below are two such activities.

Rabbits

What you need

Paper, pencils.

What to do

Explain to the children that the following is a model of the way that rabbits reproduce; that is, it isn't exactly what happens, but gives us a structure which we can use to predict rabbit numbers.

When rabbits are one month old, they are too young to have baby rabbits, but a pair of two-month old rabbits will have a pair of babies. They then have a pair of baby rabbits *every* month. How many rabbits will there be at the end of a year, remembering that all the new rabbits will also have babies at two months and thereafter?

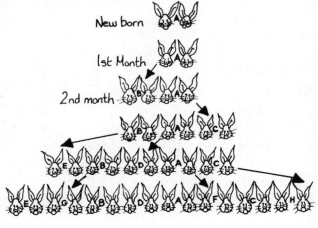

Count the pairs of rabbits each month. What happens?

NC mapping

AT3 – Level 3 PoS
  – Level 5 (a)
AT1 – Level 3 (c) (d)
  – Level 4 (b)

This idea has the disadvantage that rabbits don't really reproduce this way, so although it's fun, it's artificial. A more factual statement, though perhaps a little harder to understand, is the following activity.

Queens and drones

What you need

Paper, pencils.

What to do

Explain to the children that a queen bee can produce bees without fertilisation. These bees become drones (males). She must mate, though, to produce a female bee, who can then grow up to be another queen. So, male bees have only got one parent, whereas female bees have two. What would the family tree of a drone look like?

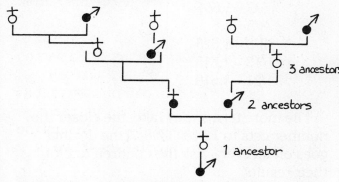

How many ancestors does a drone have in each generation?

NC mapping

AT3 – Level 3 PoS
  – Level 5 (a)
AT1 – Level 3 (c) (d)
  – Level 4 (b)

Whether the children have found the sequence using the activities from other chapters or from the activities above, they need to look for patterns and relationships within the sequence.

Fibonacci patterns

What you need

Paper, pencils.

What to do

The parts of this activity are set out in order of increasing difficulty. To begin, the children will need a list of the Fibonacci numbers up to the thirtieth. They could use a calculator, or the following short computer programs:

BASIC

```
10 LET A = 1
20 LET B = 1
30 PRINT A
40 PRINT B
50 FOR N = 1 TO 14
60 LET A = A + B
70 PRINT A
80 LET B = B + A
90 PRINT B
100 NEXT N
```

To run the program, type RUN.

LOGO

```
TO FIB :A :B
PRINT :A
PRINT :B
REPEAT 14 [MAKE "A :A + :B PRINT :A MAKE
"B :B + :A PRINT :B]
END
```

To run the program, type FIB 1 1.

The children should now be ready to work on the following problems.
• Take any four consecutive numbers from the row. For example: 3, 5, 8, 13. Multiply the two outside numbers together: $3 \times 13 = 39$. Multiply the two inside numbers together: $5 \times 8 = 40$. Try again with different groups of four. What do you notice?
• Take a group of three this time. For example: 5, 8, 13. Multiply the two outside

numbers together: $5 \times 13 = 65$. Square the middle number $8^2 = 64$. Try again with different groups of three. What do you notice?

• Write down the remainders if you divide each Fibonacci number by 4: 1, 1, 2, 3, 1, 0, 1, 1.... What happens?

• Square the first ten numbers and add pairs:
1, 1, 2, 3, 5, 8... $\rightarrow$ 1, 1, 4, 9, 25, 64...

$1 + 1 = 2$
$1 + 4 = 5$
$4 + 9 = 13$ and so on.

• There are many other patterns:

$1^2 + 1^2 = 1 \times 2$
$1^2 + 1^2 + 2^2 = 2 \times 3$
$1^2 + 1^2 + 2^2 + 3^2 = 3 \times 5$ and so on.
$2^2 - 1 \times 3 = 1$
$3^2 - 2 \times 5 = -1$
$5^2 - 3 \times 8 = 1$
$8^2 - 5 \times 13 = -1$ and so on.

NC mapping

AT3 – Level 4 (a) and PoS
     – Level 5 PoS
     – Level 6 (a)
AT1 – Level 5 (c)
AT2 – Level 3 (b) (c)

Fibonacci function machine

What you need

No special requirements.

What to do

The function machine to generate Fibonacci numbers is more complicated than those met hereto, and will introduce children to multiple functions:

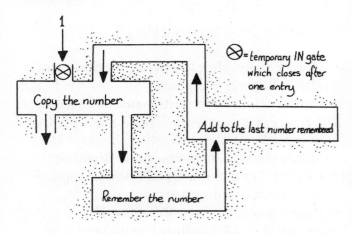

Go through the machine with the children, checking that they are able to keep records of the output. Can they change the machine to make different sequences?

Such work can be developed using the computer program *Numerator* (1989, Cambridge: Longman/Logotron) (see Appendix A), which enables children to model operations from simple addition, to more complex arrangements like the one above, through to A level mathematics.

NC mapping

AT3 – Level 5

Fibonacci fractions

What you need

Paper, pencils, calculators.

What to do

Ask the children to take the Fibonacci numbers in adjacent pairs, dividing the larger one by the smaller one, and repeating for other pairs. What do they notice?

$1/1 = 1$
$2/1 = 2$
$3/2 = 1.5$
$5/3 = 1.667$
$8/5 = 1.6$
$13/8 = 1.625$
$21/13 = 1.615$
$34/21 = 1.619$

The more terms they take, the closer the number gets to 1.61803398... (the decimal goes on forever). Ask the children to plot their results.

NC mapping

AT3 – Level 6 (c)
AT1 – Level 5 (b) (c)
AT2 – Level 4 (d)

The golden ratio

The number which the fractions in the last activity were approaching, 1.61803398, was well known to the Ancient Greeks. The ratio 1:1.61803398... is called the golden ratio, and was frequently used in Ancient Greek architecture. If you draw a rectangle with sides 1:1.61803398... it is called the Golden Rectangle. This shape is to be found in the proportions of the Parthenon, on the Acropolis in Athens, and in many other ancient Greek buildings.

This rectangle is thought to be the most pleasing aesthetically. If you survey a large group of people and present them with several rectangles to choose from, for example, picture frames, the majority will choose the Golden Rectangle. Try it!

During the Renaissance, mathematical proportions took on a great deal of significance in painting and sculpture. It was believed that an ideal human figure followed given geometrical rules, which were God-given. The golden ratio became known during this period as the *divine proportion*.

Spirals and the Fibonacci sequence

The Fibonacci sequence most deserves study, however, because of its appearance in nature. Sunflower heads contain seeds set in spirals. There are 21 clockwise spirals and 34 anticlockwise spirals. These are consecutive numbers in the Fibonacci sequence.

Pine cones have their seeds arranged so that there are eight seeds in each of the clockwise spirals and 13 seeds in each of the anticlockwise spirals. So does the pineapple!

The number of petals of many flowers are also Fibonacci numbers:
• 3 petals – lilies and irises;
• 5 petals – buttercups, some delphiniums;
• 8 petals – some delphiniums;
• 13 petals – corn marigolds;
• 21 petals – some asters;
• 34, 55 and 89 petals – daisies.

Do not be surprised if you pick a flower which does not obey these rules – they are only typical values. Children may be interested in conducting a statistical survey to find the averages for the different flowers.

That this pattern appears so much in nature is not an accident. Growth obeys mathematical rules, whether for living things (such as microbes or plants) or lifeless objects (such as crystals or snowflakes). Growth will tend to be in the direction offering the most space, and this leads approximately to the Fibonacci distribution.

The ratio of the distances from the centre of a snowflake to the first pattern ring and second pattern ring is the golden ratio.

Spirals seem to crop up a good deal in our examples. This is not by accident. Try the following activity with the children.

Spiral

What you need

Large, squared paper; pencils, rulers.

What to do

Ask the children to draw two small squares side by side:

Then ask them to draw a 2 × 2 square alongside them:

They should then keep going round in the same direction (it doesn't matter which as long as it is constant) adding the next sized square needed. Point out to the children, if they don't notice it themselves, that the lengths of the sides of the squares are

Fibonacci numbers. Can the children see why? (As they draw a new square, its side is equal to the lengths of the two squares they drew immediately before.)

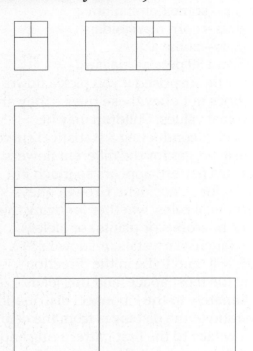

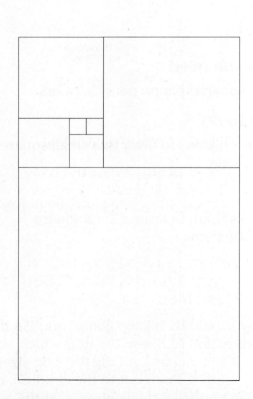

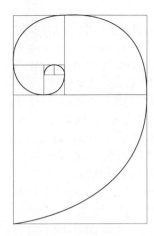

This spiral, as it grows, becomes closer and closer to the spiral found in snail shells, the nautilus and so on.

NC mapping

AT3 – Level 5 (a)
AT1 – Level 5 (a) (b)

Children who have looked at both Pascal's triangle and the Fibonacci sequence will be interested in the following activity.

Pascal meets Fibonacci

What you need

No special requirements.

What to do

Ask the children to write Pascal's triangle slightly differently, as shown below:

```
1
1  1
1  2  1
1  3  3  1
1  4  6  4  1
1  5 10 10  5  1
```

Ask them to add up the diagonals:

What do they notice?

NC mapping

AT3 – Level 5 (a)
AT1 – Level 5 (a) (b) (c)

Finally, ask the children to draw quarter-circles in each square:

146

Chapter Four
Algebra across the maths curriculum

Algebra, like Attainment Target 1 (Using and applying mathematics) and Attainment Target 5 (Handling data) is to some extent a service subject. Attainment Target 1 describes methods of working with and exploring numbers and shape and space, while Attainment Target 5 records and displays the information we can find out about numbers and shape and space. Similarly, algebra (AT3) describes the patterns, structures and relationships in numbers and shape and space. This means, therefore, that Attainment Targets 1, 3 and 5 are themselves closely linked and often inseparable.

This chapter explores these links in two ways: first through examining certain areas of the algebra attainment target – such as repeating patterns – for their relationships with statements of attainment from the other four programmes of study and second, through studying several areas of normal school activity.

Links with other attainment targets

Attribute recognition

It was stated at the beginning of Chapter One that a child cannot be expected to recognise a pattern, and hence cannot be expected to repeat or devise a pattern, unless she can recognise the attributes of the objects being considered. Therefore, logic work is an essential part of the algebra curriculum for children 'working towards' Level 1.

However, Attainment Target 5 (Handling data) also requires the sorting of objects in order that they may be counted and the number of objects under different categories displayed in a variety of ways. Attribute recognition is therefore listed in the National

Curriculum under this attainment target:

- AT5 Level 1 Programme of Study – **'selecting criteria for sorting a set of objects and applying them consistently'**;
- AT5 Level 2 Programme of Study – **'using diagrams to represent the results of classification using two different criteria, for example Venn and tree diagrams'**;
- AT5 Level 4 Programme of Study – **'creating a decision tree diagram with questions to sort and identify a collection of objects'**.

Therefore, the logic activities worked on previously in algebra (pages 24 to 29) will also serve as an introduction for young children to data handling. For example, children can sort beads by colour (**'Sort a set of objects, describing the criteria chosen'** AT5 Level 1a Statements of Attainment).

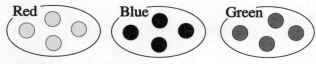

They can then make a repeated pattern by taking one bead from each set in turn (**'Devise repeating patterns'** AT3 Level 1a Statements of Attainment).

If the properties of shapes are used as criteria for sorting, then the children will also be working within Attainment Target 4 (**'sorting and classifying 2-D and 3-D shapes using words such as "straight", "flat", "curved", "round", "pointed", etc.'** Level 1 Programme of Study), and hence across three attainment targets:

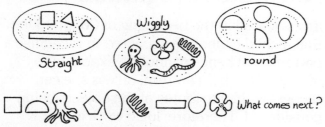

Repeating patterns

Repeating number patterns have been dealt with extensively in Chapter One, and mappings to Attainment Target 2 are to be found in the activity pages. Repeating patterns also have a role in the recognition of movement types (**'recognising types of movement: straight [translation], turning [rotation]'** AT4 Level 2 Programme of Study). The potato printing pattern below demonstrates translation. Through discussion, children need to appreciate that the shapes are all the same size, the same shape, and all point in the same direction.

Children should also make repeating patterns by turning the shapes.

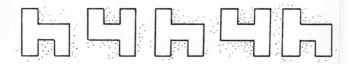

This effect can be reinforced if the children are asked to draw details on their patterns. The pattern below turns through a right angle (**'understanding turning through right angles'** AT4 Level 2 Programme of Study):

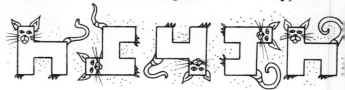

Partitioning

Partitioning activities, such as those met on pages 73 to 76 encourage children to explore possible number bonds. Hence they discover the number's properties, that is, its structure. For small numbers, this also reinforces addition and subtraction (**'knowing and using addition and subtraction facts up to 10'** AT2 Level 2 Programme of Study, and **'learning and using addition and subtraction facts to 20'** [including zero] AT2 Level 3 Programme of Study).

As the children learn to cope with larger numbers, partitioning reinforces the meaning of the digit in the 'tens' column (**'reading, writing and ordering numbers to at least 100 and using the knowledge that the 10s digit indicates the number of 10s'** AT2 Level 2 Programme of Study) for example:

$34 = 10 + 10 + 10 + 4$, that is, 'three 10s plus 4'.

The following calculator activity provides such practice.

Noughts and ones

What you need

Calculators, Multibase equipment, Multibase boards (can be drawn out on paper).

What to do

Work through the following example with the children. Write 54 on a piece of paper and explain to the group that they are going to make 54 on their calculators by only pressing 0s, 1s, + and =. How do they think it could be done? You can help by showing them + 10 = and + 1 =, and if necessary the solution to this first problem. How many times do they think they will have to press + 10 = ? Work together, and at each + 10 = put a Multibase 'long' block on the board. When the children have 50, add + 1 = four times and add four unit blocks to the board.

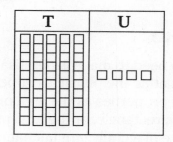

Decide if the children need the reinforcement with Multibase material to help them and let them work in the same way to make 45, 23, 32, 61, 16, 48 and 84.

NC mapping

AT3 – Level 3 (a)
AT1 – Level 3 (a)
AT2 – Level 2 PoS

Mental methods

As the above activity helps children to see the partition of numbers into tens and units, it will also help them to solve larger mental additions than 20. For example,
24 + 15 = 20 + 4 + 10 + 5 = 30 + 9 = 39 (**'adding and subtracting mentally two two-digit numbers'** AT2 Level 4 Programme of Study).

Changing 'Noughts and ones' slightly will enable children to practise the use of the 'hundreds' column. For example, to make 324, the children will need to press + 100 = three times, + 10 = twice and + 1 = four times (**'reading, writing and ordering numbers to at least 1000 and using the knowledge that the position of a digit indicates its value'** AT2 Level 3 Programme of Study).

The following activity can be used as a follow-up to 'Noughts and ones'. It can be used to reinforce the concept of subtraction as the inverse of addition.

Space invaders

What you need

Calculators, three dice per pair of children.

What to do

Ask the children in each pair to take turns throwing the dice. They must take the three digits and make a number with them on their calculators. They can then take turns to 'shoot' down the number of their opponent using ammunition marked –100, –10 or –1. The first child to make their opponent's number zero is the winner. For example, if the children throw 3, 5, 1 with the dice the game may look like this:

Player 1	Player 2
351	531
–100→	–100→
251	431
–100→	–10→
151	421
–100→	–10→
51	411
–10→	–10→
41	401
–10→	–10→
31	391
–10→	–100→
21	291
–10→	–100→
11	191
–10→	–100→
1	91
–1→	–10→
0	81

This game reinforces the value of the digits. The actual number the children choose to make will not affect the result. The game can be varied by 'charging' the children per shot, the hundreds costing the most to shoot down and the units being the cheapest. After several games, the total costs can be found. The child with the smallest bill is the overall winner. This introduces an element of strategy.

NC mapping

AT3 – Level 3 (a)
AT1 – Level 3 (a)
AT2 – Level 3 PoS

Sequences

The behaviour of numbers and the relationships between properties in mathematics are often investigated by children through looking for patterns. For example, children can best find the effect of multiplying or dividing by 10s or 100s by doing so on a calculator and describing what happens (**'understanding and using the effect of multiplying whole numbers by 10 or 100'** AT2 Level 4 Programme of Study).

The ×10 machine (or ×100)

What you need

No special requirements.

What to do

Draw a '×10' function machine. Ask the children what will happen if you feed in 1 or 2. Ask them to use their calculators to fill in the following table:

IN	OUT
1	10
2	20
3	
4	
5	
6	

Can the children explain in their own words what happens when they multiply by 10? What happens if they multiply by 100?

Provide a different table, where the numbers do not form a sequence, and ask the children to complete it; for example:

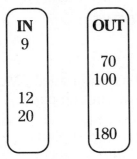

IN	OUT
9	70
	100
12	
20	180

NC mapping

AT3 – Level 3 (a)
    – Level 4 (a)
AT2 – Level 4 (b) and PoS

Similar activities to 'Space invaders' and 'The ×10 machine' will lead children to make generalisations about dividing by 10s and 100s (**'multiplying and dividing mentally single-digit numbers of powers of 10 with whole number answers'** AT2 Level 5 PoS).

Formulae

Children also need to make generalisations when investigating the physical properties of shapes. Such properties as the area or perimeter of a rectangle, or the area or circumference of a circle, are unchanging relationships and hence provide a good introduction to the concept of a formula. Such formulae are required in Attainment Target 4:
• AT4 Level 5 Programme of Study – **'finding the circumference of circles practically, introducing the ratio p'** (the circumference of a circle, c = pd, where d is the diameter);
• AT4 Level 5 Programme of Study – **'finding areas of plane figures (excluding circles), using appropriate formulae'**;
• AT4 Level 5 Programme of Study – **'finding volumes of simple solids (excluding cylinders), using appropriate formulae'**;
• AT4 Level 6 Programme of Study – **'finding areas of circles using the formulae'**.

The fact that the formulae for these properties are unchanging (for example, that the volume of a cylinder will be $V = \pi r^2 h$ no matter which cylinder we choose to look at) is best established through practical exploration. The following activity is an example of how children can find the relationships for themselves.

Circumferences

What you need

A variety of objects with a circular cross-section, for example coffee jar lids, tins of baked beans, rolls of sticky tape and so on; string, rulers, pencils, paper, calculators.

What to do

Ask the children to measure the distance around the curved surfaces (the circumferences) of various objects using string and a ruler. Also ask them to measure the distance across the circular cross-section. What do they notice? Encourage the children to record their results on a mapping diagram, or on a table, for example:

	Circumference	Diameter
Coffee mug	25cm	8cm
Sticky tape	31cm	10cm
Magnifying glass	20cm	6.4cm

Can they seen any connections? If not, ask them to make a further column with circumference divided by diameter:

	Circumference	Diameter	C ÷ D
Coffee mug	25cm	8cm	3.125
Sticky tape	31cm	10cm	3.1
Magnifying glass	20cm	6.3cm	3.174

Introduce the children to the number π, the Greek letter used to denote the relationship circumference divided by diameter. Explain that the true value of π is a decimal which goes on forever, but that we can get very good results using 3.14 (or 3.142 is even better). Ask the children to remeasure their objects. Can they get closer to π?

NC mapping

AT3 – Level 5 (b)
AT4 – Level 5 PoS

Co-ordinates

As has been seen in Chapter One, co-ordinates are vital to algebra work as a way to show graphically the relationship between IN and OUT numbers (later becoming x and y numbers). By plotting the co-ordinates and joining them with a straight line or a curve we produce a picture of how a function behaves. However, co-ordinates are also used in Attainment Target 4 to represent position:
• AT4 Level 4 Programme of Study – **'specifying location by means of co-ordinates in the first quadrant and by means of angle and distance'**;
• AT4 Level 5 Programme of Study – **'specifying location by means of co-ordinates in four quadrants'**.

As algebra involves the search for patterns and rules, one way to link these two areas of co-ordinate work is to ask the children to find rules for what happens to the co-ordinates of shapes when the shapes are transformed.

Transformations of two-dimensional shapes (translations, reflections, rotations and enlargements) are met at various stages through AT4:
• AT4 Level 2 Programme of Study – **'recognising types of movement: straight (translation), turning (rotation)'**;
• AT4 Level 3 Programme of Study – **'recognise reflective symmetry in a variety of shapes in two and three dimensions'**;
• AT4 Level 4 Programme of Study – **'recognising rotational symmetry'**;
• AT 4 Level 6 Programme of Study – **'enlarging a shape by a whole number scale factor'**.

Such work has been touched on already in Chapter One (page 64) and the following investigation develops the theme, giving children more freedom to explore.

Guess and plot

What you need

Squared paper, pencils, rulers, tracing paper.

What to do

Ask the children to draw and label axes from

−10 to 10, and then draw a very simple shape in the first quadrant. The exercise will be most meaningful if the children draw a shape with no symmetry. You may wish to provide one in the first instance. For example:

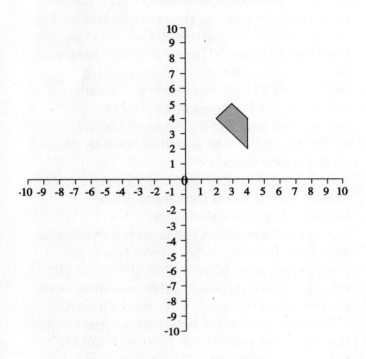

Ask the children to write down the co-ordinates of their shapes; for example, for the above shape they are (4,2) (4,4) (3,5) (2,4).

There are two ways to approach this investigation. Either the children can transform their shapes, perhaps with the help of tracing paper, and see what the co-ordinates of the new shape are, or they can transform the co-ordinates and see what new shape this produces.

How could they change their co-ordinates? Encourage simple suggestions to begin with, such as 'Add a number to *x*', 'Make y negative', 'Multiply both co-ordinates by a small number' and so on. The children need to experiment with these changes, and come to some conclusions, before they allow themselves any wild speculations!

You may wish instead to provide the children with a list of possible changes for them to try; for example:

• Adding only to *x* to produce a translation along the *x* axis (4,2) (4,4) (3,5) (2,4) → (9,2) (9,4), (8,5) (7,4).

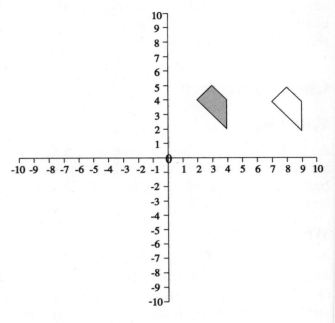

• Adding only to y to produce a translation along the y axis.
• Changing all the *x* co-ordinates to negatives to reflect the shape in the y axis – (4,2) (4,4) (3,5) (2,4) → (−4,2) (−4,4) (−3,5) (−2,4).

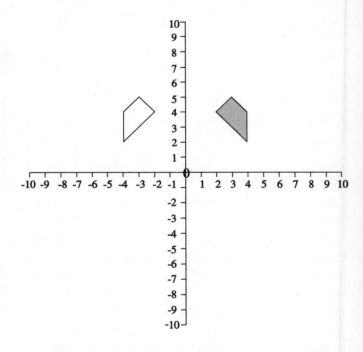

• Changing all the y co-ordinates to negatives to reflect the shape in the *x* axis.
• Multiplying all the numbers by two, to double the size of the shape – (4,2) (4,4) (3,5) (2,4) → (8,4) (8,8) (6,10) (4,8).

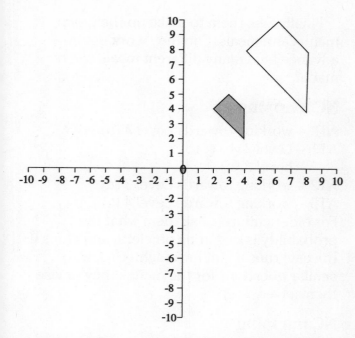

The changes needed to make a rotation are less simple. Either provide the children with the changes and ask them to find out what they do, or ask them to draw a rotation, using tracing paper, and then list the co-ordinates of the new shape. Swapping the x and y in each co-ordinate, and then making the new x negative, rotates the shape through $90° - (4,2)$ $(4,4)$ $(3,5)$ $(2,4) \rightarrow (-2,4)$ $(-4,4)$ $(-5,3)$ $(-4,2)$.

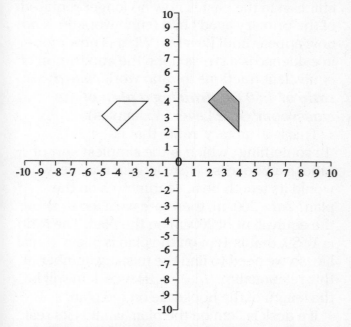

Ask the children to try combinations and variations of the above transformations.

NC mapping

AT3 – Level 5 PoS
AT1 – Level 5 (b) (c)

– Level 6 (a)
AT4 – Level 4 PoS
– Level 5 PoS
– Level 6 PoS

Spatial arrangements

In the section on spatial arrangements in Chapter Two, the Cartesian product model of multiplication was referred to as an alternative to 'repeated addition'. Both models need to be understood and *used* by children if they are to have a full grasp of the underlying structure of multiplication. As an example of the Cartesian product model, let us return to the example of dressing bears (page 105). A bear may have a red hat or a blue hat, red boots or blue boots. In how many ways can we dress the bear? Initially, children are able to list or draw the possibilities, but should be guided with time to show them as a mapping.

The initial stage of listing all possibilities is also a preparation for later probability work (**'listing all possible outcomes of an event'** AT5 Level 4, Programme of Study). This is necessary in order to work out probabilities (**'Knowing that if each of n events is assumed to be equally likely, the probability of one occurring is 1/n'** AT5 Level 5 Programme of Study). For example, for our bear there are four outfits, and therefore a red hat and blue boots is one possible outcome from four possibilities, that is $^1/_4$ or 0.25. What is the probability that the bear will wear an outfit with matching hat and boots? (Two out of four, that is $^1/_2$ or 0.5.)

Children need to meet several such examples, with varying numbers of items, so that they can reach the conclusion that the total number of possibilities is the multiplication of the number of varieties. For example, if the bear has three different hats, four different coats and two different pairs of boots, then he has $3 \times 4 \times 2$ different outfits, in other words 24 possibilities. The probability of any one combination is therefore $^1/_{24}$.

We have already met the probabilities of two combined events in the discussion of Pascal's triangle in Chapter Three. The multiplication rule above shows why we got the results in that chapter; for example, with tossing three coins (see page 3). As we saw, there are eight possible outcomes which derive from $2 \times 2 \times 2$ ('**identifying all the outcomes when dealing with two combined events which are independent, using diagrammatic, tabular or other forms**' AT5 Level 6 Programme of Study).

The probability of getting three heads is therefore $\frac{1}{8}$, of two heads and a tail is $\frac{3}{8}$, of two tails and head is $\frac{3}{8}$ and of three tails is $\frac{1}{8}$. The numerators are 1, 3, 3, 1 – one of the lines of Pascal's triangle.

Hence the spatial arrangements from algebra can help children understand simple probability.

Menus

What you need
Paper, pencils.

What to do
Ask the children to suggest three ideas for the main course of a meal in a café, and two ideas for a pudding. Draw up a list; for example:

Menu
<u>Main course</u>
Spaghetti
Omelette and chips
Chilli and baked potato
<u>Pudding</u>
Ice-cream
Cheesecake

Ask the children to draw all the possible meals which could be eaten at this café.

Finally, ask them to make up their own menus and meals. Can they work out in advance how many different meals can be made?

NC mapping
AT3 – working towards Level 3 (a)
AT1 – Level 2 (b) (c)
    – Level 3 (c)
AT2 – working towards Level 3 (c)
AT5 – working towards Level 4 PoS
For older children, ask them what the probability is of getting omelette and chips if the café runs a 'pot luck night' ($\frac{1}{6}$), with similar questions for the menus they devise themselves.

NC mapping
AT5 – Level 5 PoS

Equivalent fractions

The equivalent fractions met in algebra have an obvious link with any fraction work met in Attainment Target 2 (Number). However, the manipulation and calculation with fractions which caused so much pain to so many children in the past is now no longer required of the primary-aged child (such work does not now appear until Level 8). What *is* now more in evidence is a stress upon the application of equivalent fractions to ratio work: '*use a ratio of 1:50 for drawing a plan of the classroom*' (AT2 Level 5 Examples).

This is a 'unitary' ratio, that is '1 : something', which is the simplest sort of ratio. If a bookcase is 2m long in real life, what would its length be in centimetres on the plan? 2m = 200cm, therefore we need to show the equivalent of 200cm on the plan. The ratio is 1 : 50, that is 1cm on the plan is 50cm in real life, so we need to find the missing number in this relationship: $\frac{1}{50} = \frac{?}{200}$. Hence 4cm will be the length of the bookcase on the plan.

If a desk is 3cm on the plan, what is its real length? ($\frac{1}{50} = \frac{3}{?}$)

Through work with equivalent fractions, children will have learned that whatever is done to one part of the fraction, must be done to the other – an old-fashioned rule, but one that works! This can be seen, for example, from shading fractional parts of a rectangle:

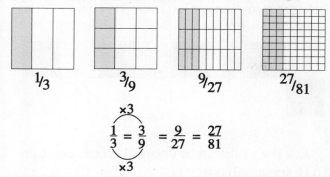

$$\frac{1}{3} = \frac{3}{9} = \frac{9}{27} = \frac{27}{81}$$

The children should check their answers using a calculator: $1 \div 3 = 3 \div 9 = 9 \div 27 = 27 \div 81 = 0.33333...$ (**'understanding and using equivalent fractions and equivalent ratios and relating these to decimals and percentages'** AT2 Level 6 Programme of Study). What percentage of each shape is shaded?

Bedsit

What you need

Cardboard, glue, squared paper, scissors, furniture catalogues, calculators, paints or coloured pens.

What to do

Tell the children that they are going to design a bedsit for a student or single adult. Decide together on the size of the room (to avoid the designing of mansions!) and what the essentials would be (for example, a cooker, sink and bed). Non-essentials can be decided upon by individuals.

Ask the children to draw scale plans (overhead views) of their bedsits on squared paper. The scaling should be agreed upon as a class and kept constant. For example, the class might agree on a 4m by 3m room scaled down to a 40cm by 30cm plan (ratio 10 : 1) or scaled down to a 20cm by 15cm plan (ratio 20 : 1).

Finally, once the children are satisfied with the layout of their plans, they should try to make three-dimensional models of their bedsits.

NC mapping

AT3 – Level 5 PoS

AT1 – Level 5 (a)
AT2 – Level 5 (b)
AT4 – Level 5 (a)

Algebra in everyday mathematical topics

Teachers are adept at linking mathematical activities into class topics. What happens more rarely, however, is a topic being chosen *purely* to extract a mathematical concept.

This section provides examples of such mathematical topic choices which can also be used to explicitly emphasise algebra.

Key Stage 1

Picture books

Picture books often provide sources of visual, numeric and linguistic sequences.
• Pat Hutchins' book *The Wind Blew* (Picture Puffin, 1978), has a picture on each page which shows a growing sequence of objects – blown away by the wind – for children to try to remember. Hence the children are introduced to a repeating pattern (AT3 Level 1 PoS).
• *A Bun for Barney*, by Joyce Dunbar (Picture Corgi Books, 1987) provides a 'counting back' sequence and a repetitive phrase in the language, for example, 'an iced currant bun with two cherries on is better than a bun with none' (AT3 Level 2a SoA).
• Mitsumasa and Masaichiro Anno's book, *Anno's Mysterious Multiplying Jar* (Bodley Head, 1982), shows how quickly numbers can grow if you keep multiplying by a growing number and introduces children to a powerful sequence (the mathematics is at Level 5, but the growth of the numbers will be of interest to younger or less-able children).
• Pat Hutchins' book, *The Doorbell Rang* (Bodley Head, 1986), provides children with an introduction to sharing and also contains a repetition in the language: 'No one makes cookies like Grandma!' Reading this book with the children can be followed up by asking

them to see which numbers *could* be shared in this way.

Playground songs/skipping songs

Many traditional children's songs are concerned with trying to learn something, be it counting ('This old man'), counting backwards ('There were ten in a bed'), time sequences ('Today's Monday') or whatever. There is a fear today that these traditions are disappearing, and so you may well wish to teach the children more formally during lesson time.

One version of skipping is based on listening to the number of syllables in a phrase or word. Children must jump into the rope on the first syllable and out again on the last. For example, if using the words 'win-dow pane', they would skip in on 'win', out on 'pane'. Ask the children to think of other three-syllable words or phrases and then four-syllable ones. Can the children make their own skipping sequences based on syllables?

Construction

Free play is important for young children, but a good deal of mathematics can be extracted from an activity through teacher questioning and encouragement along particular lines.
• Ask the children to build a bridge with red and yellow Multilink cubes like this:

You can then ask how many red cubes there are and how many yellow ones. Can the children make their bridges longer, but still keep the colour pattern?

How many red cubes are there now? How many yellow ones? Can they make their bridges even longer?

Ask the children to count the colours. Can they see a pattern?
• Ask the children to build walls with LEGO. How many different patterns can they put in their walls?

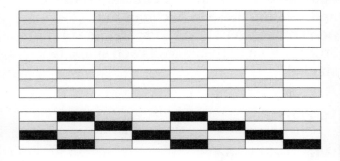

Ask them to draw their patterns (or write sentences describing them).

Shops

Setting up a class shop gives children an opportunity to use both shape and number patterns. Can they design some bunting for the shop which follows a pattern? Can they arrange the shop items in a 'pleasing' pattern? Why do they think it should be pleasing? Can they sort different types of items by price or by size? Can they make a display of items of decreasing size? In how many ways can they pay for an item? In how many ways can they give change (partitioning)? The scope for algebra-related activities is almost endless!

Home corner

Decorating the home corner can bring frieze patterns and wallpaper patterns into realistic use. Sorting items on the shelves and in the cupboards provides a good opportunity for discussing attributes. Setting the table provides an example of multiples; for example, asking how many plates are needed for four people or how many cookies will they have each, what order they can set the table in, what order they can get dressed in, and so on.

Sand

Let the children make some wet-sand patterns, using combs, templates, biscuit cutters and so on.

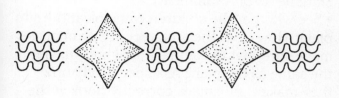

The children can also make sand-castles with paper cups and make flags to go on top of them. Can they make a pattern with the flags?

The street

When the class is venturing out for a school visit, encourage the children to look for number patterns in the environment, such as house numbers and car number plates and so on, and shape patterns, such as brick bonds, manhole covers, railings, fire escapes and so on.

If the children are walking two by two, they could look to see whether everyone has got a partner. If not, then why do they think this is?

Birthdays, parties and festivals

Birthdays

Ask the children to find out whose birthday it is that month. Who has already had a birthday? Who hasn't had a birthday yet? The children can then add together their results on a calculator. Do they get the number of children in the class? How do the numbers compare with those from last month (partitioning)?

Arrange all the birthdays on a number line. The month you are in should be classed as

zero. The children should then be able to tell you who had a birthday one month or two months ago. Who will have a birthday in one month or two months' time? Record the answers on a number line, to give the children experience of negative numbers. For example, Christopher's birthday was two months ago, so he goes to –2.

Christopher	Alex	Mary Jas	Tom	Michael Helen
–2	–1	0	1	2
February	March	April	May	June

Parties

Let the children help with the organisation of a party. How many drinks will they need? How many biscuits? They can use a calculator for the large numbers. Also ask them to make frieze patterns to decorate the classroom and hats with shape patterns on them. Also help the children to make wrapping paper for presents.

Festivals

Festivals provide a good opportunity to explore patterns from different religions and cultures. Involve friends or members of the school – including adults – who belong to the particular culture or practise the particular religion. Invite them in to show the children any special clothing, food, presents or items of special significance. Put the festivals on a time-line.

The Chinese calendar consists of 12 years, which occur in a cycle. Each year is named after an animal. Put the animals on a time-line, making the present year zero. Each child can then count back to find the animal for the year of his or her birth, or those of their brothers and sisters and so on. If the children look at the animal signs for some adults, they will be working with multiples of 12 and remainders. They are usually very interested to find adults who have the same animals as themselves and to guess how old the adults might be.

Key Stage 2

With the advent of the National Curriculum,

many schools have decided that they are unable to provide the full breadth of the curriculum required through traditional topic teaching. Rather than abandon a proven and enjoyable teaching method, some have chosen to divide their school year into topics which have particular subject bias. For example, a school may choose to take the topic of 'Romans' in order to fulfil the needs of the humanities curricula, but would follow this with 'The weather' in order to cover science, and to some extent mathematics, requirements. With a cycle of topic types, the school can provide children with a varied curriculum, drawing cross-curricular links which are not artificial, and satisfy the National Curriculum.

If mathematics is to fit this model, and not become purely an 'add on' subject provided by published schemes, then there is a need to develop mathematics topic teaching. There follows two topics which could be chosen for a term where mathematics is the major emphasis. However, only ideas which link to algebra are included, although there are many more mathematical and, of course, cross-curricular links within each topic.

Buildings

Arrange a visit to a building site (bearing in mind appropriate safety procedures) and ask the children to make the following investigations.

• Ask the children to find out what jobs are done by the different employees (for example, bricklayer, electrician and so on). Which of these people are on the site all the time and which only part of the time? Can they describe to the children the order in which they do things? Who do they have to wait for before they can do their jobs (for example, the plasterer has to wait for the electrician to finish some jobs, then the electrician has to wait for the plasterer to finish before adding sockets, and so on)?

Back at school, the children can draw a flowchart showing the sequence of work done on site (working towards AT3 Level 7) and try to find the most efficient flowchart – a 'time and motion' study.

• Ask the children to find out which tools are used by different employees. They could then design a board game or card game (for example, something similar to 'Happy families', but collecting tool groups) where the knowledge of the sets of tools needed by each employee is required (AT1 Level 4a Statements of Attainment). They should discuss the fairness of their game and work out any simple probabilities involved (AT5 Level 3 Programme of Study, Level 4d Statements of Attainment).

• See whether the children can look at the site plans. How does the architect or site manager make sure that the actual building turns out the same as the plan? Ask specifically how they make right angles correctly (look at the right angles and the shapes in the ceiling joists).

Back at school, introduce the children to the Ancient Egyptian method of ensuring they had right angles in their buildings. This is the famous triangle '3, 4, 5'; that is, if a rope is knotted in equal sections and then a triangle is made of 12 sections – one side with 3 sections, one with 4, and the third with 5 – then there will be a right angle opposite the longest side.

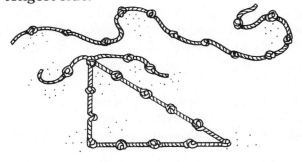

Although used by the Ancient Egyptians, this useful fact is known as Pythagoras' Rule, after a Greek mathematician. Children working at Level 7 of the National Curriculum need to have some understanding of why this rule works, but for junior children it is enough that they experiment with it and check that it does in fact work. Can they find other triangles with whole number sections of string and right angles? Children working at Levels 5 and 6 can be shown the relationship $3^2 + 4^2 = 5^2$. Using a spreadsheet, they could try to find similar connections using 'trial and improvement' methods (AT3 Level 6

Programme of Study). Do they agree with those found by practical investigation?

• Ask the children to find out why triangles are used in ceiling joists. They should experiment with geostrips to show that triangles are the strongest structure:

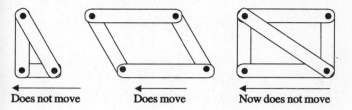

The diagram shows that a structure made of triangles will not move and hence is strong enough for construction work. The investigation asks children to make triangles within a growing shape and look for the number patterns.

This can lead to an investigation for any straight-sided shape. For example, in the diagram below how many struts will be needed to stop movement?

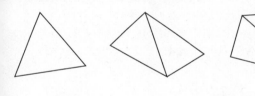

Number of sides	Number of extra struts	Number of triangles
3	0	1
4	1	2
5	2	3

Can the children say how many struts would be needed for a shape with 100 sides and how many triangles this would make?

Can they write a generalisation in their own words and then using symbols? For example, if s = sides, e = extra struts and t = triangles, then $e = s - 3$ and $t = s - 2$. How are e and t connected?

• Ask the children to measure the school buildings and work together to produce a scale diagram (AT2 Level 5 Programme of Study). They should divide up the plan into a grid, labelled either with letters and numbers or numbers and numbers. They can then use the grid to devise a maths trail or a treasure hunt (AT3 Level 4c Statements of Attainment).

• Ask the bricklayers on the building site about brick bonds. Are there different bonds in use on the site? Why do the bricklayers use the bonds they do? Building firms may lend out pictures or samples of brick bonds to look at more closely in school.

Back at school, ask the children to design their own bonds (repeating patterns). They should devise a test for strength and compare the bonds they have made, for example, using LEGO bricks.

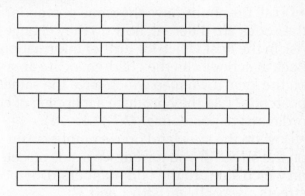

Which of their bonds are the strongest? Which bonds are used in the school walls? Can the children find a way of using numbers to record bond patterns? Can they draw the bonds on a computer?

• Similarly, ask the joiners if they are going to lay any wooden floors. Do they ever do parquet flooring? If so, what designs do they use?

Back at school, look for any floor designs and copy them (AT3 Level 1, but ongoing).

• Ask the bricklayers about the proportions of the materials they use to make mortar. What might happen if they get the mixture wrong? Similarly, find out the mixture for concrete.

Back at school, ask the children to make up some 'mixture problems'. They could also design a poster to show the equivalent fractions of the whole for each ingredient in the mortar or concrete mixtures (AT3 Level 5).

• Ask the children to build their own scale models of buildings – perhaps their 'ideal homes'? They could produce an 'Ideal home exhibition'. They will need to design and make their own wallpaper with repeating patterns (using computer print out if possible), weave strips of paper to make carpets, design and print material for curtains, plan arrangements of flowers for the garden and so on. They should then describe their patterns mathematically (the latter can become a real activity if the school grounds are to be planted with bulbs). Can they use the '3, 4, 5' triangle to check they get a right angle?

The high street

Arrange a journey to your local shops, where the children can make the following enquiries.
• Do all the shops have the same postcode? If the codes are different, how do they change? Ask in the Post Office for further information. Back at school, can the children locate areas on the local town map which have the same postcode? Can they produce a mapping of co-ordinates to postcodes? (AT3 Level 4).
• How do the shop and house numbers run on the street? If you turn down a side street, on which side are the odd numbers? Do streets always begin with 1 and 2?

Back at school, mark on the town map where the children live and their house/flat numbers. Ask the children to look at other numbers in their streets on the way to school next day, and add them to the plan. Build up a picture of how the numbers are allocated. Is there a pattern or a rule? (AT3 Level 4a Statements of Attainment; AT1 Level 4d Statements of Attainment.)
• Can the children discover how the traffic lights at junctions are triggered? Time the intervals between the changes of the lights and work out the sequence of the traffic flow. Are there pedestrian lights at the junction as well? Is there a difference in the pattern if the pedestrian-light button has been pushed?

Back at school, ask the children to draw a flowchart of the traffic flow (working towards AT3 Level 7). Can they describe the sequence using a number pattern?
• Visit shops which sell food; for example, a butcher's and a greengrocer's. Do they use metric weights, imperial weights or a mixture? Do they have any problems with the fact that we have two systems? What system do the wholesalers use? Do they ever use a conversion chart?

Back at school, tell the children the conversion factor between metric and imperial weights (1 kilogram approximately equals 2.2 pounds). Ask the children to find the imperial equivalents of some metric weights (AT3 Level 5a Statements of Attainment) and to draw mapping diagram:

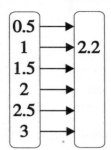

The children should then draw a conversion graph (AT3 Level 6c Statements of Attainment; AT5 Level 5):

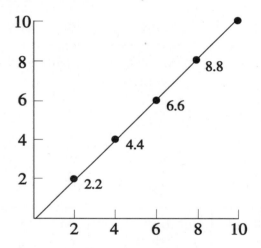

Ask the children such questions as: 'How many kilograms would 6lb be?' so that they use the conversion chart in both directions.

(This activity can be repeated for liquid measures: 1 litre is approximately 1.75 pints.)
• Ask the children to look for patterns in the high street. These will mainly be shape patterns: patterns in paving stones, manhole covers, brickwork, window displays, advertisements and so on. Can the children find any number patterns or sequences? (AT3 Level 1, but ongoing)
• Ask the children to interview a postie, a newsagent and a police officer. What routes do they take in the course of their jobs? How many possible different routes are there?
• Let the children design some street signs without using any words.

Chapter Five
Algebra across the whole curriculum

A great deal of the primary curriculum – and especially that for Key Stage 1 – is concerned with process; that is, the actions of finding out information or producing effects, drawing inferences and conclusions, and seeing further possibilities. As algebra is a method of describing what has been discovered or produced, it is not surprising that there are many links to be drawn between algebra and the rest of the curriculum.

This chapter, as with Chapter Four, shows the cross-curricular links in two ways: first through direct relationships with statements of attainment from other curriculum areas and second through considering some specific themes.

Links with other National Curriculum documents

Attribute recognition

The recognition of the attributes of objects enables children to form patterns where one or several attributes are changing. Therefore, attribute recognition is vital to algebra. Children will show more interest and meet many more types of attributes if the experience comes from cross-curricular work.

Art

The National Curriculum for art requires attribute recognition at the earliest stage – Attainment Target 1: Investigating and making, at Key Stage 1, states: **'collect and sort images, objects, and source material'** (PoSiii); *'make a collection of pebbles and arrange them in order, eg from light to dark'* (Examples). Therefore, the sorting of, for example, types of pasta for collage work or the sorting of pictures into predominant colour types will provide children with practice of attribute recognition. This could be extended to producing repeating patterns. Similarly, producing repeating patterns of objects (Maths AT3 Level 1) will also satisfy this art attainment target.

Science

The science document also recognises the importance of this early groundwork – Attainment Target 1: Scientific investigation, at Key Stage 1, states: **'encourage the sorting, grouping and describing of materials and events in their immediate environment, using their senses and noting similarities and differences'** (PoS). For example, attributes such as 'will/won't let light

through', 'will/won't float' and 'will/won't slide along the table' provide practice of attribute recognition. Specimens can be ordered by how much light gets through, and so on. Such activity is very important for later science exploration, where one attribute should be varied and the effect of that change monitored, as in scientific investigation, at Key Stage 2: **'These activities should: involve variables to be controlled in the development of "fair tests"'** (PoS).

Attainment Target 2: Life and living processes, requires at Key Stage 2 that children **'investigate and measure the similarities and differences between themselves, animals and plants and fossils'** (PoSii) and Attainment Target 3: Materials and their properties, also mentions the sorting of materials. Interestingly, the fourth and final attainment target, Physical processes, at Key Stage 2 suggests that children should investigate the strength of structures, which ties in nicely with the brick bonding experiment of the last chapter (see page 159).

Technology

In the technology document, children are expected to learn **'how to store, select and analyse information using software, *for example using a simple database package'*** (KS1 PoS). In storing an item on a database, the children must recognise the attributes of the information. This usually takes the form of answering questions. For example, in a database about fruit they might be asked: 'Does it have seeds?', 'Are the seeds inside?', 'Do we eat the skin?' and so on. The database *Our facts* is quite accessible to junior children and the *Branch: Information handling pack* which accompanies it is an excellent start to sorting information (see Appendix A).

Repeating patterns

Music

There are lots of different ways to link music to number patterns, some of which have already been discussed (see pages 26 to 27).

This produces a sequence growing with a factor of two (in other words, doubling).

At a higher level, the structure underlying musical composition can be very mathematical. At a recent pre-Prom talk given at the Albert Hall by Sir Peter Maxwell Davies, the composer described the 'architecture' of his latest symphony as being built upon the Fibonacci sequence!

Interestingly, the piano keyboard is divided into Fibonacci numbers. An octave contains 13 semitones, 8 white and 5 black notes – 5, 8 and 13 are all Fibonacci numbers.

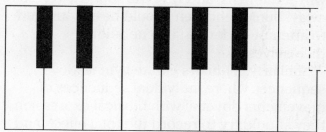

The actual statements from the document which underlie those activities are – Attainment Target 1: Performing and composing:

• **'memorise and internalise short musical patterns and simple songs, and imitate and recall simple rhythms and melodies'** (KS1 PoSi); *'sing a song, staying silent during a phrase within it; echo short rhythm patterns clapped by the teacher'* (KS1 Examples);

• **'read simple signs and symbols and perform from them'** (KS1 PoSii); *'perform a simple rhythmic pattern from symbols'* (KS1 Examples);

• **'communicate simple musical ideas'** (KS1 PoSx); *'create a musical pattern to match a movement pattern and teach it to another child'* (KS1 Examples);

• **'record their own compositions'** (KS1 PoSxii); *'invent a repeated pattern and notate it, or use a cassette player to record it'* (KS1 Examples).

Look at the duration of musical notes:
• semiquaver – $\frac{1}{4}$ beat;
• quaver – $\frac{1}{2}$ beat;
• crotchet – 1 beat;
• minim – 2 beats;
• semibreve – 4 beats.

More simply, children should try to describe the patterns underlying their own music mathematically. Attainment Target 1 for music at Key Stage 2 states that children should:

• **'maintain a part as a member of a group in a round or simple part song'** (PoSv);

• **'develop musical ideas through improvising, composing and arranging'** (PoSxi); *'improvise a solo section in a class piece based on a rondo form (ABACADA) or a vocal "verse" alternating with a given "chorus"'* (Examples);

• **'create music in response to a range of stimuli, using appropriate musical structures'** (PoSxii); *'create a piece in response to a rhythmic pattern, movement,...'* (Examples).

Take a very simple round, such as 'London's burning', and allocate numbers to its sections:

1. London's burning
2. London's burning
3. Draw nearer
4. Draw nearer
5. Fire! Fire!
6. Fire! Fire!
7. Call the engines!
8. Call the engines!

The pattern of sound can then be written:

```
1 2 3 4 5 6 7 8
  1 2 3 4 5 6 7 8
    1 2 3 4 5 6 7 8
      1 2 3 4 5 6 7 8
        1 2 3 4 5 6 7 8
          1 2 3 4 5 6 7 8
            1 2 3 4 5 6 7 8
              1 2 3 4 5 6 7 8
```

When is *everybody* singing? Can the children hear the crescendo? Can they see why it happens, and why the sound level dies away? Junior children should be encouraged to attempt to devise such notations themselves.

Similarly, if juniors create gymnastic sequences where individual sequences of movements dovetail with musical expression, they should try to record the total effect, and numbers are an excellent method. For example, taking the sequence 1, 2, 2, 3, 1, 2, 2, 3, 1, 2, 2, 3 where:

1 = stretch upwards and strike a triangle;
2 = jump on the spot and strike a wooden bar;
3 = forward roll and shake a tambourine.

Another child could choose to change the meanings of the numbers, for example:

1 = curl in a tight ball;
2 = backward roll;
3 = stretch sidewards.

PE

Combining sequences can produce interesting effects. Such work is reflected in the physical education Programme of Study (General) for Key Stage 2: **'Pupils should be enabled to remember, select and repeat a range of movements and perform more complex sequences alone and with others'**.

For physical education, the statements relating to number patterns are at Key Stage 1 in the Programme of Study for gymnastic activities: **'Pupils should: be given opportunities to link together a series of actions both on the floor and using apparatus, and be able to repeat them'**.

An activity can be devised, therefore, which will meet the requirements of all three learning programmes (music, physical education and maths) through encouraging the children to devise a repeating number pattern where each number represents both a sound and a movement.

English

There are also links between this activity and English in the Programme of Study for Attainment Target 1: Speaking and listening, at Key Stage 1: **'giving and receiving simple explanations, information and instructions; asking and answering questions'**; and also in Attainment Target 1 at Level 1(c): **'respond appropriately to simple instructions given by a teacher'** and in the corresponding example: ***Follow two consecutive instructions such as "Choose some shells from the box and draw pictures of them"***; and in Attainment Target 1 at Level 2(e): **'respond appropriately to a range of more complex instructions given by a teacher, and give simple instructions'** and in the example: ***Follow three consecutive actions...'***. For example, 'Choose a colour for Paddington bear's hat. Choose a different colour for his boots. Draw your bear. Try again with some other colours. In how many different ways can you dress the bear with four colours?'

At a higher level, rhyming poetry can be a source of number patterns. Many of these

Monday | Tuesday
Wednesday | Thursday
Friday | Saturday
Sunday

poems have names, such as heroic quatrains which go abab, cdcd... and heroic couplets (aa bb cc...); for example, the traditional nursery rhyme 'Monday's child':

Monday's child is fair of face.
Tuesday's child is full of grace.
Wednesday's child is full of woe.
Thursday's child has far to go.
Friday's child is loving and giving.
Saturday's child works hard for a living.
But the child that is born on the Sabbath day
Is bonny and blyth, good and gay.

Children need not be aware of these technical terms, but they should be encouraged to look for the structures; for example, in the traditional rhyme 'Mary, Mary quite contrary' the lines rhyme in the pattern a a b, c c b, d d b, e e b.

Children may also notice that the spacing of the beginning of lines often follows a number pattern. Ask the children to make up their own rhyming poetry, deciding on a pattern at the outset.

Even handwriting can be improved by using number patterns. Children who have difficulty in differentiating between certain letters are often given rather dull handwriting practice to remedy the problem. If asked to make patterns with the letters, they may find the work more stimulating. From the English document, Attainment Target 5: Handwriting, states at Level 2(b) that children should: **'produce letters that are recognisably formed and properly oriented and that have clear ascenders and descenders where necessary'**. The example suggests *'b and d, p and b'*. Show the children patterns with b and d, for example: b d b b d b b b d b b d b d.

The children can then make up some repeating patterns for themselves.

Art

Repeating patterns are very common in art and craft work, and can be seen in the artefacts of other cultures.

The study of such examples is required by the National Curriculum for art – Attainment Target 2: Knowledge and understanding, states at Key Stage 1: **'look at and talk about examples of work of well-known artists from a variety of periods and cultures'** (PoSiii); *'...in African tribal art...'* (Examples). In Attainment Target 1: Investigating and making, children at Key Stage 1 are encouraged to make their own patterns: **'explore and recreate pattern and texture in natural and made forms'** (PoSvii).

For example, the children can use pictures of basketwork found in books to help them to

165

recreate these patterns with real rushes or strips of paper. In pottery they can recreate traditional designs.

The children can then make their own clay pots or tablets and inprint their designs upon them.

In such ways, children come to appreciate that information can be stored and communicated through a variety of media.

Technology

The technology document states that children should know that information can be stored as words, numbers, pictures and sounds. The previous examples of poetry (words), art (pictures), music (sounds) and maths (AT3) (number) provide examples of this. Also, the science document suggests that at Level 1 of Attainment Target 4 the children experiment with the sounds made by musical instruments.

Using modelling or posters to display information can be easily adapted for any subject or theme. The following are three examples from algebra.

Make a mobile

What you need

Stiff wire (or strips of wood or dowelling), weights or weighted models (see below), paper, coloured pens, scissors, adhesive, string.

What to do

Make a simple mobile for the children, for example:

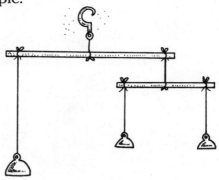

Use heavy weights, so that the weight of the wire is negligible, and the left-hand weight is equal to the sum of the other two, equal weights. Ask the children why they think the mobile balances. What would happen if any one weight was removed? The mobile can be made into a sum (or a partitioning) by sticking numbers on to represent the weights.

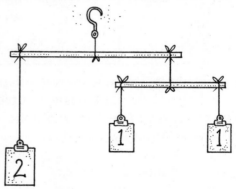

Ask the children to show some other partitions using mobiles.

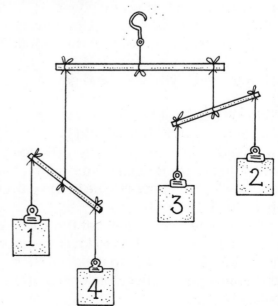

NC mapping

AT3 – Level 2 (a)
AT2 – Level 2 (a)

Technology KS1 PoS **'Pupils should be taught to:**
• **know that a system is made of related parts which are combined for a purpose;**
• **join materials and components in simple ways;**
• **represent and develop ideas by drawing, models, talking, writing, working with materials.'**

Make a function machine

What you need

Junk modelling materials, paper, coloured pens, scissors, adhesive, string.

What to do

Ask the children to make their own function machines to carry out a mathematical function they have been learning. They should make labels to explain what their machines do. They will need to think about how objects can go in and out; for example, the objects could be on a cardboard tray which pulls through the function machine with string.

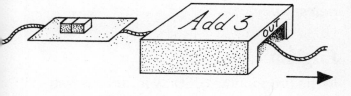

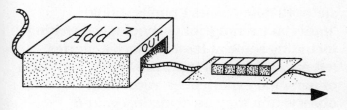

NC mapping

AT3 – Level 2 (a)
AT2 – Level 2 (a)

Technology KS1 PoS: **'Pupils should be taught to:**
• **know that a system is made of related parts which are combined for a purpose;**
• **join materials and components in simple ways;**
• **represent and develop ideas by drawing, models, talking, writing, working with materials.'**

Make a poster

What you need

Large paper, coloured pens, scissors, old magazines and catalogues.

What to do

Ask the children to make a poster to 'teach' others what they themselves have been learning in maths.

NC mapping

AT3 – various
AT2 – various
Technology KS1 PoS: **'Pupils should be taught to:**
• **represent and develop ideas by drawing, models, talking, writing, working with materials.'**

Sequences

The number sequences we have met in mathematics have all followed particular rules. The order of the members of the sequence is important and the rule can be expressed in words, in a formula or in a sequence of instructions. Sequencing can be seen as a facet of logical thought and, as such, is to be found in almost all human endeavours. Writing the instructions of a sequence as a flowchart is not mentioned in the maths National Curriculum until Level 7: **'constructing and interpreting flow diagrams with and without loops'** (AT3 PoS). However, simple sets of instructions as flowcharts can be followed by much younger/less-able children and they will benefit from this early experience. For example, here are instructions to prepare a bowl of cereal:

Are the instructions in the right order? Is anything missing? Ask the children to make up similar instructions which are incorrect, for others to sort out.

Sets of instructions are found throughout the primary curriculum, as the following examples show.

History

In history, Attainment Target 1: Knowledge and understanding of history, states that at Level 1 children **'should be able to a) place in sequence events in a story about the past'**. For example, using the children's own family histories, they could be asked for some important events in their families or things they themselves can remember well and then organise them in time order.

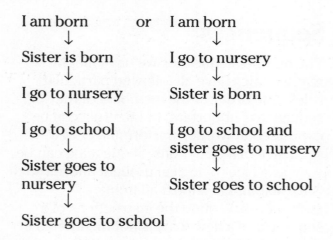

PE

In PE, the Programme of Study (General) for Key Stage 1 states that: **'pupils should: be encouraged to recognise and make up simple rules, and work within them'** and gives as examples: ***'be taught the Green***

Cross Code and Water Safety Code...'. Can the children sort cards on which are written the phrases from road safety codes?

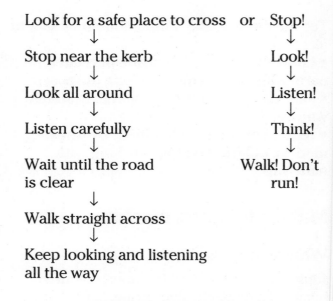

Can the children put them in the correct order? Is the order important?

Art

In art, the Programme of Study relating to Attainment Target 1: Investigating and making, states that for Key Stage 2: **'pupils should: respond to memory and imagination using a range of media'** (PoSii) and gives the example: ***'make a sequence of images to illustrate an incident described in a local newspaper'***.

English

In the Programme of Study for the English attainment target for reading (AT2), children at Key Stage 1 need to be able to write such instructions, or accounts of tasks where order is important. Attainment Target 3: Writing, states that Key Stage 1 pupils should: **'undertake a range of chronological writing including some at least of diaries, stories, letters, accounts of tasks they have done and of personal experiences, records of observation they have made, *eg. in a science or design activity,* and instructions, *eg. recipes'*.** At Key Stage 2, children should: **'undertake chronological writing, *eg. reports of work in science and*** *mathematics, instructions for carrying out a task, and accounts of personal experiences, as well as imaginative stories'.*

An example from mathematics could be the sequence of tasks used to add two two-digit numbers using Multibase:

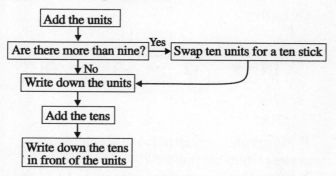

Writing mathematical procedures as connected phrases underlines the importance of order and hence helps the children to attain the statements of the English document.

Technology

Finally, in technology, according to the Key Stage 1 Programme of Study for information technology capability, children should know: **'how to give instructions to electronic devices,** *such as programmable toys and computers'* and at Key Stage 2: **'know that the order in which instructions are presented, and the form in which they are given to a computer is important,** *for example investigate the effect on a computer-controlled model of changing the order of the instructions'* and **'write a simple computer program for a particular purpose...'.** One example which links the technology document to algebra is the set of instructions to put a constant function in a calculator:

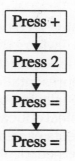

Now try this:

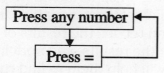

What happens?

Programmable toys such as the 'Roamer' floor turtle provide an excellent introduction to LOGO and also reinforce the technology statement. The LOGO commands listed below can be written on card and the children can use the cards to find out where 'Roamer' goes when using different combinations of cards.

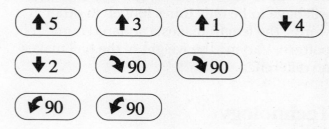

Generalising

Science

The science curriculum is the obvious place for children to gain further experience of generalising events. In Attainment Target 1: Scientific investigation, activities for children at Key Stage 2 should:

• **'involve variables to be controlled in the development of "fair tests"';**
• **'encourage systematic listing and recording of data, for example, in frequency tables and bar charts';**
• **'promote the search for patterns in data'.**

For example, in an experiment to find out how long a pendulum takes to swing, the children should identify four variables: the length of the string, the weight of the ball, the height at which the ball is held when the pendulum is released and the time it takes to make one swing.

In devising an experiment, they must decide which of these variables they will change, and record the results of that change. Looking at the results, and noticing any patterns, will help them to find rules for how a pendulum behaves. For example, the time taken to make one swing lengthens as the length of string is increased. If they make the string long enough for the time to double, the length of the string will be found to be four times as long as the original length. If they lengthen the string so that the time taken is three times as long, the length of the string will have to be nine times longer. In other words, the length makes a squared number pattern. Varying the weight of the ball makes no difference.

Technology

In technology, Attainment Target 5 states that at Key Stage 2 children should be able to **'analyse the patterns and relationships in a computer model to establish how its rules operate; change the rules and predict the effect, for example considering the way an adventure program responds to the choices made by the user'** (PoS). In its simplest form, this statement can be accomplished through using simple function machines or through setting up rules on a calculator (AT3 Levels 3 and 4). For example, the children could find the sequence made when the counting numbers go through this double machine:

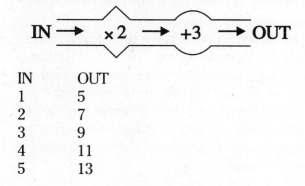

IN ⟶ ×2 ⟶ +3 ⟶ OUT

IN	OUT
1	5
2	7
3	9
4	11
5	13

The children could then explore what happens if the machines are swapped around:

IN ⟶ +3 ⟶ ×2 ⟶ OUT

Or if the numbers only were switched:

IN ⟶ ×3 ⟶ +2 ⟶ OUT

Or both:

IN ⟶ +2 ⟶ ×3 ⟶ OUT

Putting rules (constants) in a calculator was described on page 20.

Interpreting computer programs (AT3 Level 5 Examples) is an excellent way of delivering this technology requirement. To introduce children to how a program works, a good first step is to look at the OUT numbers when counting numbers are fed in, for example in BASIC:

```
10 FOR N = 1 TO 20
20 PRINT 2*N + 3
30 NEXT N
40 END
```

In LOGO:

```
TO MAC :NUM
REPEAT 20 [PRINT :NUM*2+3
MAKE "NUM :NUM+1]
END
```

Can the children explain what the program is doing and what each line does? Encourage them to change parts of the program to explore its working.

Co-ordinates

As was seen in Chapter 4, co-ordinates in Attainment Target 3 – where they express relationships – can be reinforced through their other use as representation of position (AT4). Position is equally important in geography and physical education activities, and hence the concepts can easily be approached in a cross-curricular mode.

Geography

Early work in geography, introducing children to the concept that position can be represented on paper, prepares them for co-ordinate work as is laid out in the 'Geographical skills' section of the Programme of Study for Key Stage 1: **'Pupils should be taught to:**
• **follow directions, including the terms forwards and backwards, up and down, left and right...;**
• **extract information from, and add it to, pictorial maps;**
• **draw around objects to make a plan,** *for example, mathematical shapes...;*
• **make representations of actual or imaginary places,** *for example, their own bedroom, a treasure island...;*
• **follow a route on a map,** *for example, a map of the local area of the school produced by a teacher....'*

Also at this level is included: **'...observe, describe and record the weather over a short period'** (KS1 PoS), which maps nicely to the co-ordinate activity in Chapter One, page 56.

At Key Stage 2 of 'Geographical skills' within the Programme of Study we find: **'Pupils should be taught to:**
• **make representations of real or imaginary places; make and use maps of routes, and sketch maps of small areas showing the main features and using symbols with keys...;**
• **use letter and number co-ordinates and four-figure grid references to locate features on a map...;**
• **measure and record the weather using direct observation and simple equipment.'**

Hence, geography and mathematics become indistinguishable!

PE

In physical education, the Programme of Study for outdoor and adventurous activities at Key Stage 2 states that children should: **'experience outdoor and adventurous activities in different environments** *(such as school grounds and premises, parks, woodlands and sea shore)* **that involve planning, navigation, working in small groups, recording and evaluating'.** The mathematics trails and treasure trails previously mentioned in Chapter One provide a context for such work, and orienteering will help children both with their geography and with their mathematics.

Themes

The following three themes have been chosen because of their richness in possibilities and because they are popular cross-curricular themes in schools. Other mathematical concepts, and cross-curricular links, are also wide-ranging, and have been left for the teacher to plan.

Toys and games

Sets

Ask the children to write down as many toys and games as they can think of (a catalogue might help). Can they sort them in any way? How many different ways can they find? Ask the children to work in groups to produce posters of the groupings of toys they think are the most appropriate. They might use pictures cut from the catalogues, make models or draw the toys and games.

Mobiles

Mobiles which show partitioning were shown in the last section (see page 166). This activity can be repeated but instead of attaching numbers, the children could make a pleasing mobile for a baby. It will be necessary to discuss with them that it can't *really* be given to a baby because of various safety issues, but instead could be used to decorate the classroom. The weights, and hence the mathematics (partitioning/addition) will still be needed.

Teddy bears

Tubs of small coloured bears are available for mathematics work (*Count Bears*, Jonathan Press or *Compare-Bears*, LDA). These can be used for number patterns and partition work, as well as many other areas of the curriculum. Mathematical links are discussed in *Mathematics with Teddy Bears* by Elizabeth Graham (Claire Publications, 1991).

Cross-products of dressing bears has already been discussed and the computer package *Teddy Bears' Picnic* (1989, Sherston Software) is an excellent infant resource containing a good deal of mathematics, much of it problem-solving.

Chess and draughts

Children who are keen on chess or draughts may find the notation described on pages 62-63 helpful. Good chess players can play blindfold, using such shorthand. This will almost certainly be beyond any of the children! However, they can play 'telephone' or 'back-to-back' chess or draughts where each player has a board and full set of pieces and keeps their own record of the progress of the game. It helps to have a referee!

Darts

What you need

A dartboard, darts (safety darts and boards are available from school suppliers but don't usually contain doubles and trebles and therefore the game will need adapting), pencils, paper.

What to do

Ask two players to take turns to try to score as large a number as possible with three darts. Each player must total their darts and subtract the total from their running score (starting from 501). The children must get exactly the score left at the end to finish. The first to finish wins. (In the adult game, you must finish with a double, and sometimes also start with a double.) The outer ring on the board is worth double the score, the inner ring treble. The outer bullseye is worth 25 and the inner bull is worth 50.

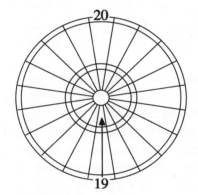

Treble 19 (i.e., 57)

A good deal of mathematics is involved in playing darts, besides the mental arithmetic. Strategies are involved, for example, in deciding which area would give a reasonable score if you missed your number, and is it worth going for that instead of a high number surrounded by low scores? If you need an odd number (to leave a double) where would you aim to have the greatest chance?

From an algebraic stance, ask the children to find which numbers can be scored using only doubles or trebles. Put the doubles or trebles in a row and look for a pattern. Make another pattern by adding together all the values in the region of a number, working

172

from the outside (that is, for 20: double 20 + 20 + treble 20 + 20). Put these region totals in order. Is there a pattern? Can the children explain it? Can they find some other patterns?

There doesn't seem to be any logic behind the way that numbers are placed on a dartboard. The children should try different arrangements and work out which would give the most skilful game.

Similar activities can be devised for other games, especially fairground games such as 'Hoopla!'.

NC mapping

AT3 – Level 3 (a)
      – Level 4 (a)

Bouncing balls

What you need

A selection of balls, brought in by the children.

What to do

Here are two scientific investigations for the children to try.

How many bounces?

Explain to the children that you want them to find out if the height from which a ball is dropped affects the number of bounces that it will make. Let them decide how to make the experiment fair and accurate.

Can they find any pattern in their results? Can they predict what the next height up would give? Ask them to check it. Ask them to draw a graph of their results.

How high?

In this experiment the children can either try to find out how the height of the drop is connected to the height of the next bounce, or they can try to measure every additional bounce. Use string stretched across a black background at equal intervals to help the children see where the ball reaches and make measuring easier.

If looking at several bounces, ask each child to concentrate on one particular bounce.

A software package designed for such

information retrieval is *Revelation* (Longman Logotron), which can be used with a video camera to get exact measurements.

Again, the children should look at the pattern of results and try to predict what will happen next. Finally, they should draw graphs of their results.

NC mapping

AT3 – Level 3 (a)
      – Level 4 (a)

Other scientific experiments can be carried out using the children's own toys from home; for example, they can compare the weights of toy cars and how far they roll after running down a ramp.

Knockout competitions

What you need

Any occasion where the children are taking part in a sports or games competition.

What to do

Use the opportunity of playing a sport to allow the children to investigate the patterns in knockout situations. They can use their findings for future occasions. For example, take the situation where the children are playing in pairs against other pairs, such as in a doubles table-tennis competition. In a class of 30 children, there will be 15 pairs. How many byes will there be? How many games will have to be played? (There were 14 games with 1 bye.)

```
A }
B }  A }
          A }
C }  C }      A }
D }              
                  A }
E }  E }              
F }      E }          
          G }          A
G }  G }                  
H }                      
                          
I }  I }                  
J }      I }              
          K }      I }    
K }  K }                  
L }          I }          
                          
M }  M }      M }          
N }                      
          O }            
O }  O }                  
```

What if the children play five-a-side football? (There would be 5 games with 1 bye.)

```
A }
B }  A }
          A }
C }  C }      
D }              
          E }
E }  E }          
F }      E }      
```

Ask the children to investigate all the situations they can think of for different class sizes. Can they see any patterns in their results tables? Can they find any generalisations?

NC mapping

AT3 – Level 4 (a) (although the number patterns are very easy, and within the ability of other children)

– Level 6 (for those who can describe symbolically)

AT1 – Level 4 (a) (b) (c) (d)

Growth

Numbers

All the sequences that were shown in Chapter One represent growth, and can be used during the topic to integrate arithmetic work. Those sequences which are developed out of spatial arrangements are obviously the most appropriate. The infinite/infinitesimal machine on page 118 shows very quick growth.

People

How does your height vary as you get older? Ask the children to bring in any measurements their parents have kept of their children's growth. Do the children know how long they were when they were born?

Can they continue the record to estimate how tall they will be when they are 20? (AT3 Levels 3 to 5). By drawing a graph, establish with the children that growth isn't uniform – a straight line graph would make them very tall indeed (AT3 Level 6 PoS)! Would it make them as tall as the tallest man in the world? They can find out his height from the *Guinness Book of Records*. Use the proportions of an adult to work out his proportions. How big were his feet? What was the circumference of his head? How long was his stride? The children could then make a model of the tallest man and find out what problems he might have had when moving around their school. Similarly, the dimensions of the fattest person and the smallest person can be explored (AT3 Level 5 PoS).

NB: It is important to explain, before tackling such an activity, the conditions which lead to growth problems so that the issue can be treated with sensitivity.

Growing squares and growing cubes have already been described, and will fit well into this topic. An alternative method of approaching growing cubes would be the following activity.

Box up

What you need

Thick card, scissors, adhesive tape, centicubes.

What to do

Ask the children to make cubes which are

What to do

Ask the children to draw a simple shape on a co-ordinate grid. Explain that they should multiply the co-ordinates of their shape by 2 and plot the new points. They should repeat for three and four times as big.

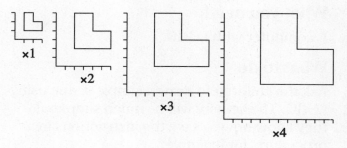

Ask the children to cut out the resulting shapes, and arrange them in an overlap.

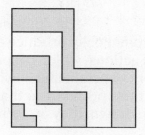

Or they can arrange them in a pattern.

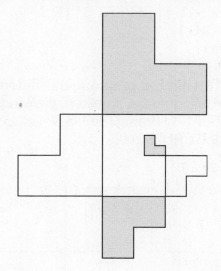

Overlapping patterns can be made if the shapes are traced on to tissue paper.

If a different number pattern from 1,2,3,4 is chosen then the growth pattern will also change. Ask the children to experiment, for example they could try ×1, ×2, ×3, ×5, ×8, ×13... the Fibonacci numbers.

$2 \times 2 \times 2$cm. They should try to find their own method of how to do this. To help any children who need direction, suggest that they first draw a net on centimetre squared paper, cut it out, stick it on to card and then cut around it. Remind them not to forget the tabs!

Next the children should see how many centicubes they can fit into their cube. They can then repeat the process for a $3 \times 3 \times 3$cm cube, and so on. The children should draw up a table of results. Can they see a pattern? Can they continue the pattern (using calculators)? Finally, the children should draw a graph. They will find that they have graphed the cube numbers.

NC mapping

AT3 – Level 5 PoS
  – Level 6 (c)
AT2 – Level 5 (d)

Transformation by enlargement was discussed on page 105, and is an obvious example of growth.

Growing shapes

What you need

Squared paper, coloured pencils, scissors, glue.

NC mapping
AT3 – Level 4 (a) or Level 5 PoS
AT4 – Level 6 PoS

LOGO growth

What you need

A computer with LOGO.

What to do

Ask the children to draw a simple shape using LOGO. The activity will be much simpler if they know how to save the instructions in a procedure, for example:

```
TO CROSS
REPEAT 4 [ REPEAT 3 [ FD
100 RT 90 ] LT 180 ]
END
```

By doing so, the children automatically produce a logical sequence of actions, which prepares them for the later work of producing flowcharts. If they can change their program so that any sized cross can be drawn, they are generalising the pattern:

```
TO CROSS :NUM
REPEAT 4 [ REPEAT 3 [ FD :NUM RT 90 ]
LT 180 ]
END
```

With this altered program, the children can produce a sequence of nested, growing crosses, just by typing CROSS 50 CROSS 100 CROSS 150 CROSS 200.

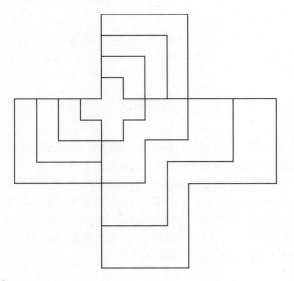

Some children may be able to cope with a growing variable within the program:

```
TO CROSS :NUM
REPEAT 4 [ REPEAT 3 [ FD :NUM RT 90 ]
LT 180 MAKE "NUM :NUM+50 ]
END
```

Typing CROSS 50 will begin this program.

NC mapping
AT3 – from Level 5 to Level 7

Exploding stars

What you need

Large sheets of paper, coloured pencils, scissors, adhesive, templates, rulers.

What to do

Ask the children to draw around a template of a regular shape (equal sides and equal angles) in the middle of their paper. They should measure the length of one side. If they continue the sides of the shape outwards, the lines will meet to make a star.

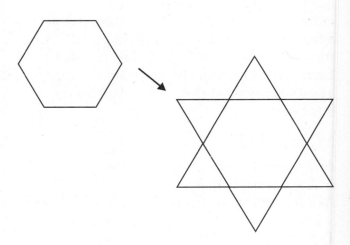

Ask the children to join the vertices (corners) of the star together. What shape do they get now? Measure the length of one side and repeat this for all the sides. Is there a pattern in the way the sides grow? How long would the tenth one be? Do the children think that they have a large enough piece of paper to check?

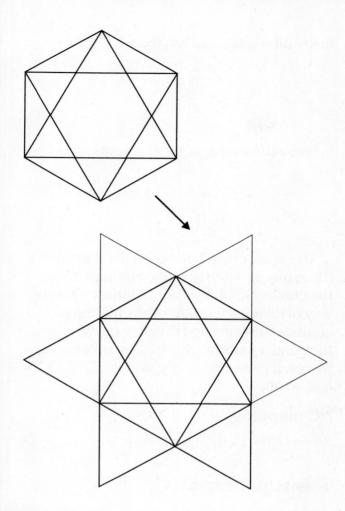

NC mapping

AT3 – Level 5 PoS

Circles, cycles and wheels

Several activities which fit into this theme have already been described elsewhere in this book, such as Passaola (on page 100), Curve stitching (on page 69), Bracelets (on page 33), Calculator bracelets (on page 87) and Circumferences (on page x51).

The concepts in 'Circumferences' can be approached in a way more fitting to the following theme.

How far with your wheel?

What you need

Bicycle wheels, a large roll of paper (hard toilet paper is good), tape measures.

What to do

Ask the children to measure the diameter of a bicycle wheel and, using a piece of Blu-Tack or sticky paper as marker, find how far the wheel rolls in one turn. They should add their results to a class results table. What do they notice? Introduce them to the concept of π.

NC mapping

AT3 – Level 3 PoS
– Level 4 (a)

How far with your pedal?

What you need

Bicycles, a large roll of paper, tape measures.

What to do

Ask the children to find out how far the wheels on the bicycles will go for one full turn of the pedal when in different gears. How many times did the wheels go round?

The children should compare their results. Are some bikes more efficient than others? Use this activity as a general introduction to gears.

NC mapping

AT3 – Level 3 PoS

Gears and cogs

What you need

A selection of working gears such as a bicycle or clock, material for making gears (wood, LEGO Technic, cardboard and so on).

What to do

The children should take part in a general investigation into gears and cogs. Ask them to look at how the cogs move as a bicycle moves or at the mechanism of a clock (geared teaching clocks are a good, simple example) and so on. The children should realise that two interlocking cogs will move in opposite directions:

Set the children such problems as:
• Which way will Cog E go in this arrangement?

• If a cog with 20 teeth is attached to a cog with 10 teeth, how many times will the 10-tooth cog go round when the 20-tooth cog goes round once? Such questions will reinforce factors and multiples.

The children should try to make their own gears from balsa wood, corrugated cardboard and so on. LEGO Technic provides good experience of the advantages of using gears. Spirographs link gear work to 'Toys and games' and are very varied in their possibilities. Which Spirograph wheels inside which rings produce very simple patterns? Which are very complicated?

NC mapping

AT3 – Level 4 PoS

LOGO circles

What you need

A computer with LOGO.

What to do

Ask the children to try to draw a circle in LOGO. This isn't as simple as it sounds! They will discover that they need a very small line length and a very small angle, plus a large number of repeats.

NC mapping

AT3 – Level 1 (a)

Pizza cuts

What you need

Paper, pencils, perhaps circular templates but these are not absolutely necessary.

What to do

Show the children a 'pizza' with one cut. How many pieces of pizza are there?

Show them a pizza with two cuts.

The pizza could have been divided into three pieces with two cuts, but impress on the children that we want the most efficient way of dividing it up. Ask the children to continue drawing and dividing pizzas. Can they find a pattern? A rule? The number of pieces, if drawn correctly, will go: 2,4,7,11,16 and so on.

NC mapping

AT3 – Level 4 (a)

Tissue patterns

What you need

Circles of tissue paper in several colours.

What to do

Ask the children the following question: 'If two circles overlap, how many darker sections are made?'

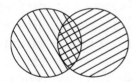

If three circles are used, what patterns can be made?

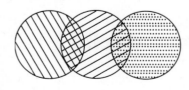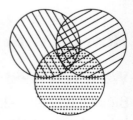

NC mapping

AT3 – Level 3 PoS
 – Level 4

Pattern blanks

Fill in the blanks.

1, 3, 5, 7, □, □, □

2, 4, 6, 8, □, □, □

5, 10, 15, 20, □, □, □

2, 6, 10, □, 18, 22, 26

20, 17, □, 11, 8, □, 2

1, 4, □, □, 13, 16, □

3, □, □, □, □, □, 21

24, □, □, □, □, □, 0

Now make some of your own.

_____

_____

_____

Blank grids

Addition square

+	1	2	3	4	5	6	7	8	9	10
10										
9										
8										
7										
6										
5										
4										
3										
2										
1										

Hundred square

1	2	3	4	5	6	7	8	9	10
11	12	13	14	15	16	17	18	19	20
21	22	23	24	25	26	27	28	29	30
31	32	33	35	35	36	37	38	39	40
41	42	43	44	45	46	47	48	49	50
51	52	53	54	55	56	57	58	59	60
61	62	63	64	65	66	67	68	69	70
71	72	73	74	75	76	77	78	79	80
81	82	83	84	85	86	87	88	89	90
91	92	93	94	95	96	97	98	99	100

10 x 10 grid

This page may be photocopied for use in the classroom and should not be declared in any return in respect of any photocopying licence.

Stamps

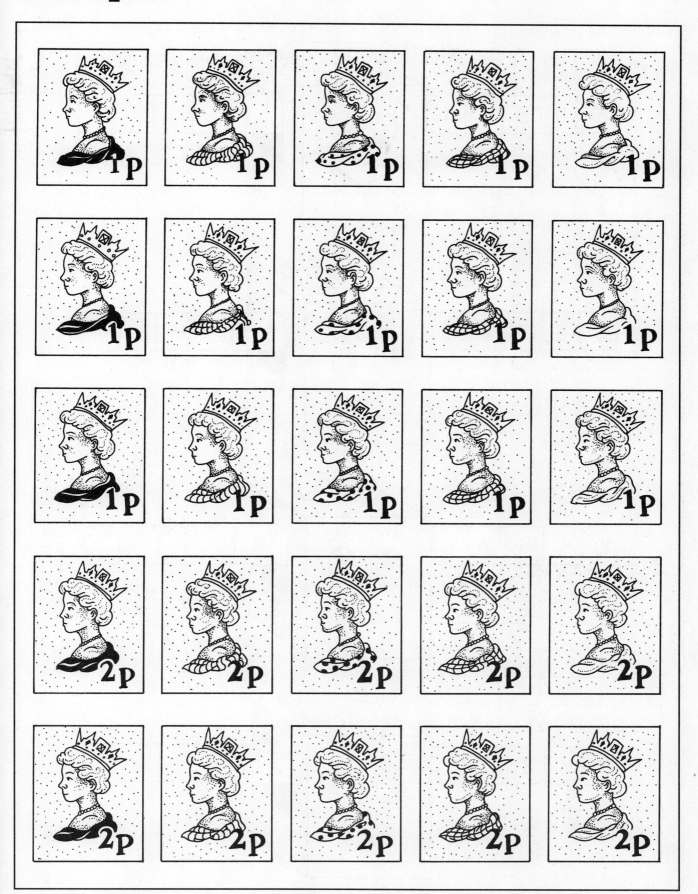

Find the OUT numbers

This page may be photocopied for use in the classroom and should not be declared in any return in respect of any photocopying licence.

Find the rule

This page may be photocopied for use in the classroom and should not be declared in any return in respect of any photocopying licence.

183

Bouncy cannon-balls

Where will these cannon-balls bounce? Write down the numbers.

This is a three cannon.

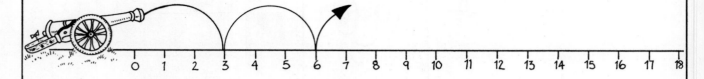

This is a five cannon.

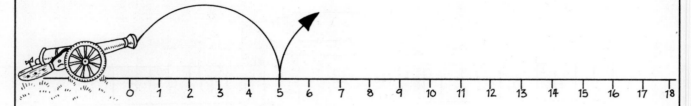

This is a four cannon.

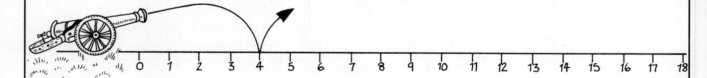

How many cannons can you find which land on 10?
Draw them on the lines.

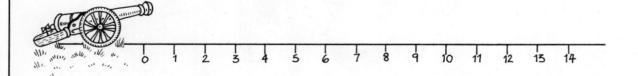

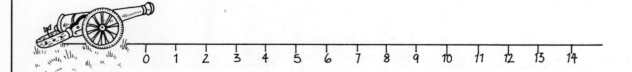

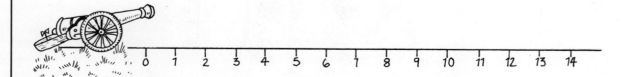

Machine tables

Complete these tables. Can you find any number patterns?

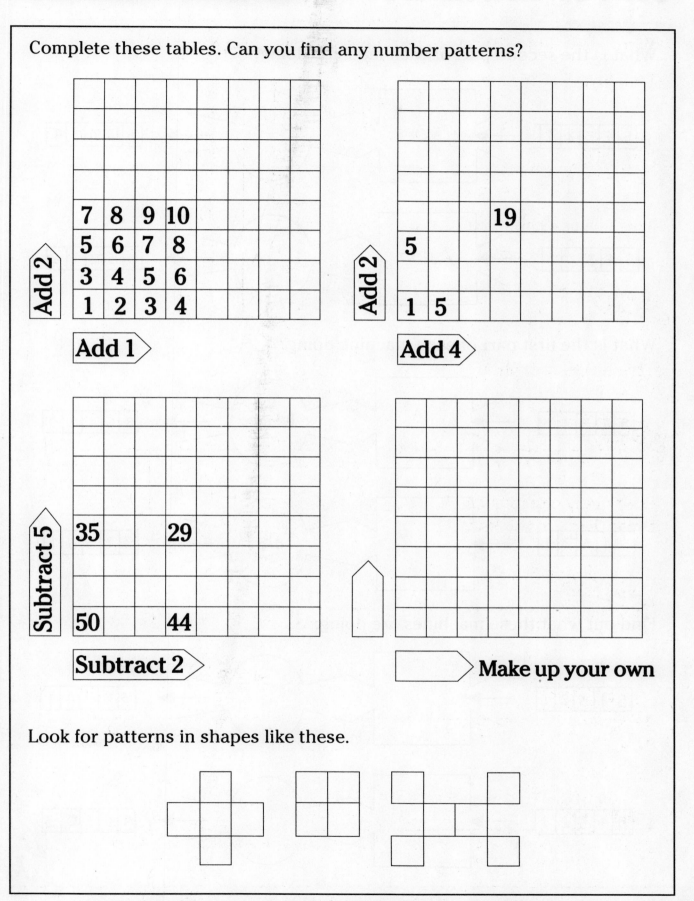

Add 2

7	8	9	10			
5	6	7	8			
3	4	5	6			
1	2	3	4			

Add 1

Add 2

			19			
5						
1	5					

Add 4

Subtract 5

35		29				
50		44				

Subtract 2

Make up your own

Look for patterns in shapes like these.

Clever machines

What is the second part of each machine doing?

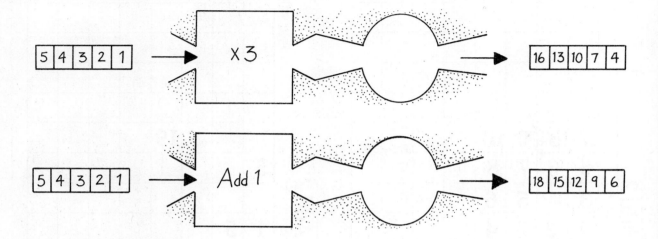

What is the first part of each machine doing?

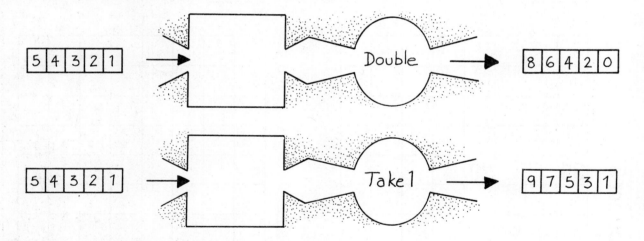

Find out what these machines are doing:

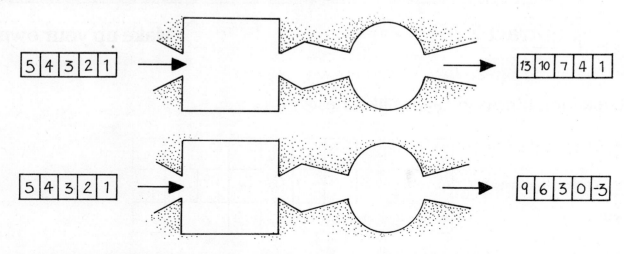

This page may be photocopied for use in the classroom and should not be declared in any return in respect of any photocopying licence.

Body puzzles

- The nurse's head is in B4. Where are her feet?

- Which letters make the guard?

- Which letters make the ballerina?

- Write down your answers then cut up the picture.

- Put the people together properly.

Towering inferno

Start here

a	b	c	d
a	b	c	d
a	b	c	d
a	b	c	d
a	b	c	d
a	b	c	d
a	b	c	d
a	b	c	d
a	b	c	d

Wobbly grids

Draw a picture here:

Copy your picture on to some different grids:

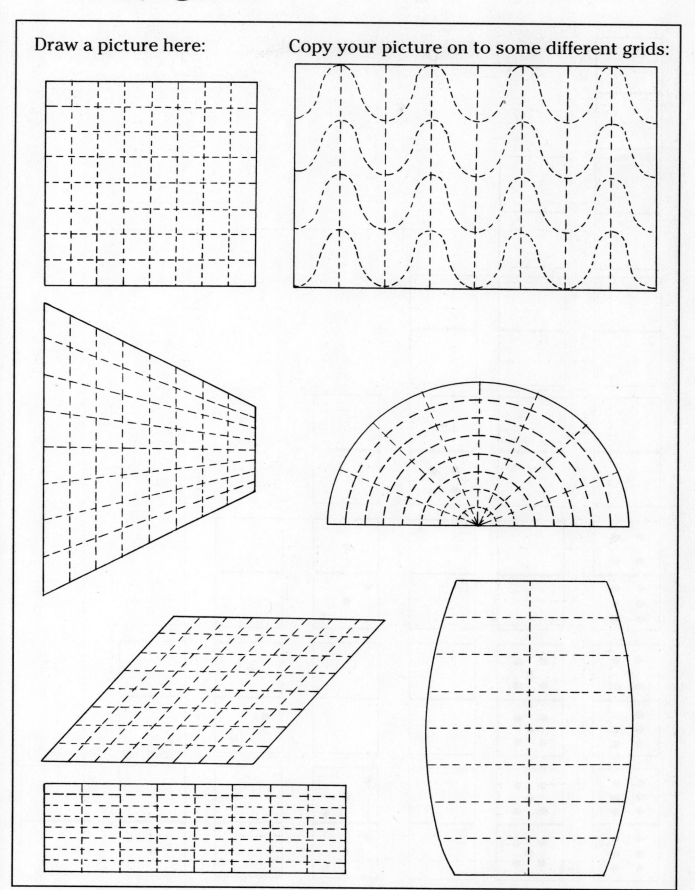

Domino triangle

Fill in the blanks.

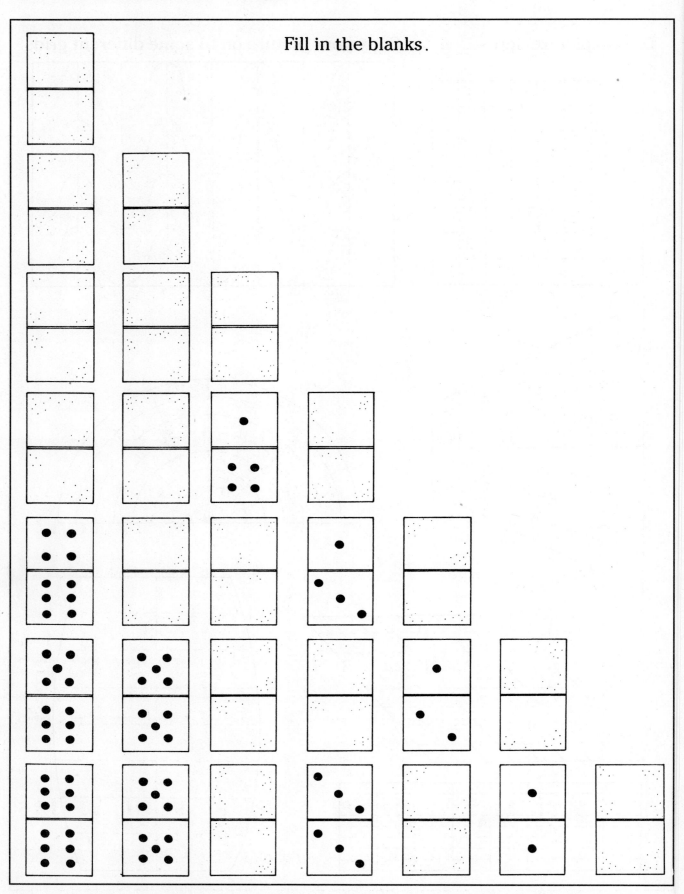

This page may be photocopied for use in the classroom and should not be declared in any return in respect of any photocopying licence.

Baby kangaroo

Help baby kangaroo get to the last stone. In how many ways can he do it?

Draw all the ways.

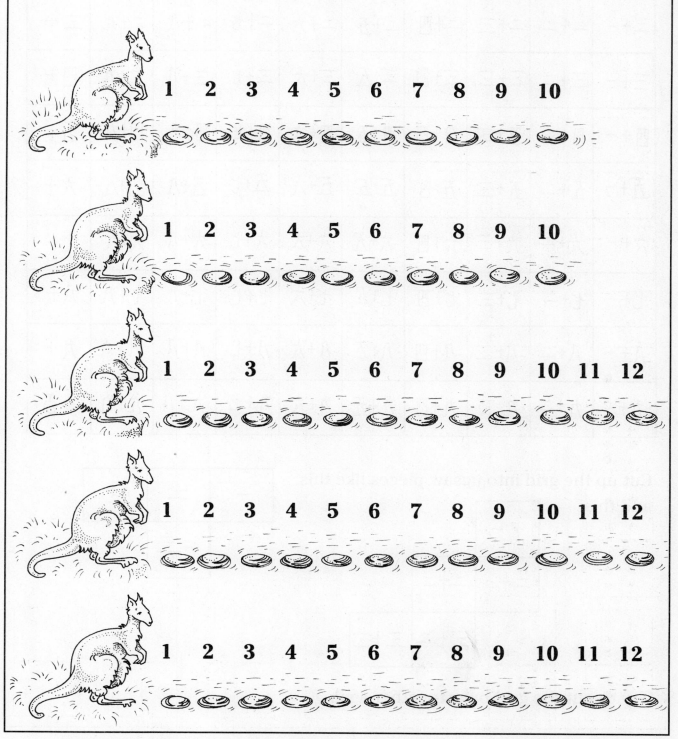

This page may be photocopied for use in the classroom and should not be declared in any return in respect of any photocopying licence.

191

The Chinese hundred square

一	二	三	四	五	六	七	八	九	十
十一	十二	十三	十四	十五	十六	十七	十八	十九	二十
二十一	二十二	二十三	二十四	二十五	二十六	二十七	二十八	二十九	三十
三十一	三十二	三十三	三十四	三十五	三十六	三十七	三十八	三十九	四十
四十一	四十二	四十三	四十四	四十五	四十六	四十七	四十八	四十九	五十
五十一	五十二	五十三	五十四	五十五	五十六	五十七	五十八	五十九	六十
六十一	六十二	六十三	六十四	六十五	六十六	六十七	六十八	六十九	七十
七十一	七十二	七十三	七十四	七十五	七十六	七十七	七十八	七十九	八十
八十一	八十二	八十三	八十四	八十五	八十六	八十七	八十八	八十九	九十
九十一	九十二	九三	九十四	九十五	九十六	九十七	九十八	九十九	一百

Cut up the grid into jigsaw pieces like this:
and this:

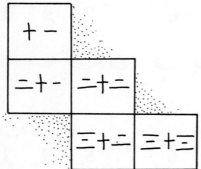

Try to put the grid back together again.

Lift off!

Fuel Tanks

Dressing bears

This page may be photocopied for use in the classroom and should not be declared in any return in respect of any photocopying licence.

Equal weights: 1

Add the weights. Fill in the blanks.

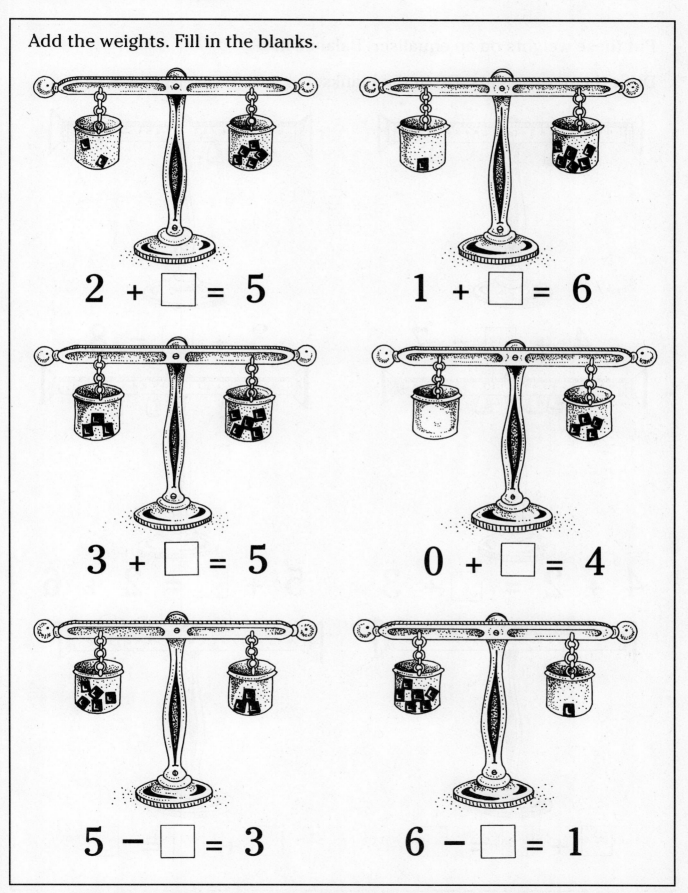

$2 + \boxed{} = 5$

$1 + \boxed{} = 6$

$3 + \boxed{} = 5$

$0 + \boxed{} = 4$

$5 - \boxed{} = 3$

$6 - \boxed{} = 1$

Equal weights: 2

Put these weights on an equaliser. Balance it.

Draw the new weights. Fill in the blanks.

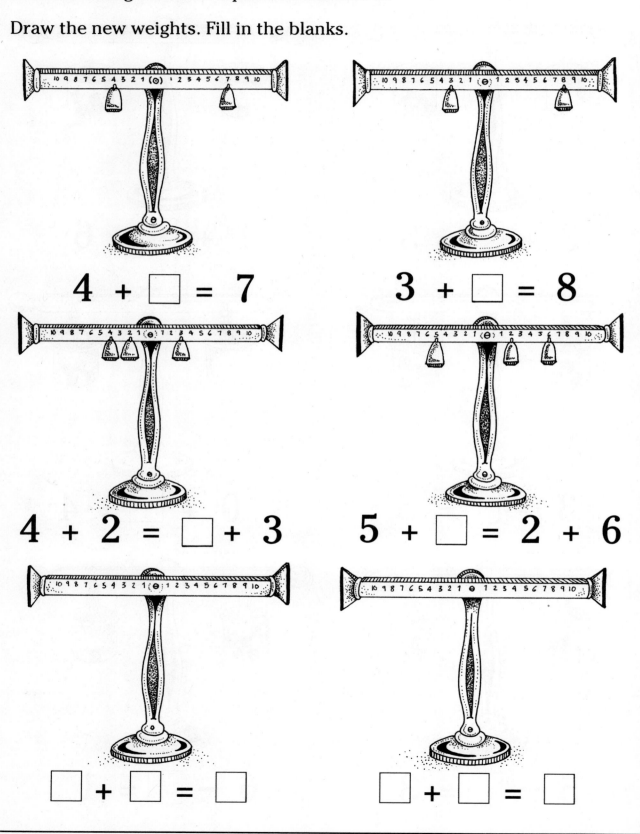

$4 + \square = 7$

$3 + \square = 8$

$4 + 2 = \square + 3$

$5 + \square = 2 + 6$

$\square + \square = \square$

$\square + \square = \square$

This page may be photocopied for use in the classroom and should not be declared in any return in respect of any photocopying licence.

'Stay the same' machines

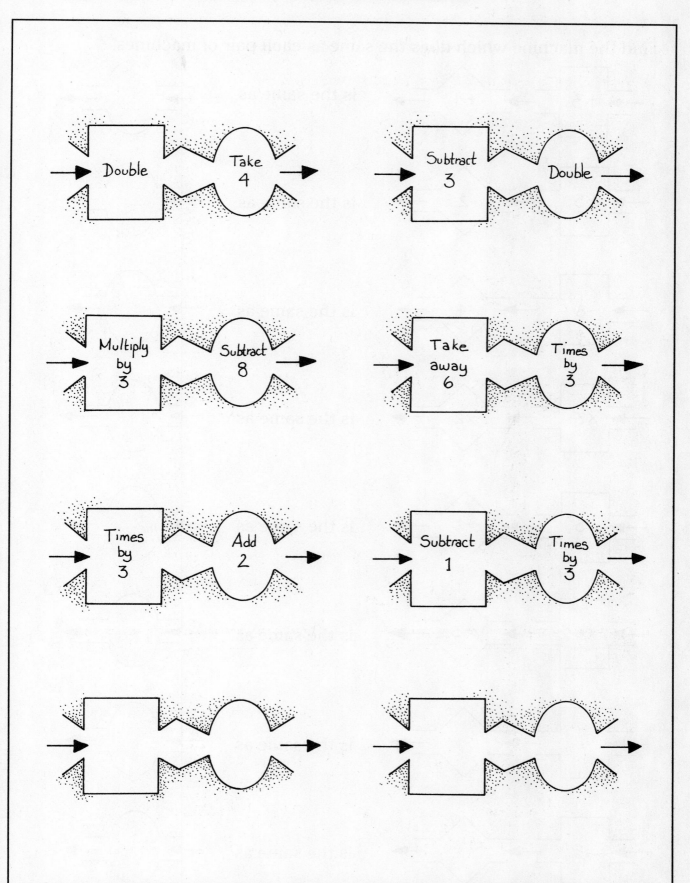

Join machines

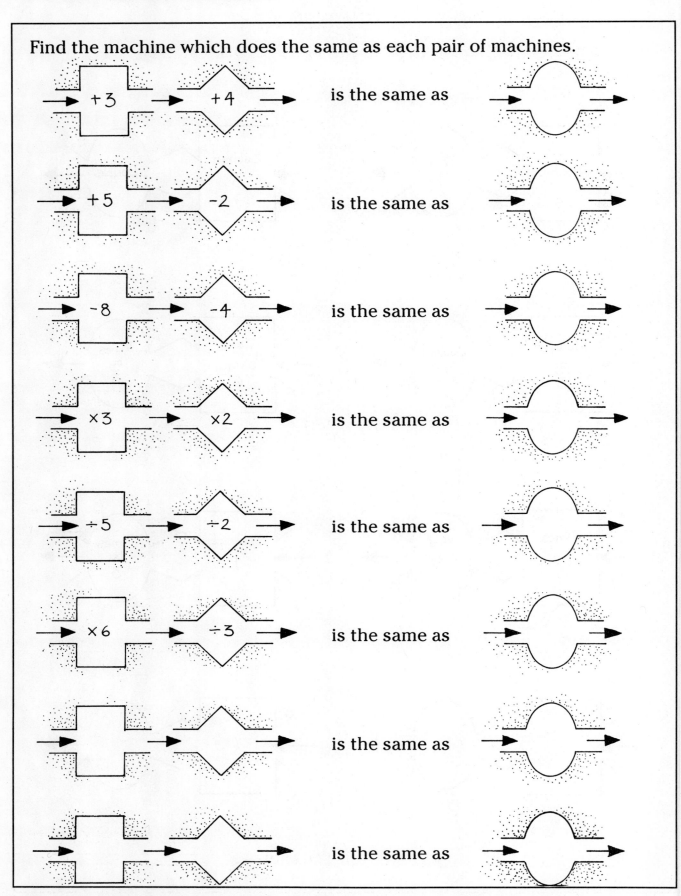

Find the machine which does the same as each pair of machines.

+3   +4   is the same as

+5   -2   is the same as

-8   -4   is the same as

×3   ×2   is the same as

÷5   ÷2   is the same as

×6   ÷3   is the same as

is the same as

is the same as

Split machines

Find the pair of machines which do the same as each machine.

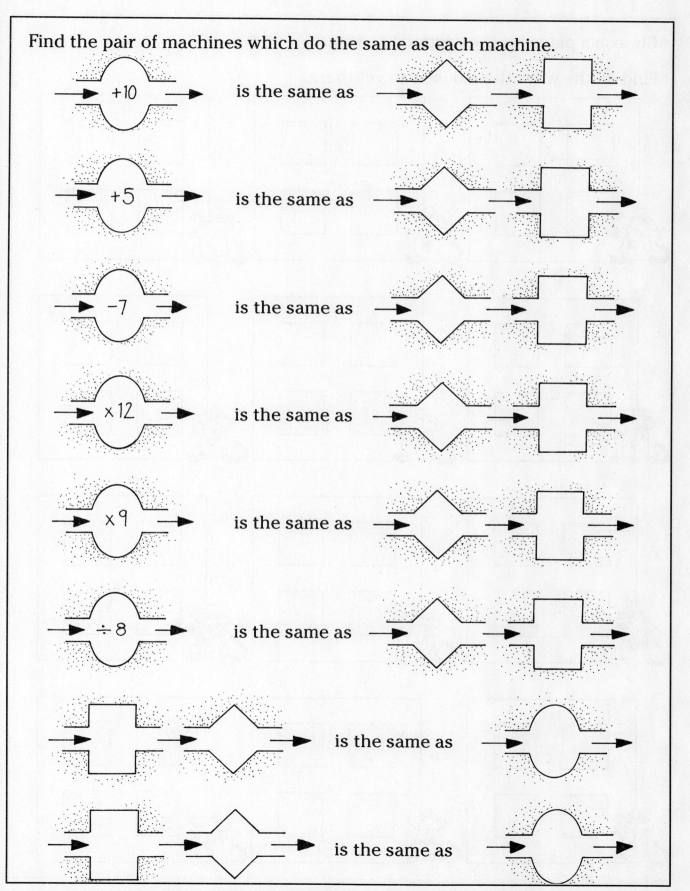

The dropped cheese puzzle

Choose a place for the dropped cheese.

Find all the ways the mouse can get there.

This page may be photocopied for use in the classroom and should not be declared in any return in respect of any photocopying licence.

Patterns in Pascal

Fill in the gaps.

This page may be photocopied for use in the classroom and should not be declared in any return in respect of any photocopying licence.

201

Complete the square

<table>
<tr><td>4</td><td></td><td>2</td></tr>
<tr><td></td><td>5</td><td></td></tr>
<tr><td>8</td><td></td><td>6</td></tr>
</table>

<table>
<tr><td>2</td><td>7</td><td></td></tr>
<tr><td>9</td><td></td><td>1</td></tr>
<tr><td></td><td>3</td><td></td></tr>
</table>

<table>
<tr><td></td><td>3</td><td>4</td></tr>
<tr><td>1</td><td>5</td><td>9</td></tr>
<tr><td></td><td></td><td></td></tr>
</table>

<table>
<tr><td></td><td>1</td><td></td></tr>
<tr><td></td><td></td><td>3</td></tr>
<tr><td>2</td><td>9</td><td>4</td></tr>
</table>

<table>
<tr><td></td><td>9</td><td></td></tr>
<tr><td></td><td>5</td><td></td></tr>
<tr><td>6</td><td>1</td><td>8</td></tr>
</table>

<table>
<tr><td>8</td><td></td><td>6</td></tr>
<tr><td></td><td></td><td></td></tr>
<tr><td>4</td><td></td><td>2</td></tr>
</table>

<table>
<tr><td>6</td><td></td><td></td></tr>
<tr><td>1</td><td></td><td>9</td></tr>
<tr><td></td><td>3</td><td></td></tr>
</table>

<table>
<tr><td></td><td></td><td></td></tr>
<tr><td>9</td><td>5</td><td></td></tr>
<tr><td></td><td>2</td><td>7</td></tr>
</table>

<table>
<tr><td>4</td><td></td><td></td></tr>
<tr><td></td><td></td><td></td></tr>
<tr><td></td><td>8</td><td>6</td></tr>
</table>

<table>
<tr><td></td><td>3</td><td></td></tr>
<tr><td></td><td>9</td><td></td></tr>
<tr><td></td><td>7</td><td>2</td></tr>
</table>

<table>
<tr><td></td><td>1</td><td></td></tr>
<tr><td></td><td>5</td><td></td></tr>
<tr><td>2</td><td></td><td>4</td></tr>
</table>

<table>
<tr><td></td><td></td><td>6</td></tr>
<tr><td></td><td></td><td>1</td></tr>
<tr><td></td><td>3</td><td>8</td></tr>
</table>

Appendix A
Software

Distributors

• Association of Teachers of Mathematics (ATM), 7, Shaftesbury Street, Derby DE23 8YB
• Inner London Educational Computing Company (ILECC), John Ruskin Street, London SE5 0PQ
• Keyboard Technology Limited, Unit 3, Gordon Road, Meadow Lane Industrial Estate, Loughborough LE11 1JX
• Kudlian Soft, 8, Barrow Road, Kenilworth, Warwickshire CV8 1EH
• Longman Logotron, 124, Cambridge Science Park, Milton Road, Cambridge CB4 4ZS
• National Council for Education Technology (NCET), Sir William Lyons Road, The Science Park, The University of Warwick, Coventry CV4 7EZ
• Newman College, Bartley Green, Birmingham B32 3NT
• Northern Micromedia, NORIC Centre, University of Northumbria, Coach Lane Campus, Newcastle upon Tyne NE7 7XA
• Research Machines Limited, Mill Street, Oxford OX2 0BW
• The Shell Centre for Mathematics Education, University of Nottingham, Nottingham NG7 2RD
• Valiant Technology Limited, Myrtle House, 69, Salcott Road, London SW11 6DQ

Packages and programs

All programs are available in formats suitable for the BBC, Nimbus and Archimedes systems unless otherwise stated.

Number patterns

Monty

Teachers can choose a variety of number grids. The children are given time to study a grid, which is then hidden. A python, called 'Monty', moves around the screen. When it stops the children must guess which numbers are hidden underneath it. (Available on *SLIMWAM2* from ATM.)

Counter

One or two numbers grow at a pace and step size set by the teacher. Digits play a tune and the children look/listen for patterns. (Available on *SLIMWAM2* from ATM.)

Patterns: 1

Multiples of one or two numbers are shaded on grids. The grid widths can be varied. The children look for patterns or try to guess the multiples. (Available on *MEP Primary Maths Pack* from local education authorities.)

Spirals

Children feed in an angle and a sequence of numbers. The computer draws the sequence lengths repeatedly, with the angle turn between each one. This is a good follow-up to 'Worm walks' (p. 31). (Available on *MicroSMILE – The first 31* from ILECC.)

Circle

The children choose how many points are spread around the circumference of a circle and how large a jump size. Lines are drawn inside the circle connecting numbers separated by the jump size. This is a good extension to 'Passaola' (p. 100). (Available on *MicroSMILE – The first 31* from ILECC.)

Pattern-generating investigations

All of the following programs are available on *Mathematical Investigations* by Anita Straker, available from ILECC.

Polygon

This is a good resource to use alongside the structures investigations in Chapter Four (page 159).

Diagonal

How many squares does the diagonal of a rectangular grid cross?

Bounce

A ball is rolled at 45° on a rectangular grid. The pattern it traces depends upon factors and multiples of the length and width.

Routes

This provides a computer model of the 'Mouse and cheese' investigation in Chapter Three (page 28) of this book.

Co-ordinates

All of the following programs are available on *MicroSMILE – The first 31* from ILECC.

Elephant

An elephant is lost in New York. The children guess the location by entering co-ordinates. They are told the direct distance (that is, 'as the crow flies') from the elephant.

Lines

This is a more complex version of noughts and crosses, where the children feed in co-ordinates for their O and X. It is a good follow-up for p.67.

Locate

The way that the grid axes are labelled is varied; for example, beginning in the top right-hand corner. The children have to identify the position of a marker by trial and improvement.

Rhino

A rhinoceros is lost in New York. The children guess the location by entering co-ordinates. They are told the walking distance (that is, along the grid lines) from the rhinoceros.

Properties of numbers

Factor

This is a strategy game in which the children need to identify which numbers have many factors and which have very few. (Available on *MicroSMILE – The first 31* from ILECC.)

Define

The children are given a list of numbers and asked to define one of them uniquely, using terms such as factor, multiple, square and so on. (Available on *MicroSMILE - The next 17* from ILECC.)

Identify

Here, the computer has chosen the number and the children must ask questions such as, 'Prime number?' or 'Greater than' to identify it. (Available on *MicroSMILE – The next 17* from ILECC.)

Number

This is an information package on the properties of numbers, including odd/even, prime, powers, factorials, triangular and Fibonacci. (Available on *Teaching Maths with a Micro: Maths 5* from The Shell Centre for Mathematics Education.)

Spreadsheets

Datacalc

An easy to use spreadsheet with a 'pull-down' menu. Will produce barcharts, piecharts and line graphs. Limited number of columns, but excellent for all but the most-able juniors/KS2. (Available on *Datasweet* from Kudlian Soft, for Nimbus and Archimedes.)

Pigeonhole

This is designed specifically as an introductory spreadsheet for the primary school. It contains some simple functions such as totals and averages. Will draw barcharts and piecharts only. (Available from Northern Micromedia, NORIC Centre.)

Grasshopper

More powerful than 'Datacalc' or *Pigeonhole*, but more difficult to use. A good option for the most-able pupils. (Available from Newman College, for BBC and Nimbus.)

Database

For defining objects by their attributes.

Branch

Enables children to access and write their own binary trees (that is, decision trees with a 'yes/no' option). (Available on *Information Handling Pack* from NCET, BBC only.)

Functions

Predict

The children feed in a set of numbers which the computer changes by a set rule. When they know the rule, the children are given more numbers. (Available on *MicroSMILE – The first 31* from ILECC.)

Numerator

This program enables children to set up on screen their own function machines. As a piece of 'content-free' software, the level of difficulty varies from Key Stage 2 to Sixth form, being determined by the user. (Available from Longman Logotron.)

Trial and improvement

Guess

(Available on *MicroSMILE - The first 31* from ILECC.)

Guessed

(Available on *MicroSMILE – The first 31* from ILECC.) The computer chooses a number between 1 and 100 (or between 1 and 10 in 'Guessed'). The children then have to guess the chosen number and are given clues, 'Too big' or 'Too small' and so on. A good introduction to 'Trial and improvement' methods.

LOGO

LOGO can be loaded from disc or by fitting a chip which will enable the school to use the additional Logotron LOGO extension disc for the floor turtle, for printing and other utilities. The Archimedes and Nimbus machines can load a comprehensive LOGO system from disc. (Discs and chips for the BBC and Archimedes available from Longman Logotron. Discs for the Nimbus available from Research Machines Limited.)

Roamer

This floor turtle is easily accessible to infants and lower juniors and provides an excellent introduction to LOGO. (Available from Valiant Technology Limited.)

Contact keyboard

This simple, cheap keyboard allows very young children to enter one-step LOGO commands, as well as access other software applications. Touch window can be used as a touch sensitive screen or as a concept keyboard. (Available from Keyboard Technology Limited.)

BABYLOGO

There is no all-encompassing version of BABYLOGO as you will require it to do various functions and meet different demands. To cut down on the amount of typing, and to scale the drawing, try the following:

```
?TO D
>PR [F B L R ?]
>MAKE "DIR RC
>IF :DIR = "S [STOP]
>PR [NUMBER?]
>MAKE "NUM RC
>IF :DIR = "F [FORWARD 50*:NUM]
>IF :DIR = "B [BACK 50*:NUM]
>IF :DIR = "L [LEFT 45*:NUM]
>IF :DIR = "R [RIGHT 45*:NUM]
>(PR :DIR :NUM)
>D
>END
```
Press ESCAPE to stop.

(? *and* > *are prompts provided by the computer;* PR *means* PRINT; RC *means* READ CHARACTER *; the computer will continue to loop until S is pressed.*)

If you wish the children to use the function keys only, the following program commands the keys to take on some LOGO primitives. (You can use whichever keys you like.)

```
?TO KEY
>*KEY 1 FORWARD
>*KEY 2 BACK
>*KEY 3 LEFT
>*KEY 4 RIGHT
>*KEY 5 PU
>*KEY 6 PD
>*KEY 7 PE
>*KEY 8 ST
>*KEY 9 HT
>*KEY 0 REPEAT
>END
```

If you wish to use the function keys and scale the inputs, it will be necessary to load several short programs under one file name:

```
?TO KEY
>*KEY 1 FORWARD
>*KEY 2 BACK
>*KEY 3 LEFT
>*KEY 4 RIGHT
>*KEY 5 PU
>*KEY 6 PD
>*KEY 7 PE
>*KEY 8 ST
>*KEY 9 HT
>*KEY 0 REPEAT
>END

?TO F :LEN
>FD :LEN*50
>END
```

```
?TO B :LEN
>BK :LEN*50
>END

?TO L :NUM
>LT :NUM*45
>END

?TO R :NUM
>RT :NUM*45
>END
```

Having typed these programs in, save them by giving them a 'group' name, e.g.: SAVE "BABYL. When you load this filename, all the programs load and are ready to use. Type KEY and then you are ready to use 'F' or 'L' and so on.

Appendix B
Useful reading

Background reading

Notes on Mathematics for Children, Association of Teachers of Mathematics (1985, Cambridge University Press).

Supporting Primary Mathematics: Algebra (series: 1 of 5), John Mason (1990, The Open University).

Thinking Things Through, Leone Burton (1984, Basil Blackwell).

Investigations: number patterns and properties

Bounce To It (for 5–9 year-olds), *Leap to it* (for 9–14 year-olds), *Jump to it* (for 9–14 year-olds) (series), Gillian Hatch (Available from Gillian Hatch, c/o The Faculty of Community Studies, Law and Education, Manchester Metropolitan University, 799 Wilmslow Road, Manchester M20 8RR).

Growth, Patrick Eve *et al.* and *Spot the Pattern*, Anna Lewis *et al.* (resource packs containing book and workcards) (1992, 'Be A Mathematician' [BEAM] project, Barnesbury Complex, Oxford Road, London N1 1QH).

Ideas to Use with Younger Children: Squares/Circles/Triangles/Dice games/Playing card games/Grids (series) (Triad Publications, PO Box 22, Stowmarket, Suffolk IP14 6PQ).

Inspirations for Maths, Beryl Webber and Jean Haigh (1992, Scholastic Publications).

Mathematics with Seven and Eight Year Olds/Eight and Nine Year Olds/Nine and Ten Year Olds/Ten and Eleven Year Olds (series), Marion Bird (Available from Marion Bird, c/o

Mathematics Association, 259, London Road, Leicester
LE2 3BE

Points of Departure 1–4 (series for 9–13 year-olds),
Association of Teachers of Mathematics.

Practical Guides: Maths, Andy Bailey, Lynda Townsend and
Mike Wilkinson (1992, Scholastic Publications).

Computers

Children Learning with LOGO, Katrina Blythe (1990,
National Council for Education Technology).

The Homerton LOGO Manual, Hilary Shuard and Fred Daly
(1987, Cambridge University Press).

Simply Spreadsheets, Roger Keeling and Senga Whiteman
(1991, KW Publications, 42 Compton Drive, Streetly,
Sutton Coldfield, West Midlands B74 2DB).

Some Lessons in Mathematics with a Microcomputer
(SLIMWAM 1) (series) , Association of Teachers of
Mathematics. Ideas for using 'Monty', 'Counter' and more.

Spreadsheets for Mathematics and Information Technology,
Andrew Rothery (1991, John Murray).

Cross-curricular mathematics

100s of Ideas for Primary Maths: A cross-curricular approach,
Paul Harling (1990, Hodder and Stoughton).

*Maths on display: Creative activities for the teaching of infant
maths*, Barbara Hume and Kathie Barrs (1988, Belair
Publications).

*Will Gulliver's suit fit? Mathematical problem solving with
children*, Dora Whittaker (1986, Cambridge University
Press).

Appendix C
Glossary of terms

An **Attribute** is a property of an object, and can be used to
sort that object from others, e.g. colour, size.

A **Carroll diagram** is a grid showing two sets of attributes.
Objects or numbers are placed on the grid so that their
attributes are described in both directions. Carroll
diagrams are an early example of a co-ordinate system.
For example, the attributes here are smiling/not smiling
and hat/no hat:

Coordinates are pairs of numbers which represent a point
on a grid or map. The first number refers to the position of
the point in relation to the horizontal (x) axis, the second
number refers to the position in relation to the vertical (y)
axis. Hence co-ordinates are written (x,y).

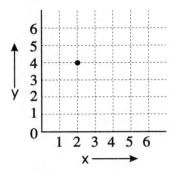

An **Equation** is a mathematical sentence which shows the
equivalence of two sets of numbers and operations. An
equation is said to 'balance'. For example:

$$2 \times 6 = 4 + 8$$

A **Factor** of a number is any number which will divide
exactly (that is with no remainders) into it. For example, 4
is a factor of 28, 5 is not.

A **Formula** is a special equation which describes the
relationship between quantities. For example, circle:

$$A = \pi r^2$$

A **Function** is a relationship or rule which forms a one-to-
one correspondence between sets of numbers. It can be
written as a rule, or generalisation (see below) or as a
mapping. For example, this is the mapping of the function
'doubling':

$$x \rightarrow 2x$$

A **Function machine** is an imaginary machine which
obeys a particular rule. **Inputs** (the starting numbers) are
changed by the machine to **outputs** (the new numbers
produced by applying the rule). Calculators and
computers can be used as 'real' function machines.

A **Generalisation** of a pattern describes the rule which is
applied to each input to produce its output. For example,
this is the generalisation of a function which doubles the
counting numbers:

$$\text{nth term} = 2n$$

Index notation/Indices are shorthand ways of showing
several multiplications of the same number. The index
number is often called the **Power** (if it is a number greater
that 1) or **Root** (if it is a number between 0 and 1). Indices
can be negative, though this is not normally used at the
primary stage. For example:

$$2^3 = 2 \times 2 \times 2 = 8 \qquad \sqrt[3]{8} = 2$$

The **Inverse** of an operation or rule is the operation or
rule which will turn each output back into its input. For
example, the inverse of doubling is halving.

A **Mapping diagram** is used to communicate a simple relationship or correspondence between sets of objects of numbers. The linked members of each set are joined by arrows. This mapping diagram shows doubling:

A **Multiple** of a number is any number into which it will divide exactly (that is with no remainders). For example, 28 is a multiple of 4., but not of 5.

Power – another word for index – see Index notation.

A **Prime** number is a number whose only factors are itself and 1. 7 is a prime number, 8 is not as 8 has factors 2 and 4, as well as 8 and 1.

Co-ordinates can represent points in the first **Quadrant**, which means that all numbers are positive, or they may represent points in the **four quadrants**, which means the x of the y co-ordinate – or both – may be negative. The points below are (-3,2) and (3,-3):

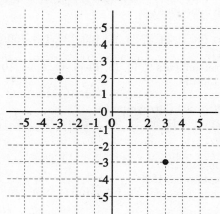

Root – see Index notation

Spatial arrangements are any arrangements of objects which can be used to explore or explain number patterns of number properties.

Spreadsheets are computer programs which enable the user to store numbers in a grid, explore their properties and manipulate them with comparative ease.

Trial and movement is a method of finding a solution to a problem or an equation instead of using analytic methods (that is, methods of using algebraic manipulation). They may be chosen because the analytic methods are beyond the pupil or because trial and improvement would be faster. The stages are:
Make a guess
Try the guess inside the rule
Compare with the required answer
Improve the guess
Continue until the accuracy is acceptable.

A **Transformation** is a movement or alteration of an object. Transformations met at the primary level are:
Translation – only position is changed. Size, shape and orientation (the direction in which each corner is pointing) are unchanged. The shape is moved by 'sliding'.
Reflection – Position and orientation changed. Size and shape are unchanged. A mirror image is produced by 'flipping over.'
Rotation – Position and orientation changed. Size and shape are unchanged. An image is produced by 'turning'.
Enlargement – Position and size are changed. Orientation and shape are unchanged. Position can be said to be unchanged if the centre of enlargement is the centre of the shape, though this is not usually the case at primary level, the origin (0,0) usually being the point measured from.

A **Variable** is a quantity which can have a range of values.

Index